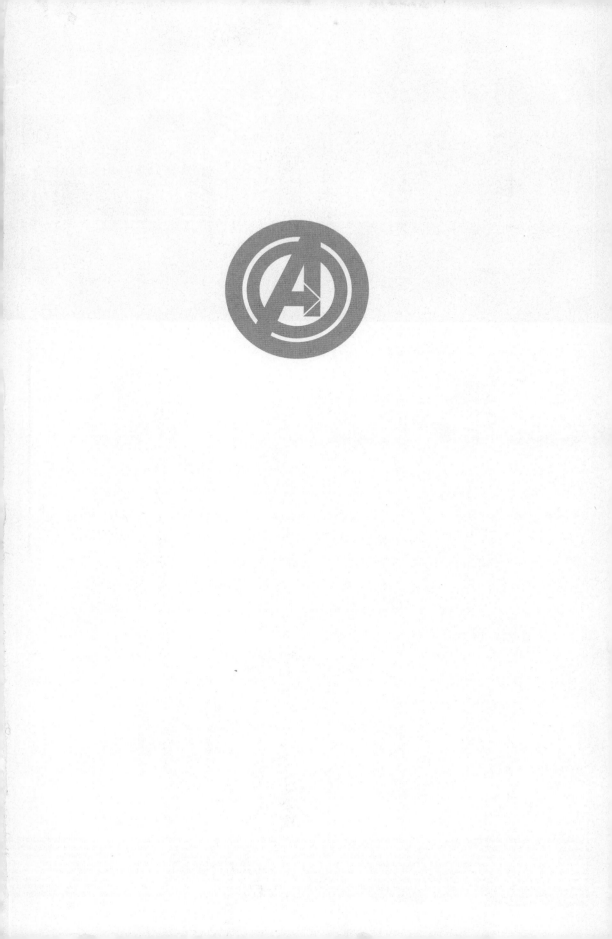

AVENGERS VOL. 2: THE LAST WHITE EVENT. Contains material originally published in magazine form as AVENGERS #7-11. First printing 2013. ISBN# 978-0-7851-6824-9. Published by MARVEL WORLDWIDE, INC., a subsidiary of MARVEL ENTERTAINMENT, LLC. OFFICE OF PUBLICATION: 135 West 50th Street, New York, NY 10020. Copyright © 2013 Marvel Characters, Inc. All rights reserved. All characters featured in this issue and the distinctive names and likenesses thereof, and all related indicia are trademarks of Marvel Characters, Inc. No similarity between any of the names, characters, persons, and/or institutions in this magazine with those of any living or dead person or institution is intended, and any such similarity which may exist is purely coincidental. **Printed in the U.S.A.** ALAN FINE, EVP - Office of the President, Marvel Worldwide, Inc. and EVP & CMO Marvel Characters B.V.; DAN BUCKLEY, Publisher & President - Print, Animation & Digital Divisions; JOE QUESADA, Chief Creative Officer; TOM BREVOORT, SVP of Publishing; DAVID BOGART, SVP of Operations & Procurement, Publishing; C.B. CEBULSKI, SVP of Creator & Content Development; DAVID GABRIEL, SVP of Print & Digital Publishing Sales; JIM O'KEEFE, VP of Operations & Logistics; DAN CARR, Executive Director of Publishing Technology; SUSAN CRESPI, Editorial Operations Manager; ALEX MORALES, Publishing Operations Manager; STAN LEE, Chairman Emeritus. For information regarding advertising in Marvel Comics or on Marvel.com, please contact Niza Disla, Director of Marvel Partnerships, at ndisla@marvel.com. For Marvel subscription inquiries, please call 800-217-9158. **Manufactured between 5/13/2013 and 6/24/2013 by R.R. DONNELLEY, INC., SALEM, VA, USA.**

10 9 8 7 6 5 4 3 2 1

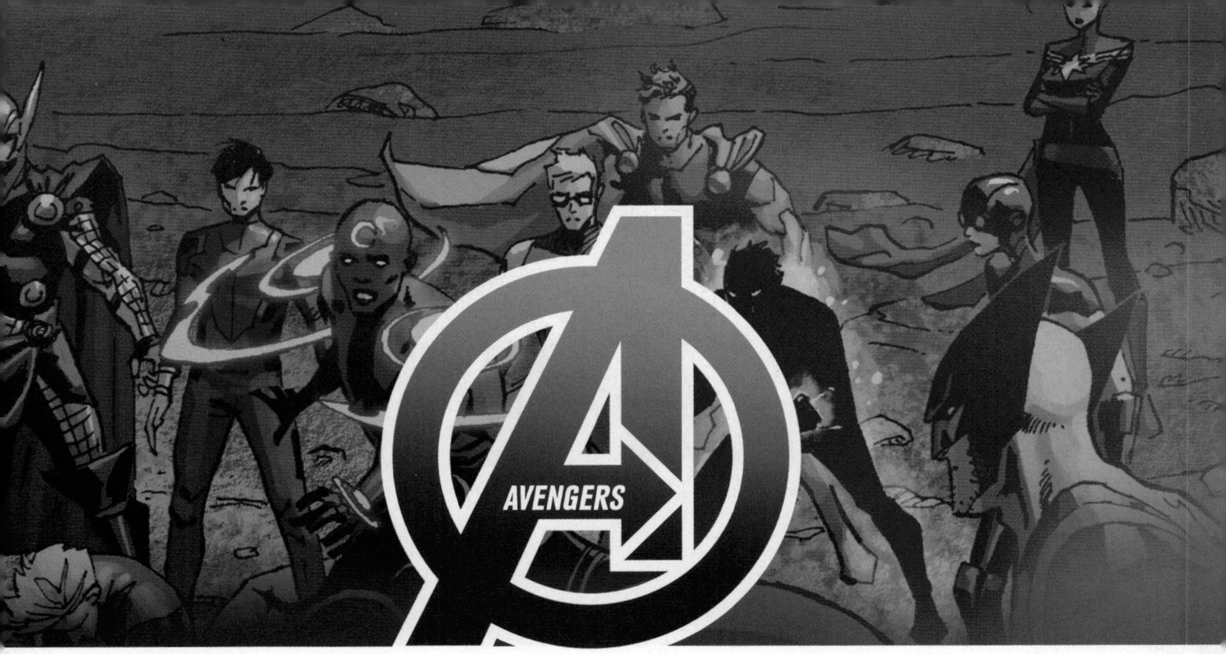
AVENGERS

WRITER: **JONATHAN HICKMAN**
ARTIST, #7-9: **DUSTIN WEAVER** WITH MIKE DEODATO [#9]
ARTIST, #10-11: **MIKE DEODATO**
COLOR ARTIST, #7-9: **JUSTIN PONSOR**
COLOR ARTIST, #10-11: **FRANK MARTIN**
LETTERER: **VC'S CORY PETIT**
COVER ART: **DUSTIN WEAVER & JUSTIN PONSOR**
ASSISTANT EDITOR: **JAKE THOMAS**
EDITORS: **TOM BREVOORT** WITH **LAUREN SANKOVITCH**

COLLECTION EDITOR: **JENNIFER GRÜNWALD**
ASSISTANT EDITORS: **ALEX STARBUCK & NELSON RIBEIRO**
EDITOR, SPECIAL PROJECTS: **MARK D. BEAZLEY**
SENIOR EDITOR, SPECIAL PROJECTS: **JEFF YOUNGQUIST**
SVP OF PRINT & DIGITAL PUBLISHING SALES: **DAVID GABRIEL**
BOOK DESIGN: **JEFF POWELL**

EDITOR IN CHIEF: **AXEL ALONSO**
CHIEF CREATIVE OFFICER: **JOE QUESADA**
PUBLISHER: **DAN BUCKLEY**
EXECUTIVE PRODUCER: **ALAN FINE**

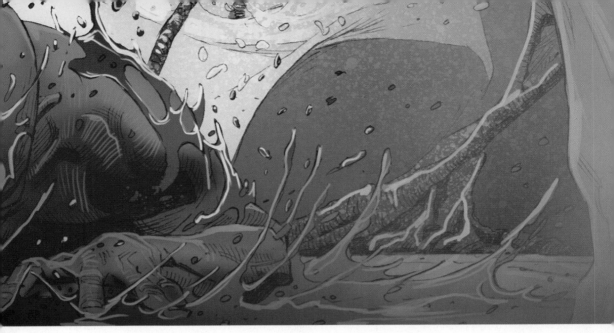

"THE LAST WHITE EVENT"

PREVIOUSLY IN AVENGERS

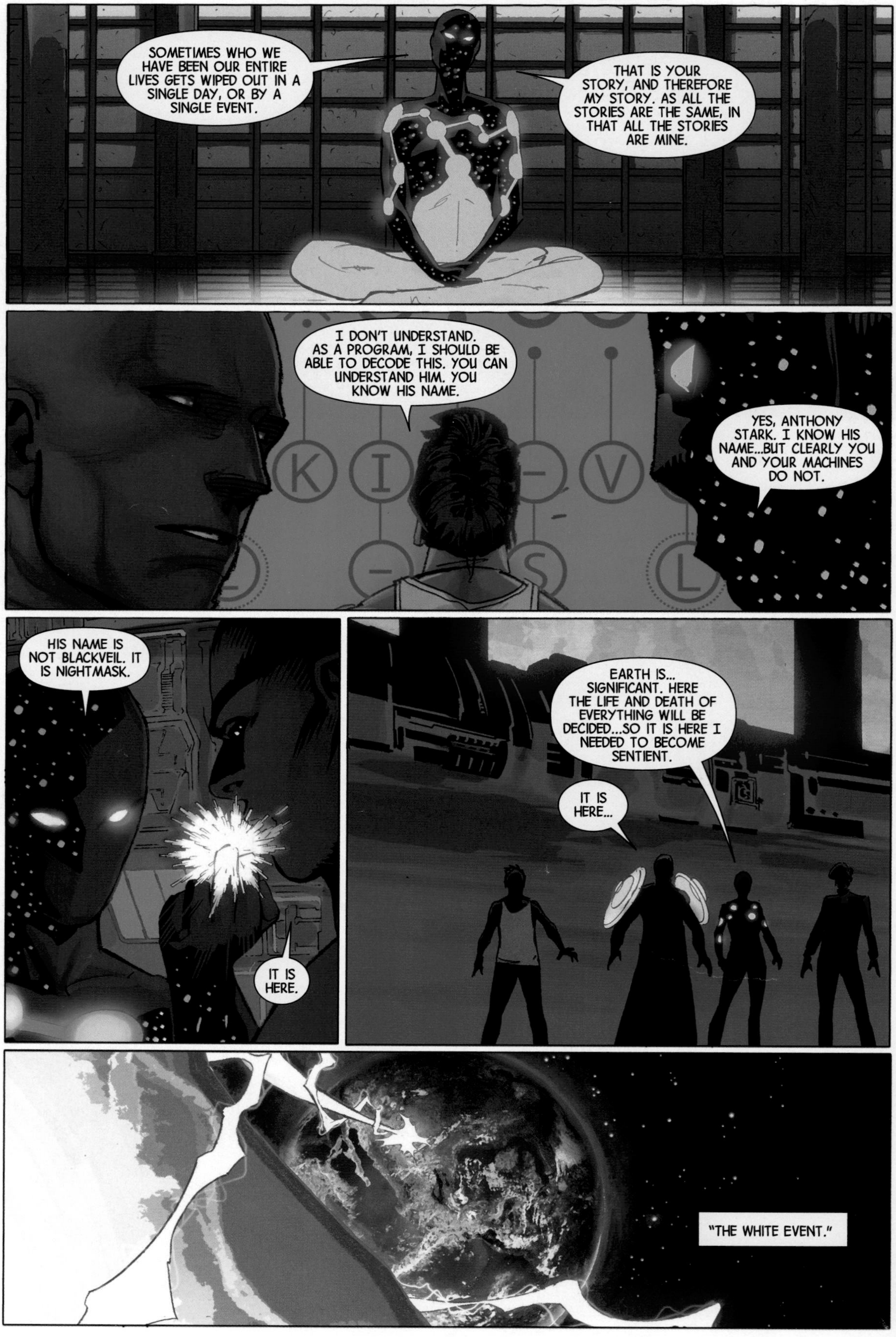

SOMETIMES WHO WE HAVE BEEN OUR ENTIRE LIVES GETS WIPED OUT IN A SINGLE DAY, OR BY A SINGLE EVENT.
THAT IS YOUR STORY, AND THEREFORE MY STORY. AS ALL THE STORIES ARE THE SAME, IN THAT ALL THE STORIES ARE MINE.
I DON'T UNDERSTAND. AS A PROGRAM, I SHOULD BE ABLE TO DECODE THIS. YOU CAN UNDERSTAND HIM. YOU KNOW HIS NAME.
YES, ANTHONY STARK. I KNOW HIS NAME...BUT CLEARLY YOU AND YOUR MACHINES DO NOT.
HIS NAME IS NOT BLACKVEIL. IT IS NIGHTMASK.
IT IS HERE.
EARTH IS... SIGNIFICANT. HERE THE LIFE AND DEATH OF EVERYTHING WILL BE DECIDED...SO IT IS HERE I NEEDED TO BECOME SENTIENT.
IT IS HERE...
"THE WHITE EVENT."

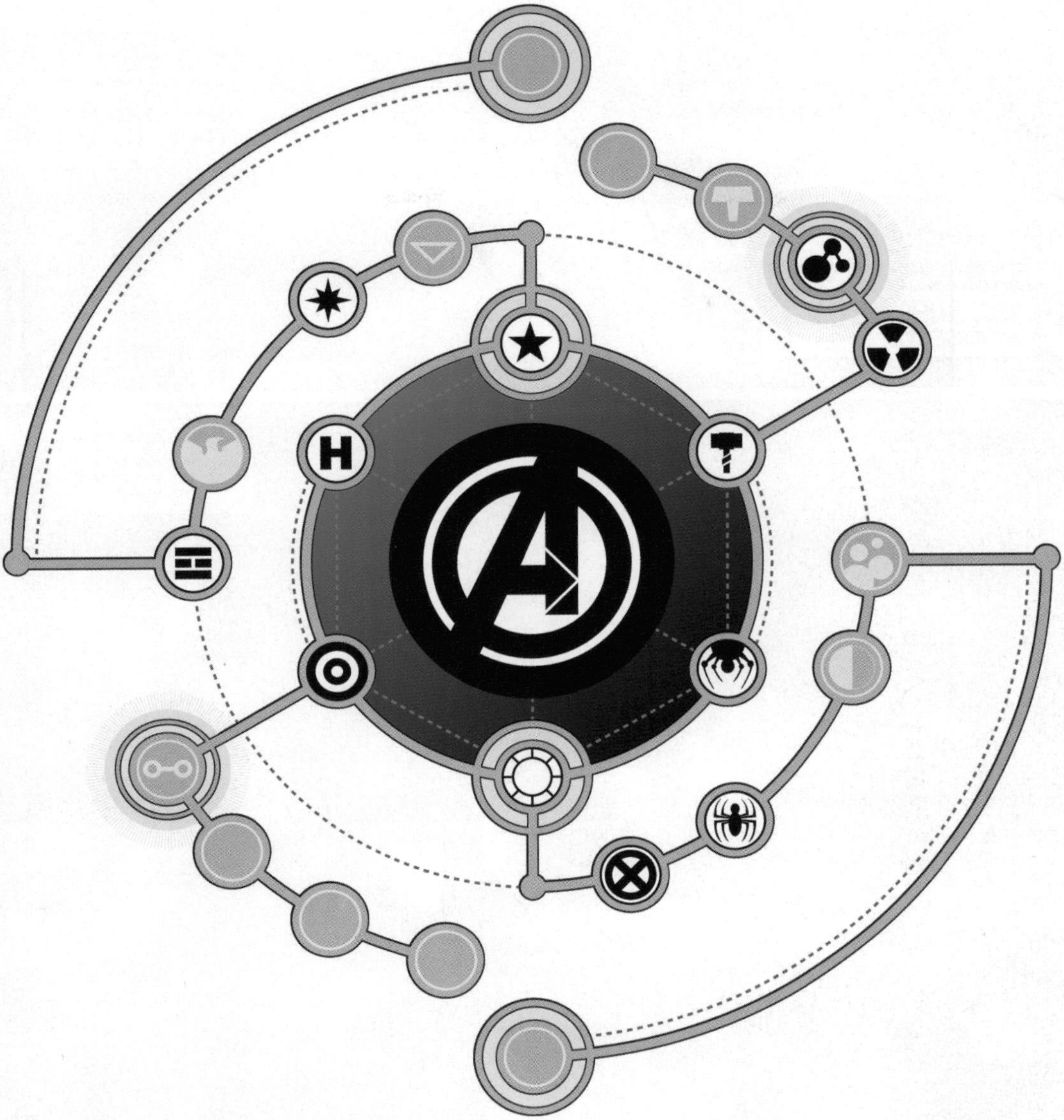

EARTH'S MIGHTIEST HEROES

CAPTAIN AMERICA · IRON MAN · THOR · HAWKEYE · BLACK WIDOW · HULK
WOLVERINE · SPIDER-MAN · CAPTAIN MARVEL · SPIDER-WOMAN
FALCON · SHANG-CHI · SUNSPOT · CANNONBALL · MANIFOLD
SMASHER · CAPTAIN UNIVERSE · HYPERION

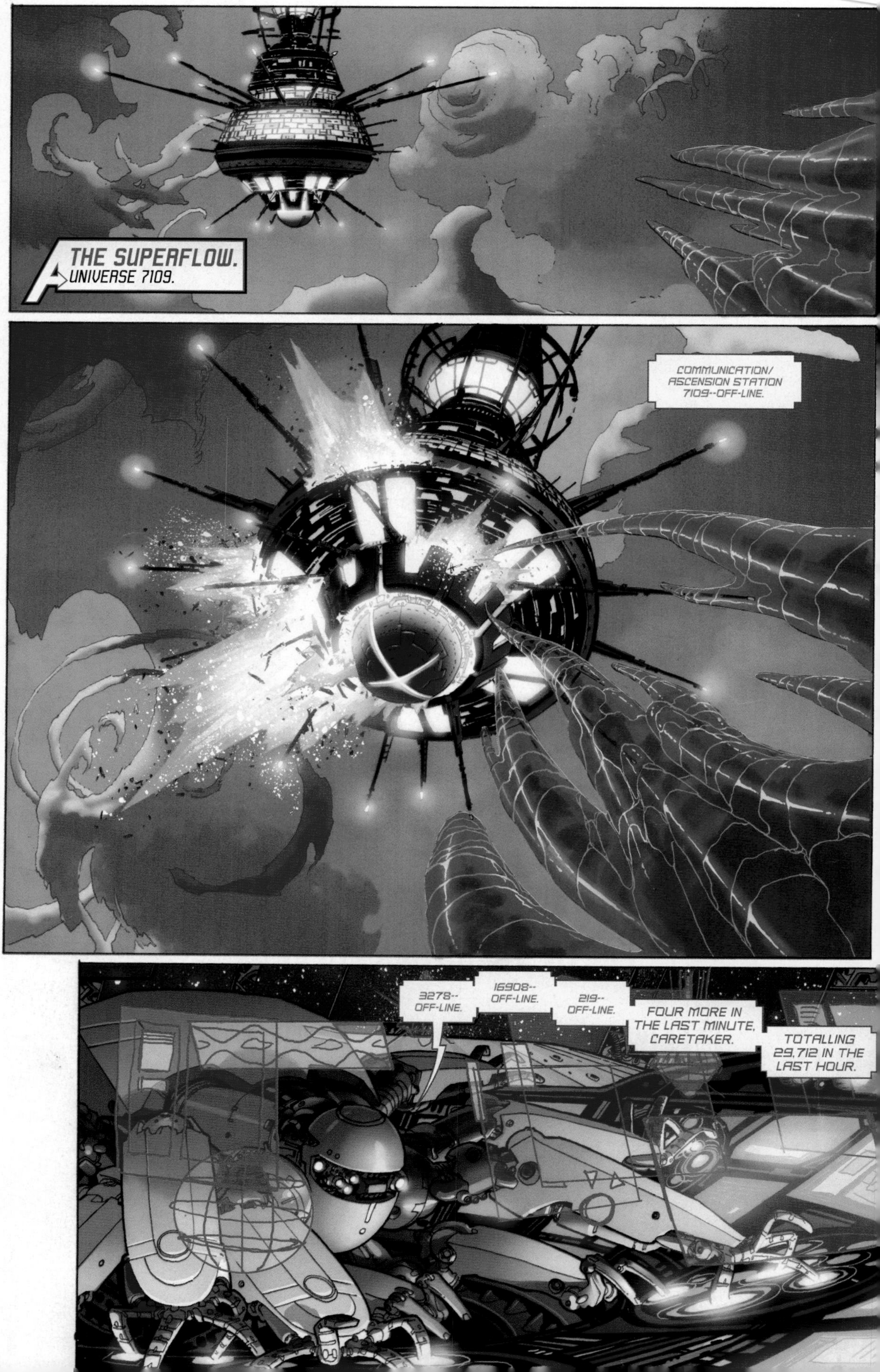
THE SUPERFLOW.
UNIVERSE 7109.
COMMUNICATION/ ASCENSION STATION 7109--OFF-LINE.
3278-- OFF-LINE.
16908-- OFF-LINE.
219-- OFF-LINE.
FOUR MORE IN THE LAST MINUTE, CARETAKER.
TOTALLING 29,712 IN THE LAST HOUR.

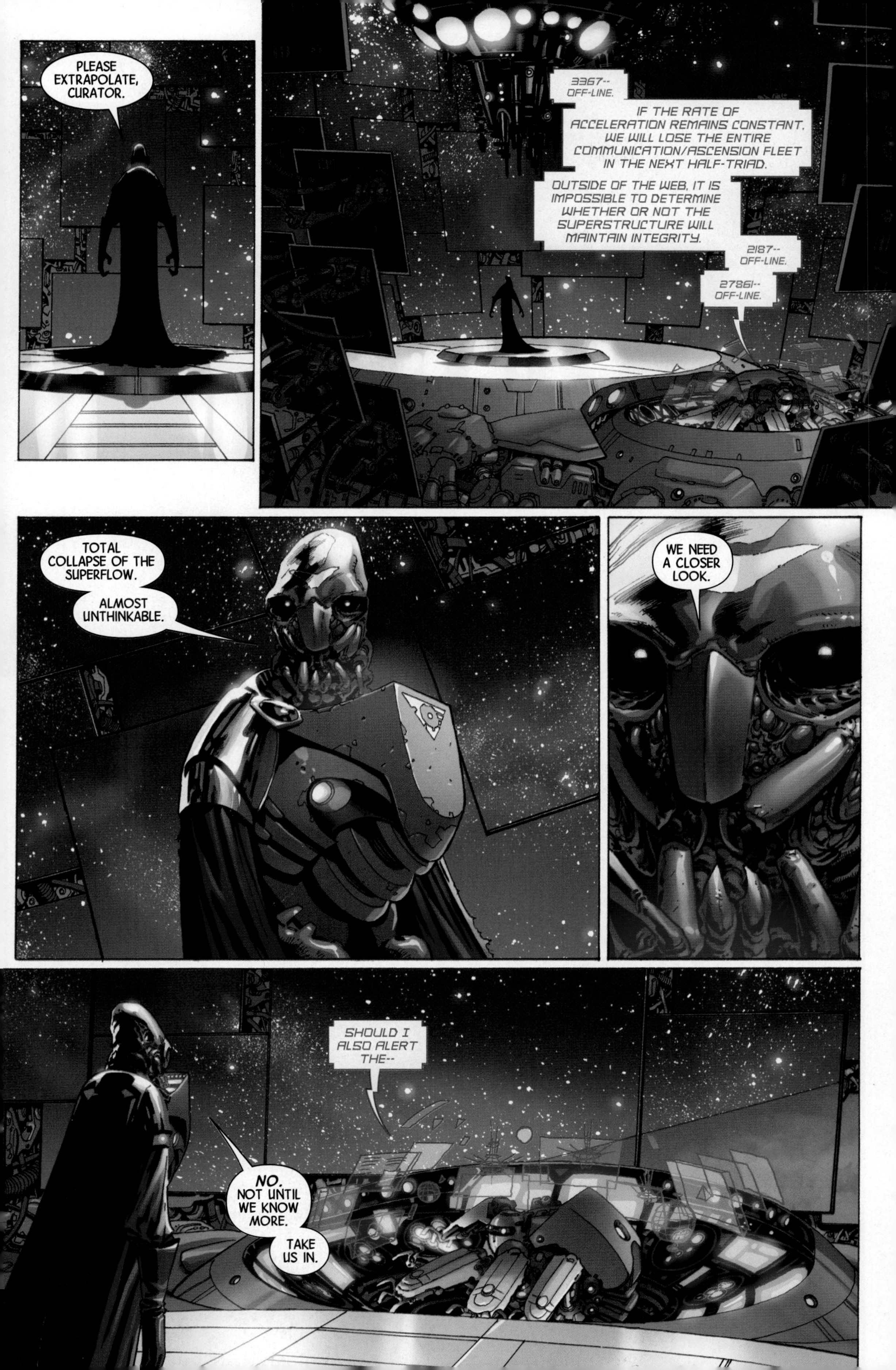

PLEASE EXTRAPOLATE, CURATOR.
3367-- OFF-LINE.
IF THE RATE OF ACCELERATION REMAINS CONSTANT, WE WILL LOSE THE ENTIRE COMMUNICATION/ASCENSION FLEET IN THE NEXT HALF-TRIAD.
OUTSIDE OF THE WEB, IT IS IMPOSSIBLE TO DETERMINE WHETHER OR NOT THE SUPERSTRUCTURE WILL MAINTAIN INTEGRITY.
2187-- OFF-LINE.
27861-- OFF-LINE.
TOTAL COLLAPSE OF THE SUPERFLOW.
ALMOST UNTHINKABLE.
WE NEED A CLOSER LOOK.
SHOULD I ALSO ALERT THE--
NO. NOT UNTIL WE KNOW MORE.
TAKE US IN.

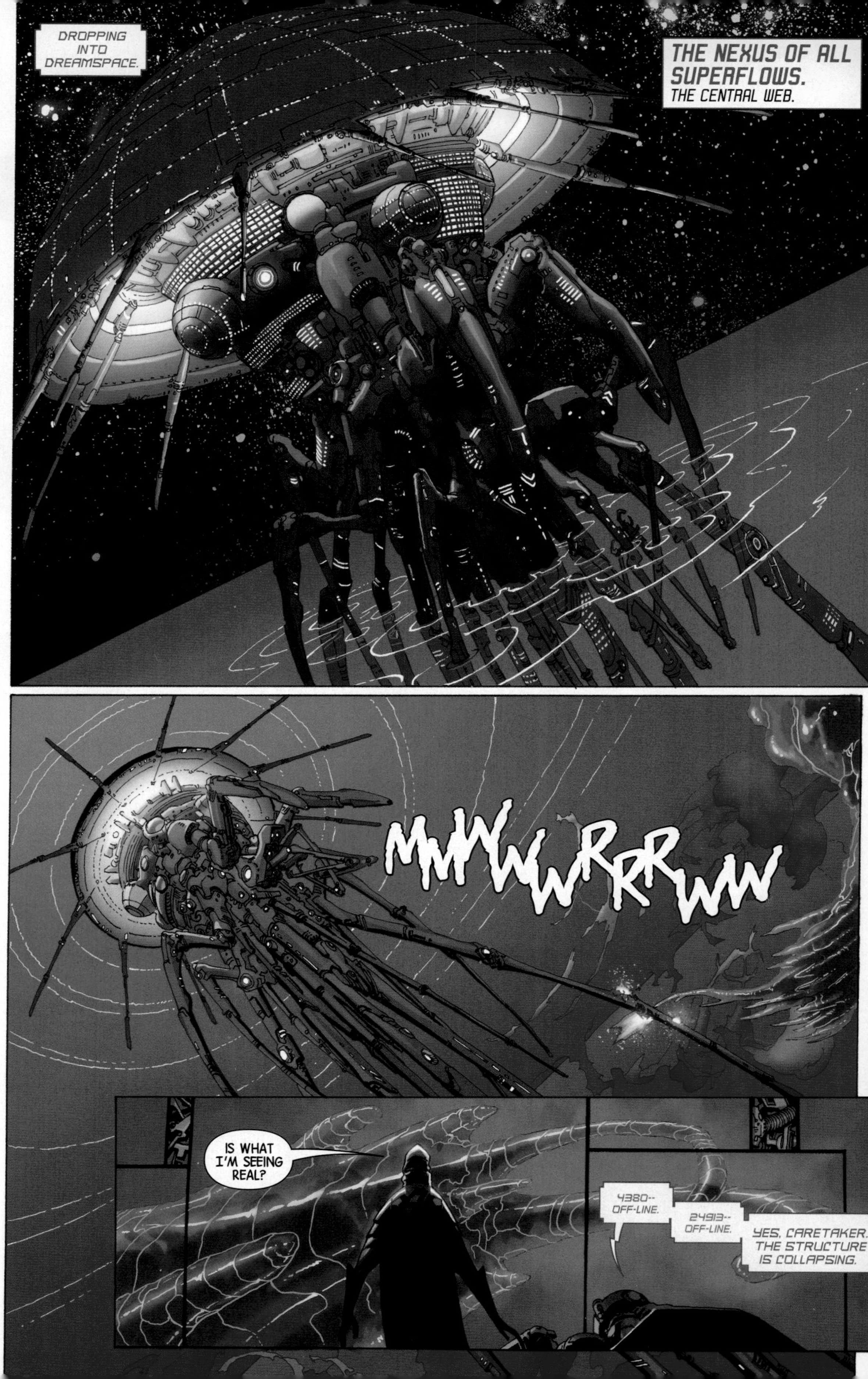
DROPPING INTO DREAMSPACE.
THE NEXUS OF ALL SUPERFLOWS.
THE CENTRAL WEB.
MMWWWRRRWW
IS WHAT I'M SEEING REAL?
4380-- OFF-LINE.
24913-- OFF-LINE.
YES, CARETAKER. THE STRUCTURE IS COLLAPSING.

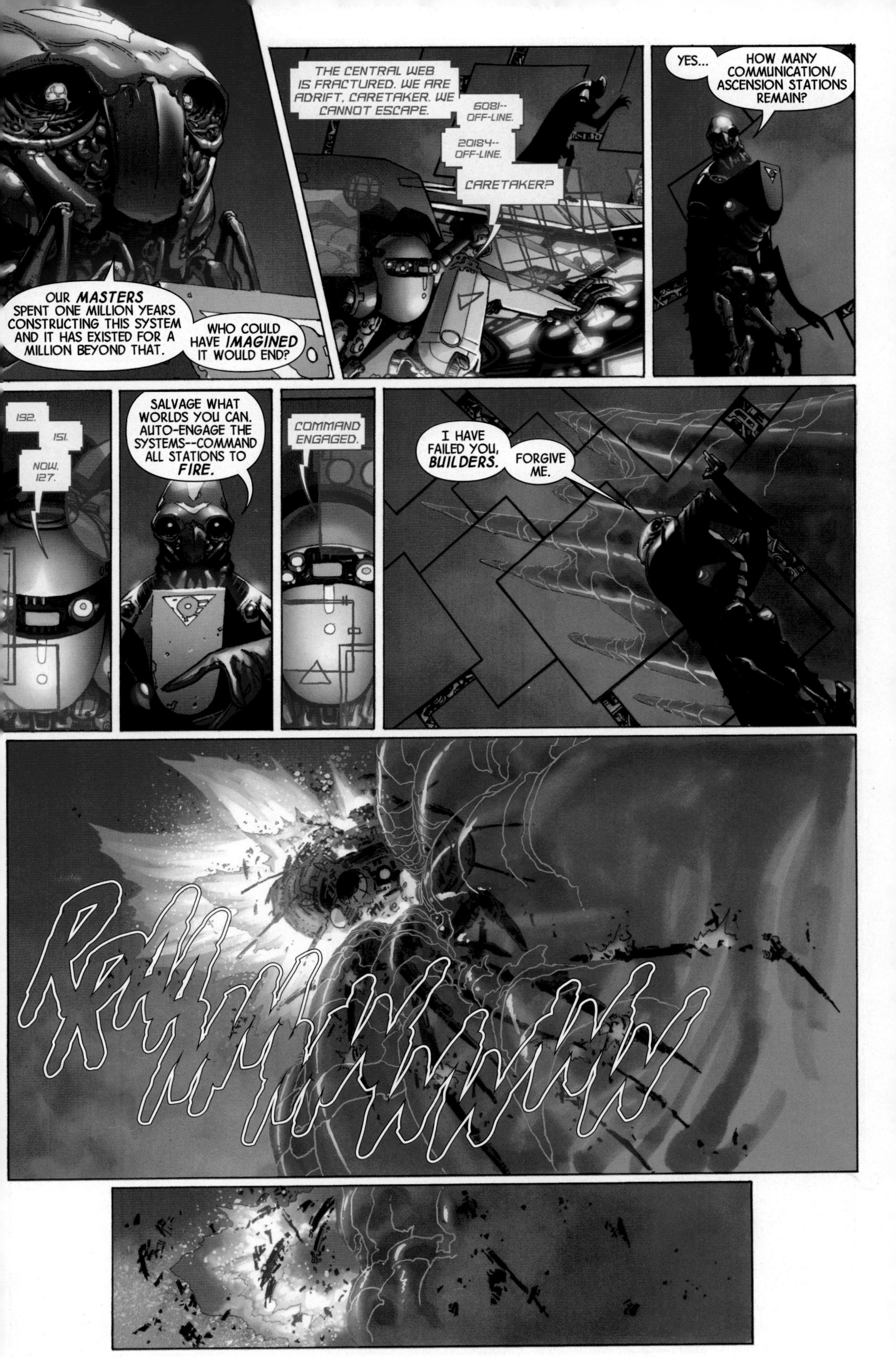
OUR MASTERS SPENT ONE MILLION YEARS CONSTRUCTING THIS SYSTEM AND IT HAS EXISTED FOR A MILLION BEYOND THAT.
WHO COULD HAVE IMAGINED IT WOULD END?
THE CENTRAL WEB IS FRACTURED. WE ARE ADRIFT, CARETAKER. WE CANNOT ESCAPE.
6081-- OFF-LINE.
20184-- OFF-LINE.
CARETAKER?
YES...
HOW MANY COMMUNICATION/ ASCENSION STATIONS REMAIN?
192.
151.
NOW, 127.
SALVAGE WHAT WORLDS YOU CAN. AUTO-ENGAGE THE SYSTEMS--COMMAND ALL STATIONS TO FIRE.
COMMAND ENGAGED.
I HAVE FAILED YOU, BUILDERS.
FORGIVE ME.

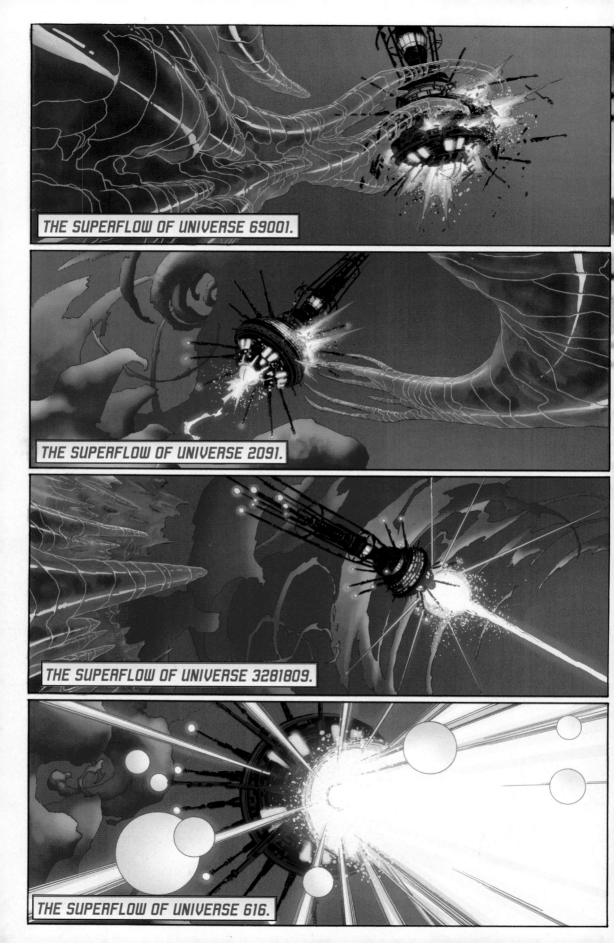

THE SUPERFLOW OF UNIVERSE 69001.

THE SUPERFLOW OF UNIVERSE 2091.

THE SUPERFLOW OF UNIVERSE 3281809.

THE SUPERFLOW OF UNIVERSE 616.

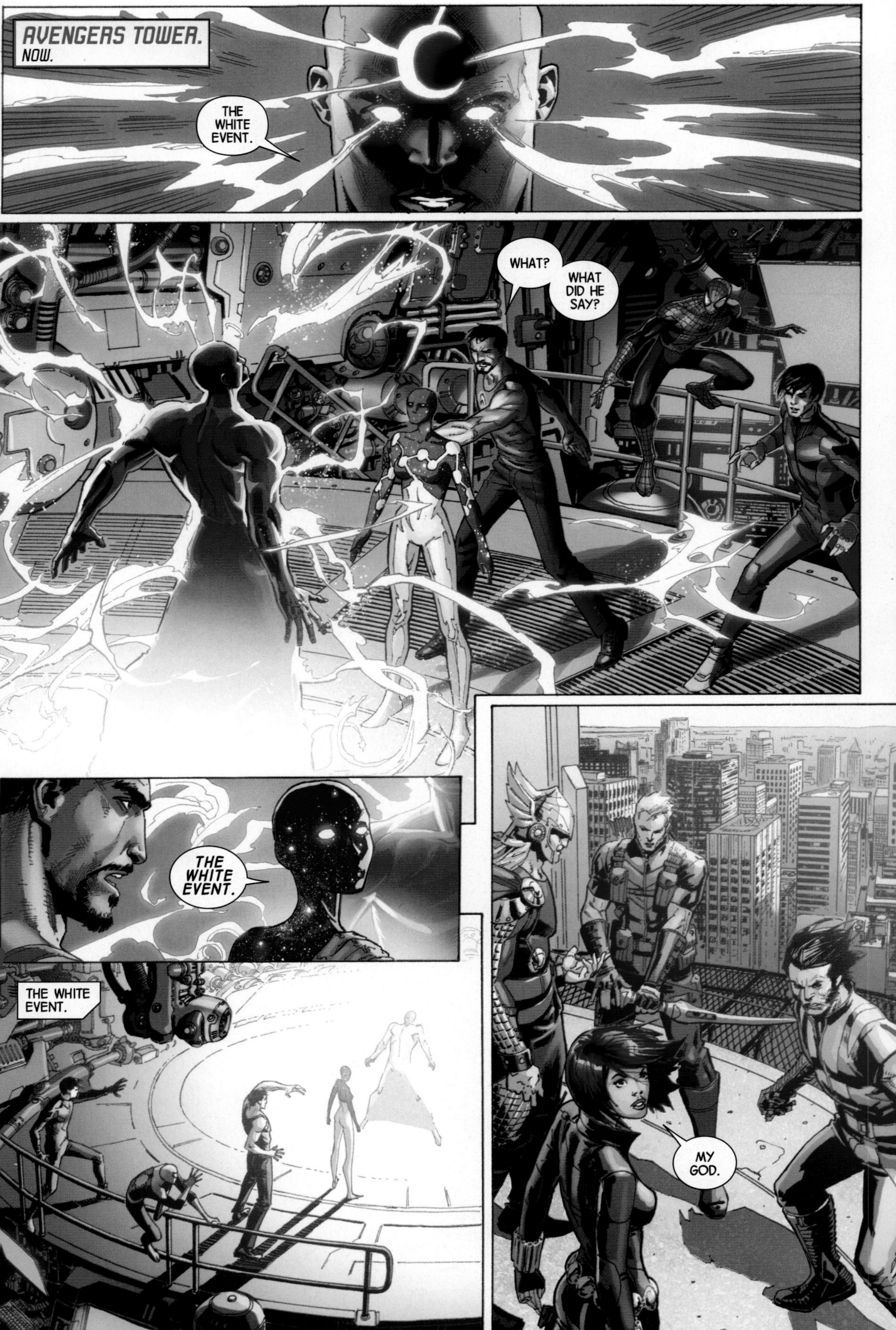
AVENGERS TOWER.
NOW.
THE WHITE EVENT.
WHAT?
WHAT DID HE SAY?
THE WHITE EVENT.
THE WHITE EVENT.
MY GOD.

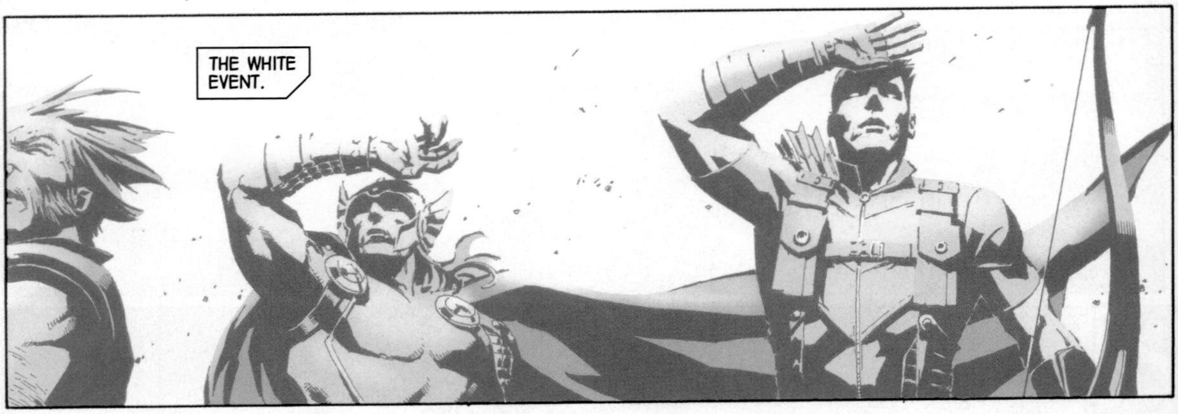
THE WHITE
EVENT.

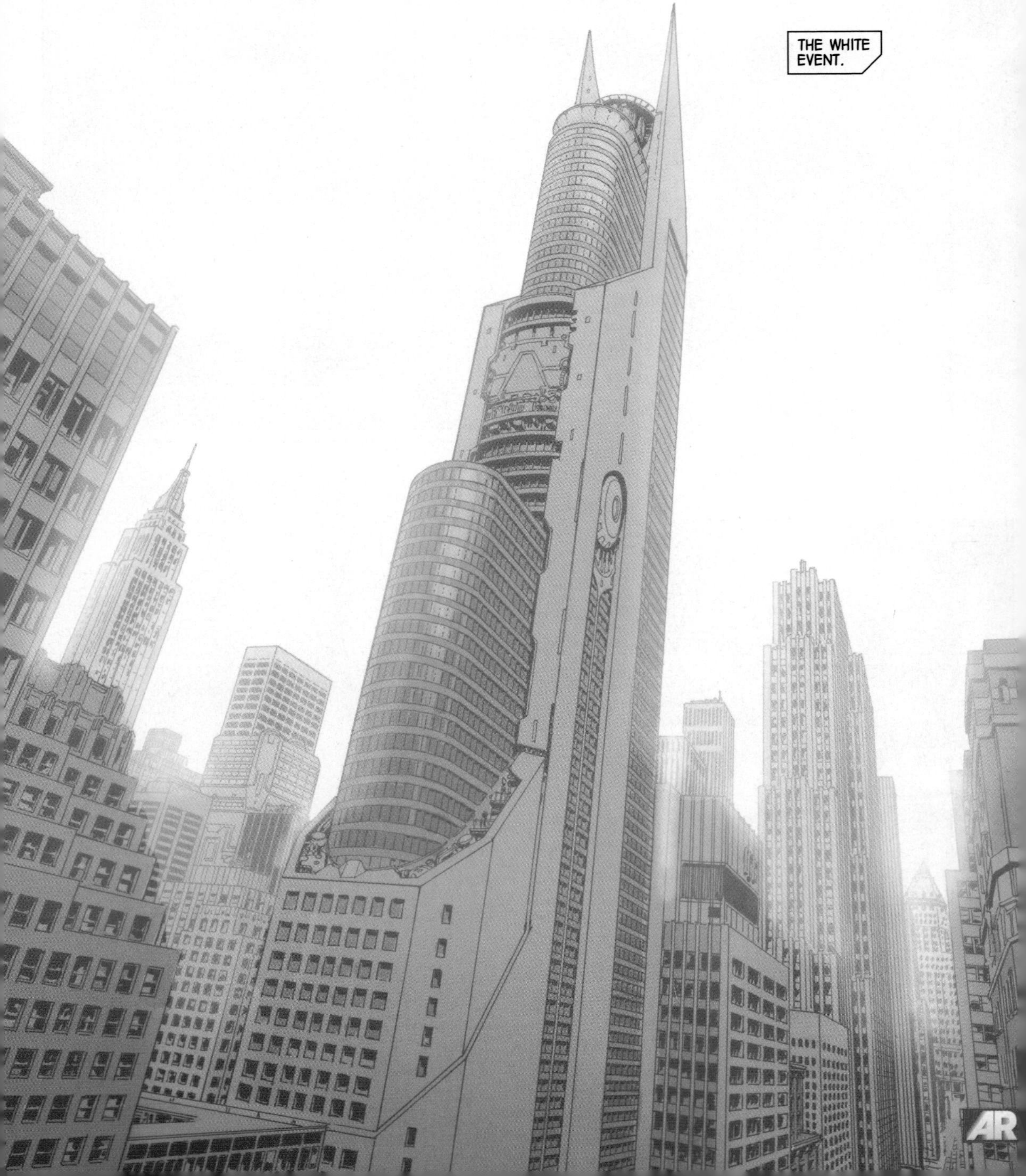
THE WHITE
EVENT.

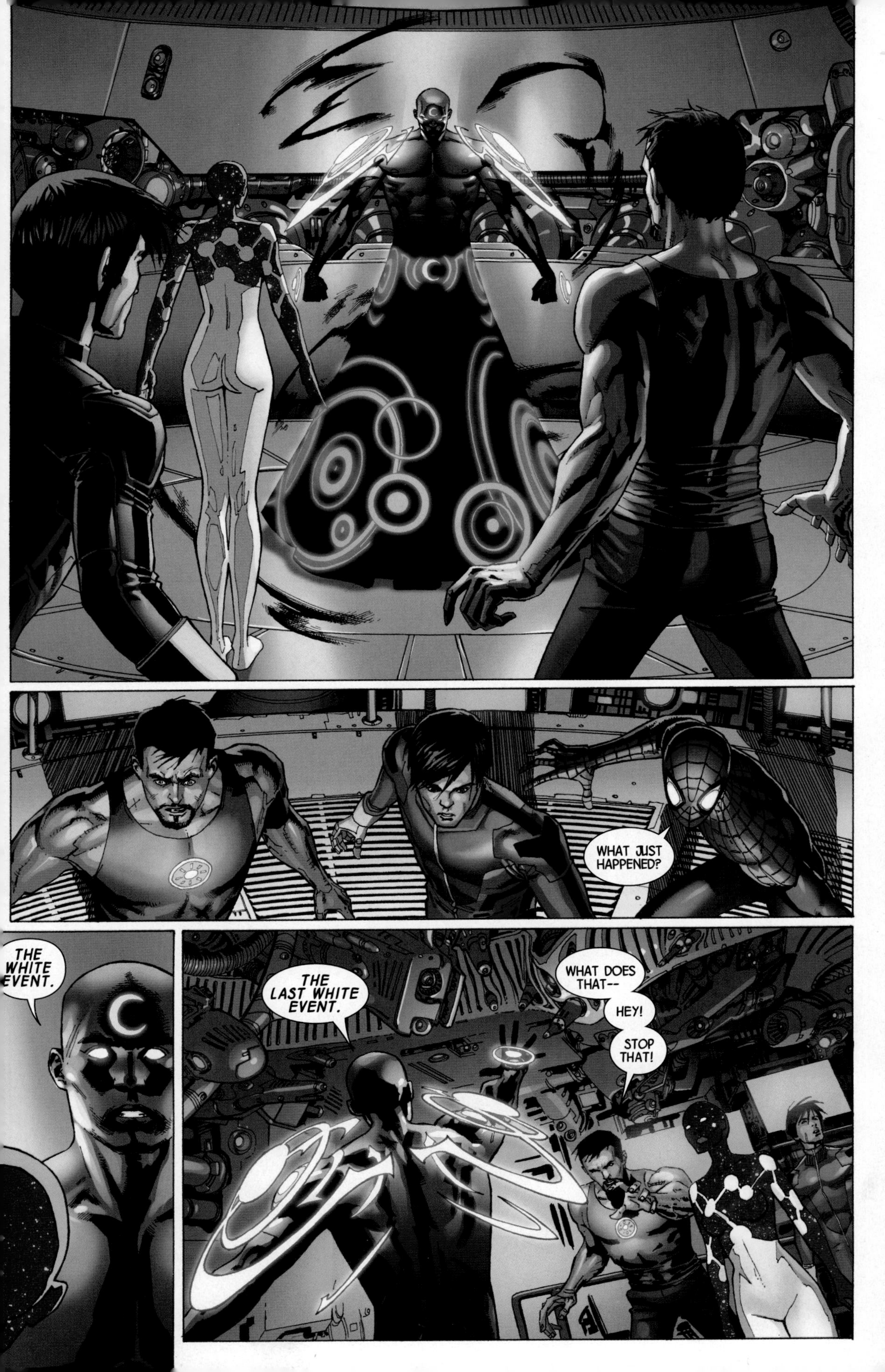
WHAT JUST HAPPENED?
THE WHITE EVENT.
THE LAST WHITE EVENT.
WHAT DOES THAT--
HEY!
STOP THAT!

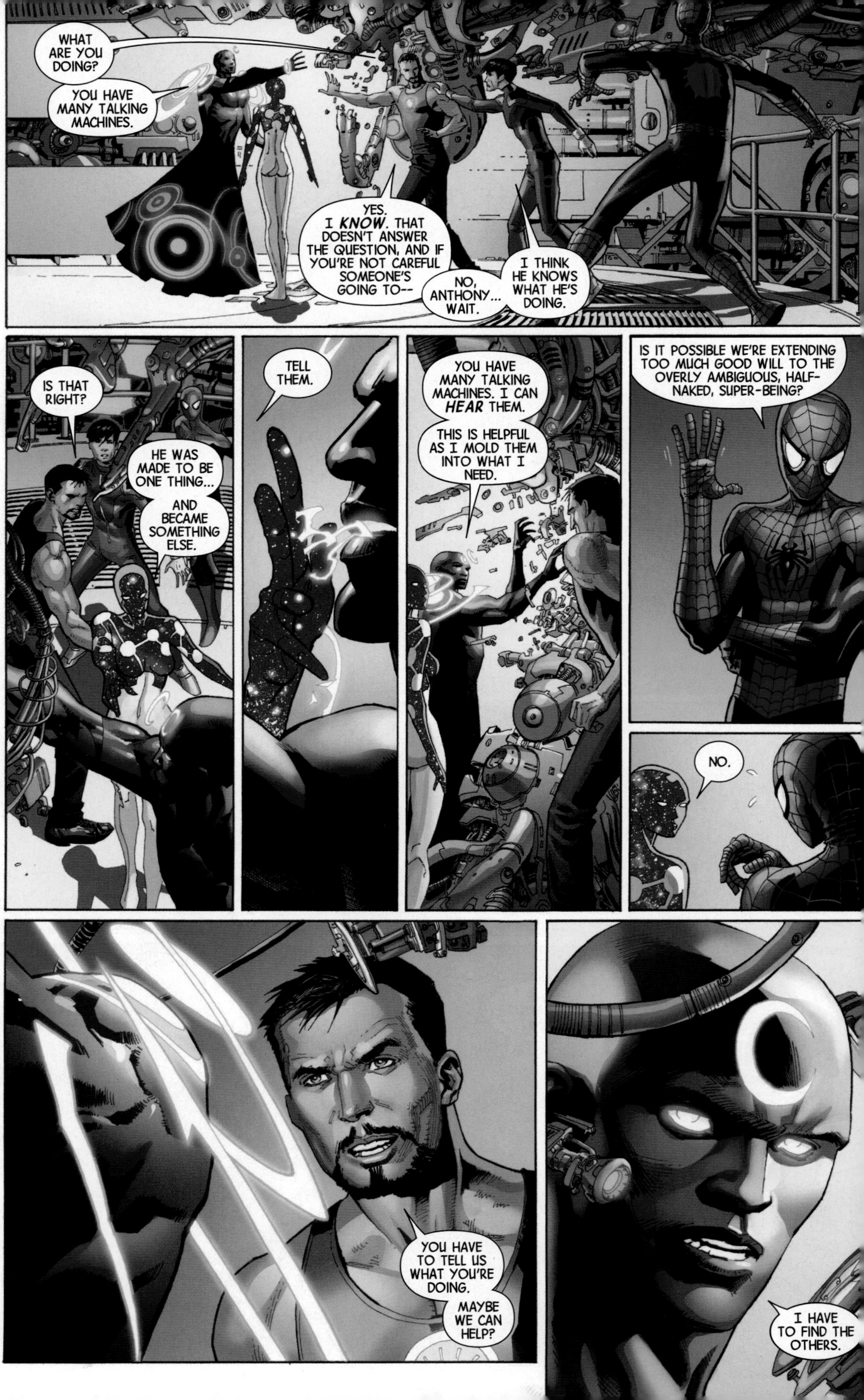
WHAT ARE YOU DOING?
YOU HAVE MANY TALKING MACHINES.
YES. I KNOW. THAT DOESN'T ANSWER THE QUESTION, AND IF YOU'RE NOT CAREFUL SOMEONE'S GOING TO--
NO, ANTHONY... WAIT.
I THINK HE KNOWS WHAT HE'S DOING.
IS THAT RIGHT?
HE WAS MADE TO BE ONE THING...
AND BECAME SOMETHING ELSE.
TELL THEM.
YOU HAVE MANY TALKING MACHINES. I CAN HEAR THEM.
THIS IS HELPFUL AS I MOLD THEM INTO WHAT I NEED.
IS IT POSSIBLE WE'RE EXTENDING TOO MUCH GOOD WILL TO THE OVERLY AMBIGUOUS, HALF-NAKED, SUPER-BEING?
NO.
YOU HAVE TO TELL US WHAT YOU'RE DOING.
MAYBE WE CAN HELP?
I HAVE TO FIND THE OTHERS.

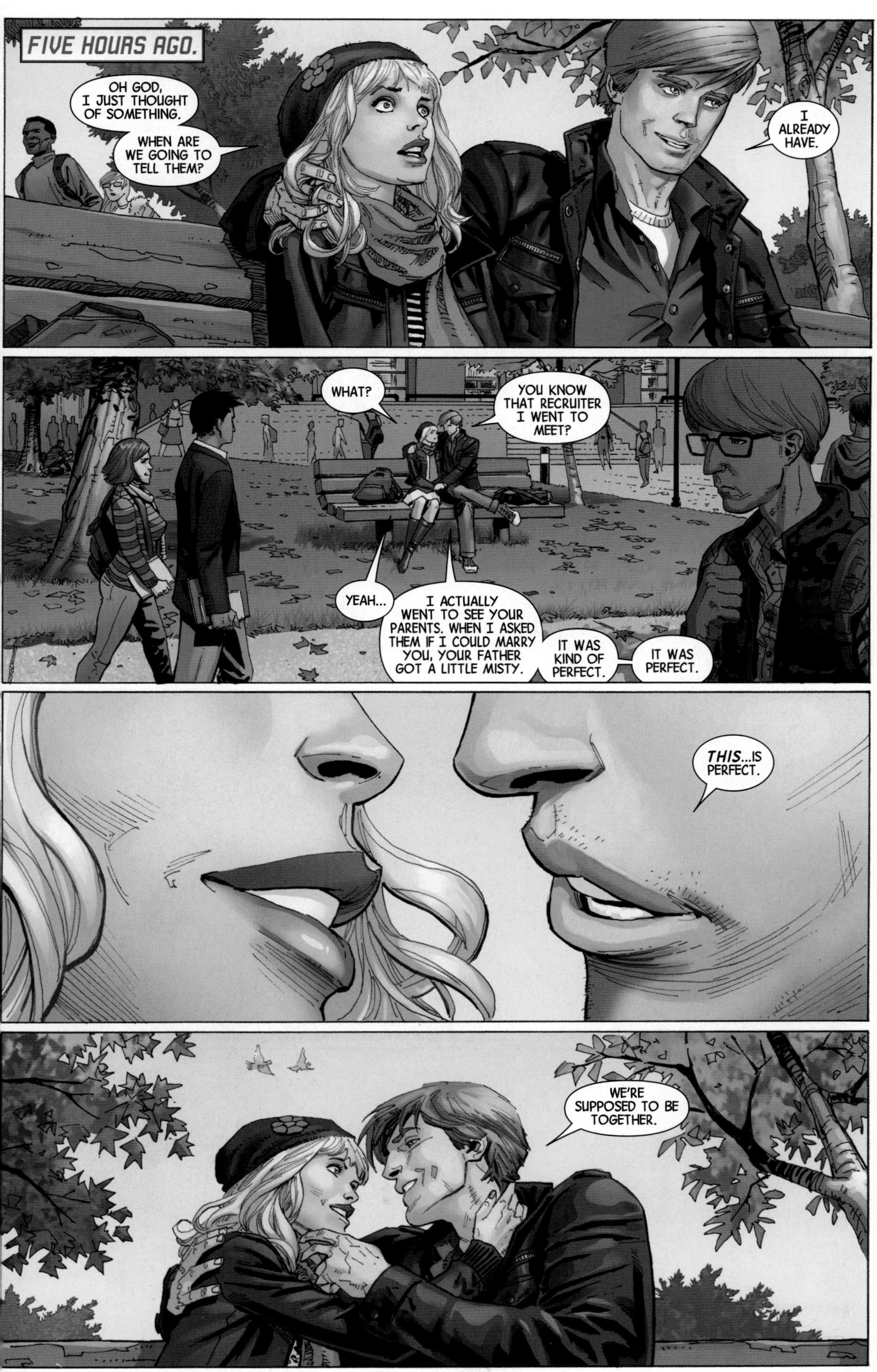
FIVE HOURS AGO.
OH GOD, I JUST THOUGHT OF SOMETHING.
WHEN ARE WE GOING TO TELL THEM?
I ALREADY HAVE.
WHAT?
YOU KNOW THAT RECRUITER I WENT TO MEET?
YEAH...
I ACTUALLY WENT TO SEE YOUR PARENTS. WHEN I ASKED THEM IF I COULD MARRY YOU, YOUR FATHER GOT A LITTLE MISTY.
IT WAS KIND OF PERFECT.
IT WAS PERFECT.
THIS...IS PERFECT.
WE'RE SUPPOSED TO BE TOGETHER.

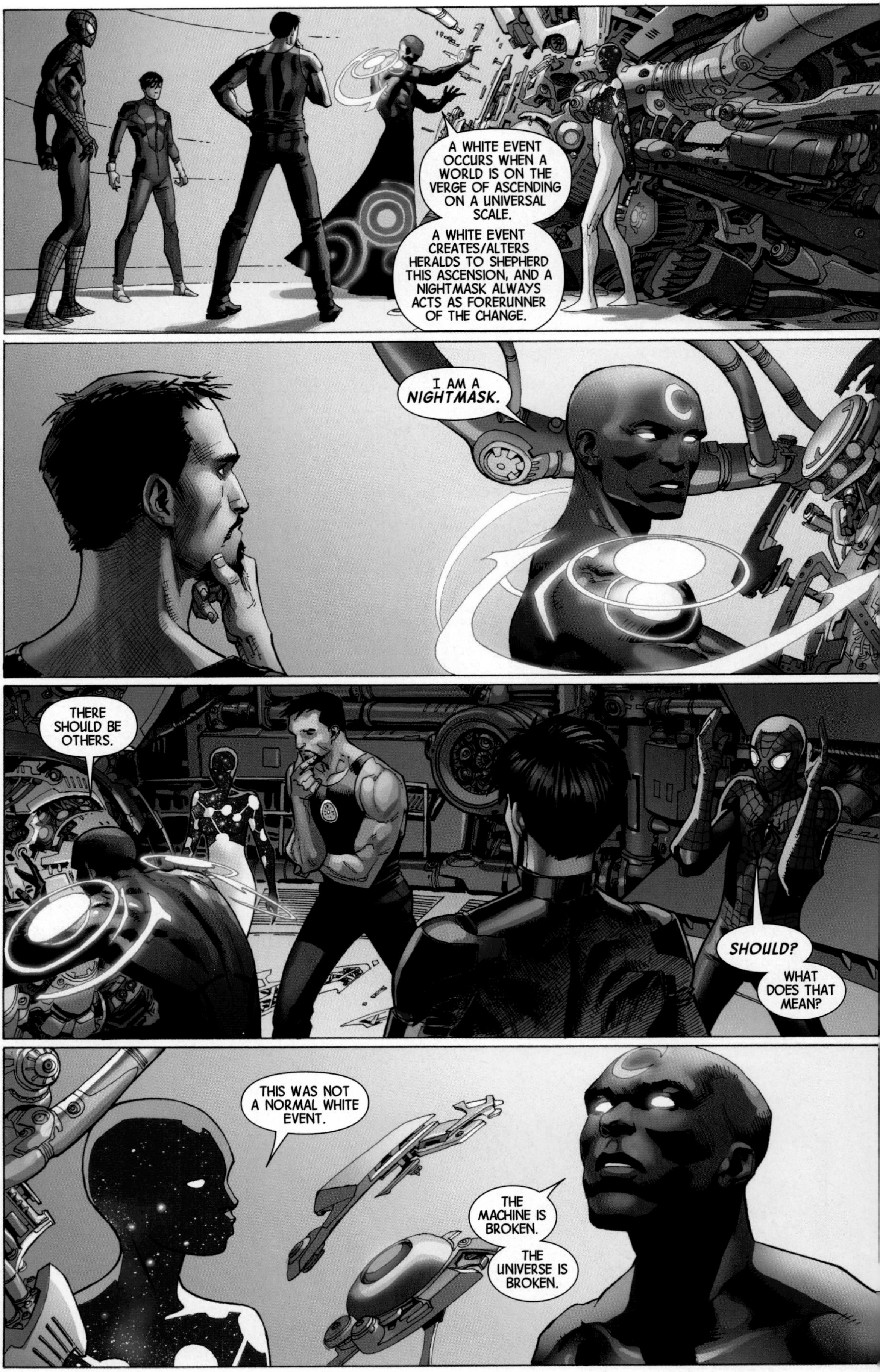
A WHITE EVENT OCCURS WHEN A WORLD IS ON THE VERGE OF ASCENDING ON A UNIVERSAL SCALE.
A WHITE EVENT CREATES/ALTERS HERALDS TO SHEPHERD THIS ASCENSION, AND A NIGHTMASK ALWAYS ACTS AS FORERUNNER OF THE CHANGE.
I AM A *NIGHTMASK.*
THERE SHOULD BE OTHERS.
SHOULD?
WHAT DOES THAT MEAN?
THIS WAS NOT A NORMAL WHITE EVENT.
THE MACHINE IS BROKEN.
THE UNIVERSE IS BROKEN.

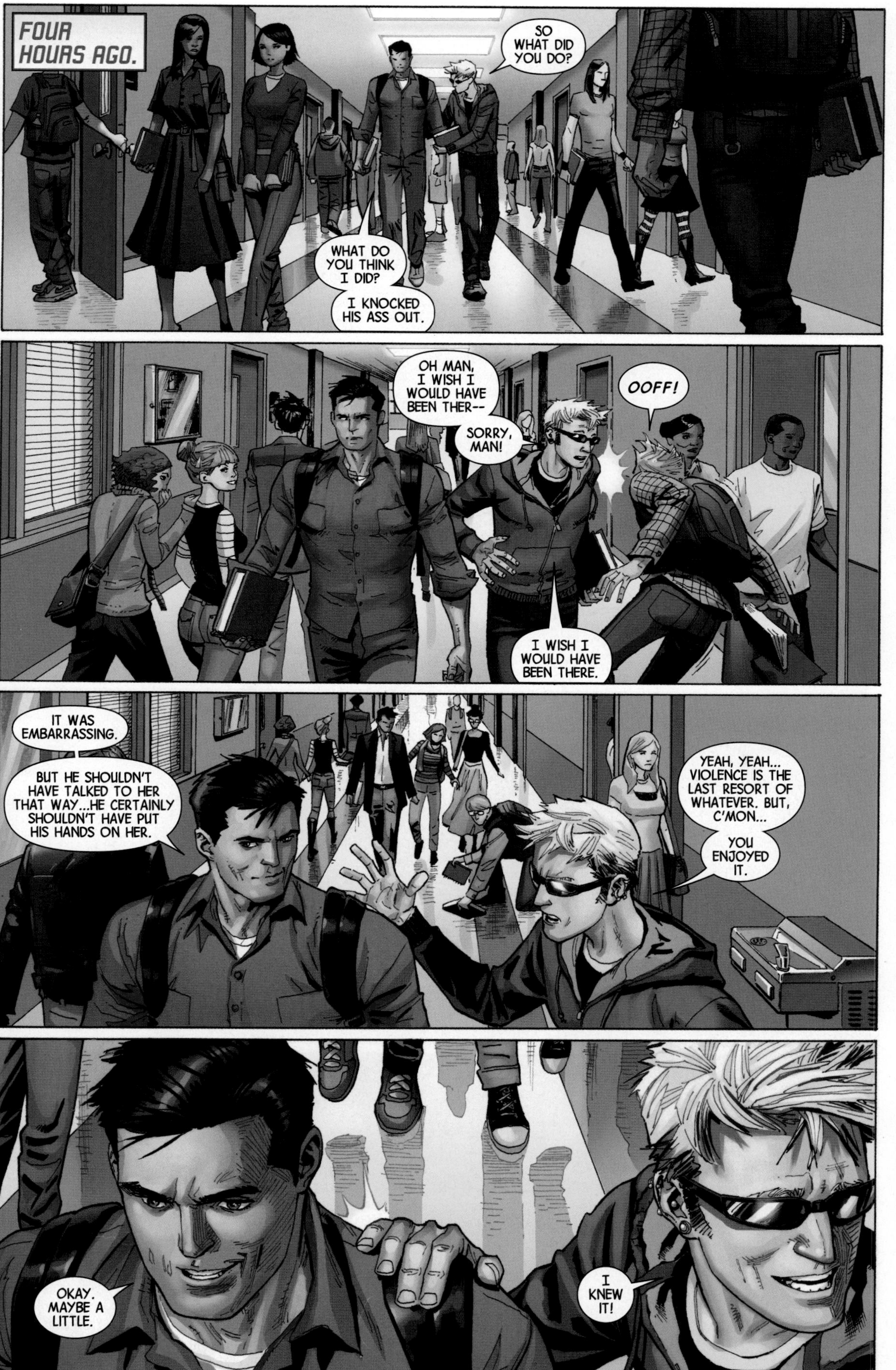
FOUR HOURS AGO.
SO WHAT DID YOU DO?
WHAT DO YOU THINK I DID?
I KNOCKED HIS ASS OUT.
OH MAN, I WISH I WOULD HAVE BEEN THER--
SORRY, MAN!
OOFF!
I WISH I WOULD HAVE BEEN THERE.
IT WAS EMBARRASSING.
BUT HE SHOULDN'T HAVE TALKED TO HER THAT WAY...HE CERTAINLY SHOULDN'T HAVE PUT HIS HANDS ON HER.
YEAH, YEAH... VIOLENCE IS THE LAST RESORT OF WHATEVER. BUT, C'MON...
YOU ENJOYED IT.
OKAY. MAYBE A LITTLE.
I KNEW IT!

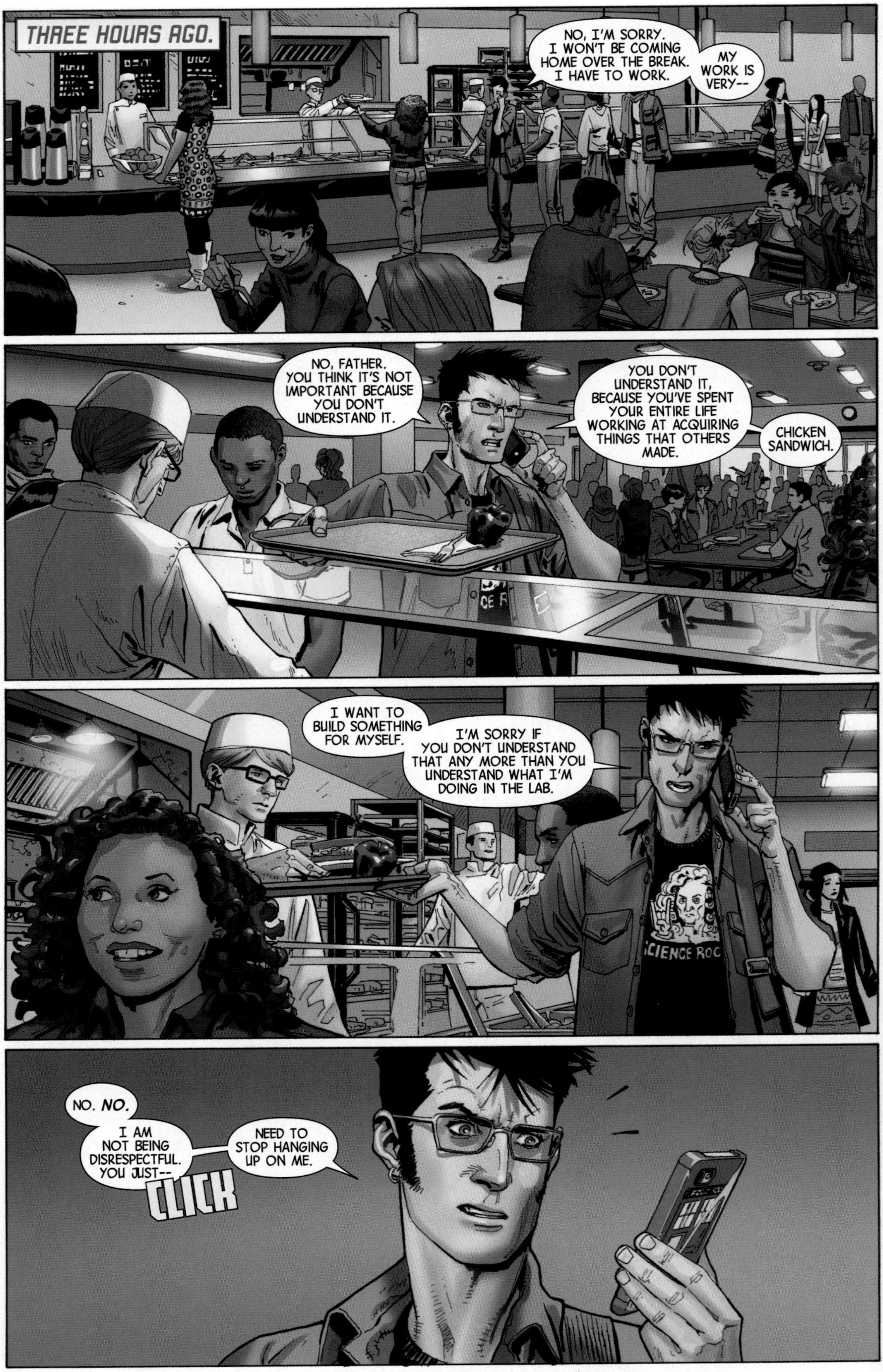
THREE HOURS AGO.
NO, I'M SORRY. I WON'T BE COMING HOME OVER THE BREAK. I HAVE TO WORK.
MY WORK IS VERY--
NO, FATHER. YOU THINK IT'S NOT IMPORTANT BECAUSE YOU DON'T UNDERSTAND IT.
YOU DON'T UNDERSTAND IT, BECAUSE YOU'VE SPENT YOUR ENTIRE LIFE WORKING AT ACQUIRING THINGS THAT OTHERS MADE.
CHICKEN SANDWICH.
I WANT TO BUILD SOMETHING FOR MYSELF.
I'M SORRY IF YOU DON'T UNDERSTAND THAT ANY MORE THAN YOU UNDERSTAND WHAT I'M DOING IN THE LAB.
SCIENCE ROC
NO. NO.
I AM NOT BEING DISRESPECTFUL. YOU JUST--
CLICK
NEED TO STOP HANGING UP ON ME.

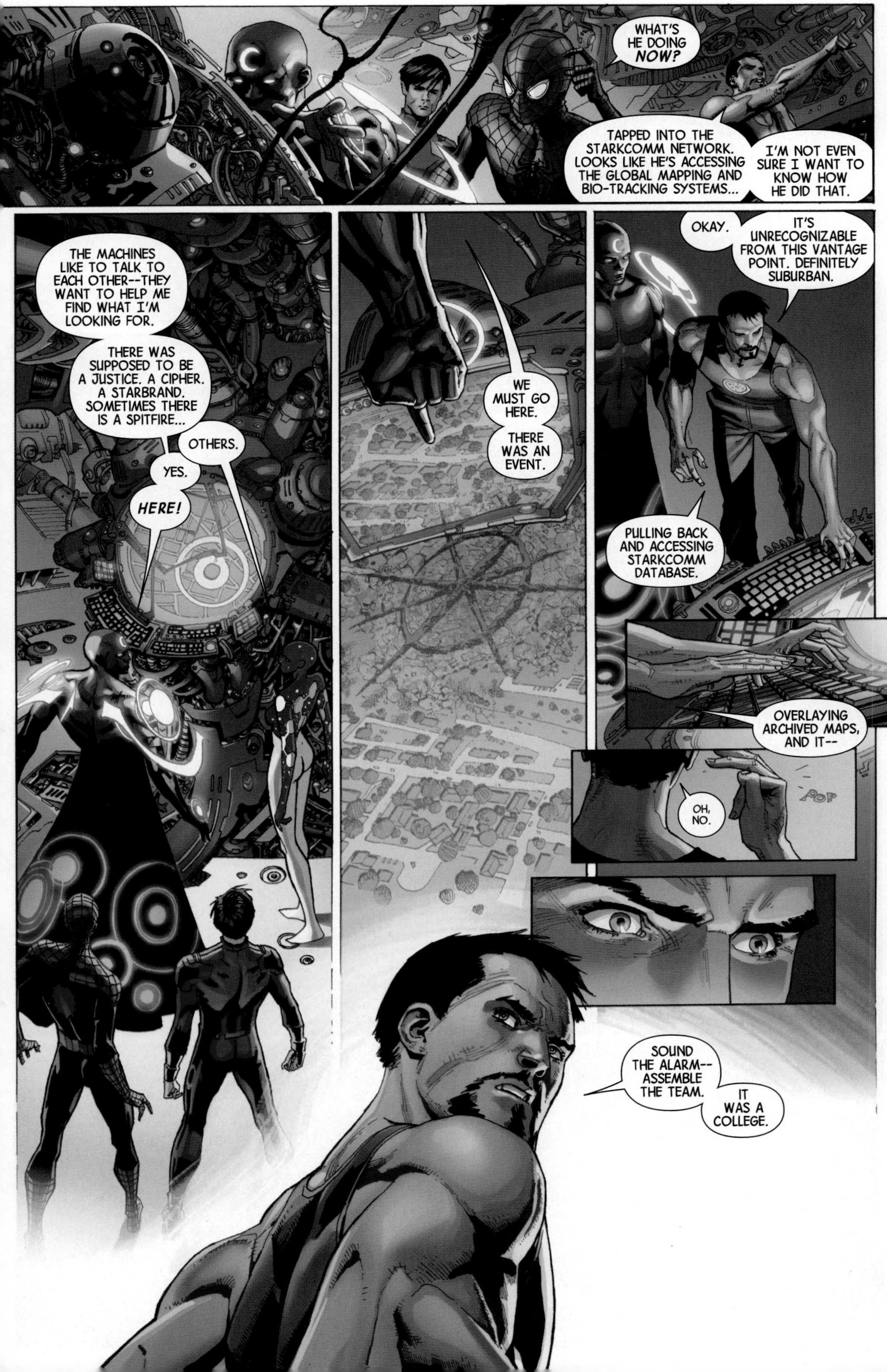
WHAT'S HE DOING *NOW?*
TAPPED INTO THE STARKCOMM NETWORK. LOOKS LIKE HE'S ACCESSING THE GLOBAL MAPPING AND BIO-TRACKING SYSTEMS...
I'M NOT EVEN SURE I WANT TO KNOW HOW HE DID THAT.
THE MACHINES LIKE TO TALK TO EACH OTHER--THEY WANT TO HELP ME FIND WHAT I'M LOOKING FOR.
THERE WAS SUPPOSED TO BE A JUSTICE. A CIPHER. A STARBRAND. SOMETIMES THERE IS A SPITFIRE...
OTHERS.
YES.
HERE!
WE MUST GO HERE.
THERE WAS AN EVENT.
OKAY.
IT'S UNRECOGNIZABLE FROM THIS VANTAGE POINT. DEFINITELY SUBURBAN.
PULLING BACK AND ACCESSING STARKCOMM DATABASE.
OVERLAYING ARCHIVED MAPS, AND IT--
OH, NO.
POP
SOUND THE ALARM-- ASSEMBLE THE TEAM.
IT WAS A COLLEGE.

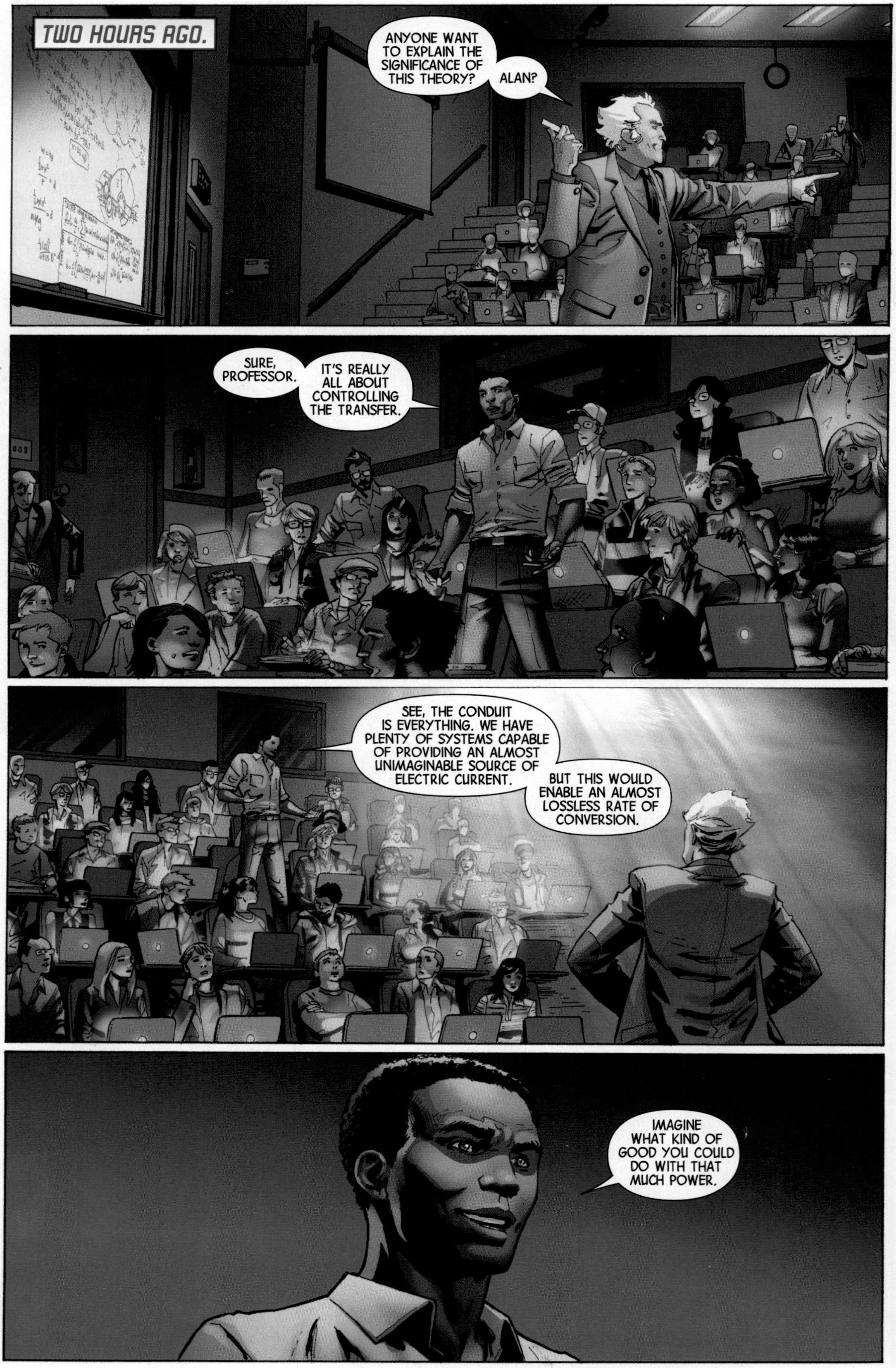
TWO HOURS AGO.
ANYONE WANT TO EXPLAIN THE SIGNIFICANCE OF THIS THEORY?
ALAN?
SURE, PROFESSOR.
IT'S REALLY ALL ABOUT CONTROLLING THE TRANSFER.
SEE, THE CONDUIT IS EVERYTHING. WE HAVE PLENTY OF SYSTEMS CAPABLE OF PROVIDING AN ALMOST UNIMAGINABLE SOURCE OF ELECTRIC CURRENT.
BUT THIS WOULD ENABLE AN ALMOST LOSSLESS RATE OF CONVERSION.
IMAGINE WHAT KIND OF GOOD YOU COULD DO WITH THAT MUCH POWER.

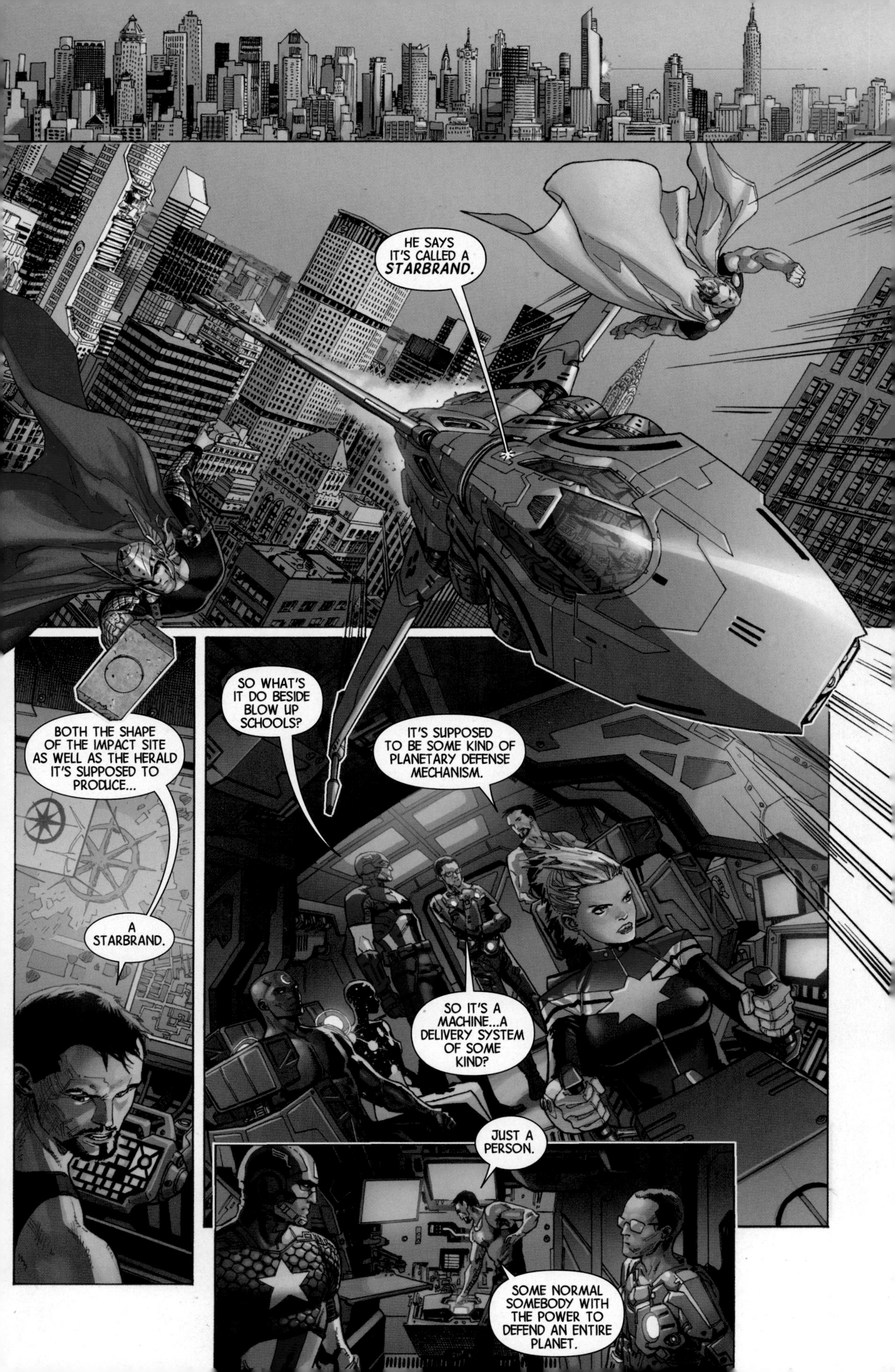
HE SAYS IT'S CALLED A STARBRAND.
BOTH THE SHAPE OF THE IMPACT SITE AS WELL AS THE HERALD IT'S SUPPOSED TO PRODUCE...
A STARBRAND.
SO WHAT'S IT DO BESIDE BLOW UP SCHOOLS?
IT'S SUPPOSED TO BE SOME KIND OF PLANETARY DEFENSE MECHANISM.
SO IT'S A MACHINE...A DELIVERY SYSTEM OF SOME KIND?
JUST A PERSON.
SOME NORMAL SOMEBODY WITH THE POWER TO DEFEND AN ENTIRE PLANET.

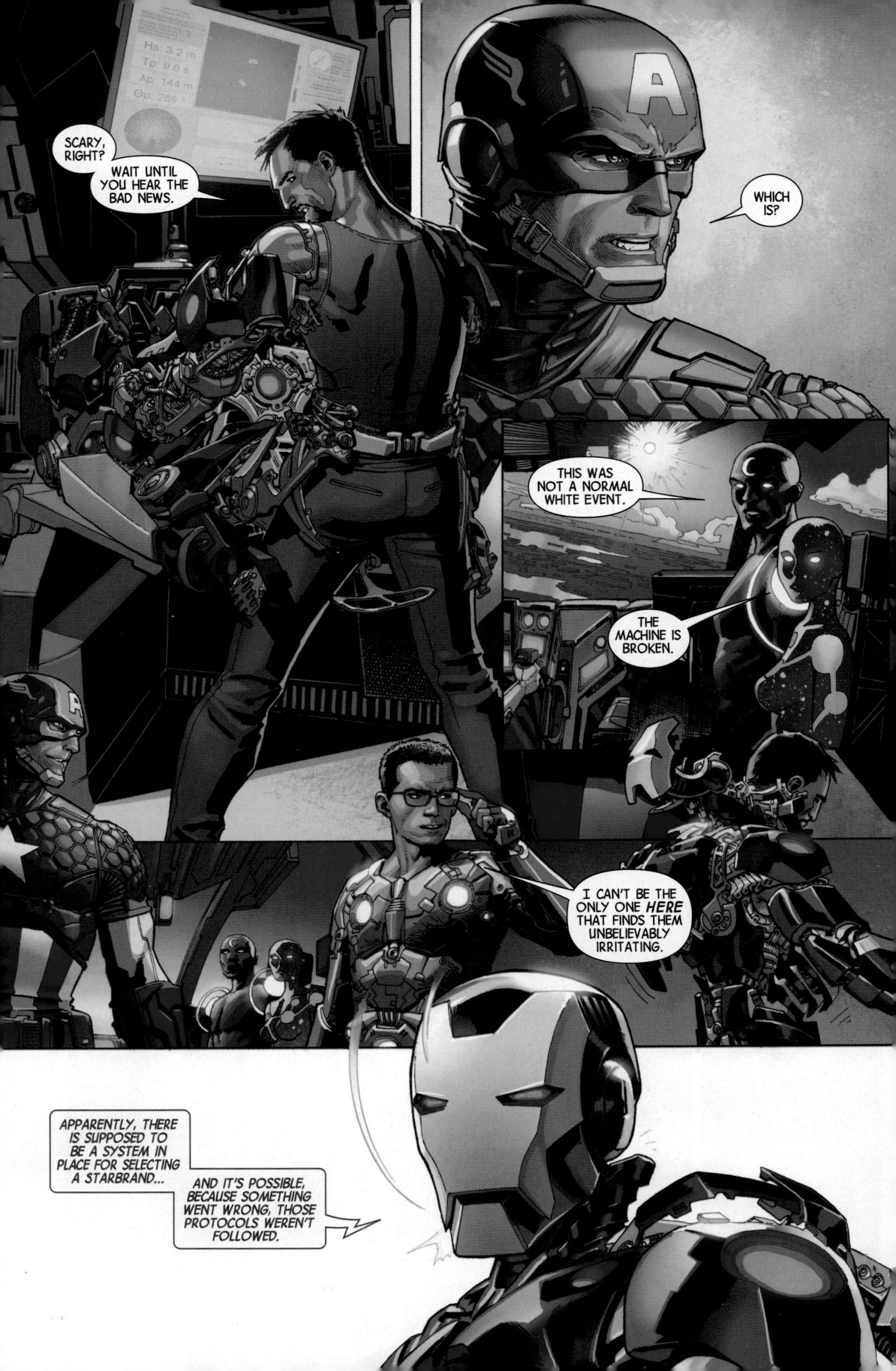
SCARY, RIGHT?
WAIT UNTIL YOU HEAR THE BAD NEWS.
WHICH IS?
THIS WAS NOT A NORMAL WHITE EVENT.
THE MACHINE IS BROKEN.
I CAN'T BE THE ONLY ONE *HERE* THAT FINDS THEM UNBELIEVABLY IRRITATING.
APPARENTLY, THERE IS SUPPOSED TO BE A SYSTEM IN PLACE FOR SELECTING A STARBRAND...
AND IT'S POSSIBLE, BECAUSE SOMETHING WENT WRONG, THOSE PROTOCOLS WEREN'T FOLLOWED.

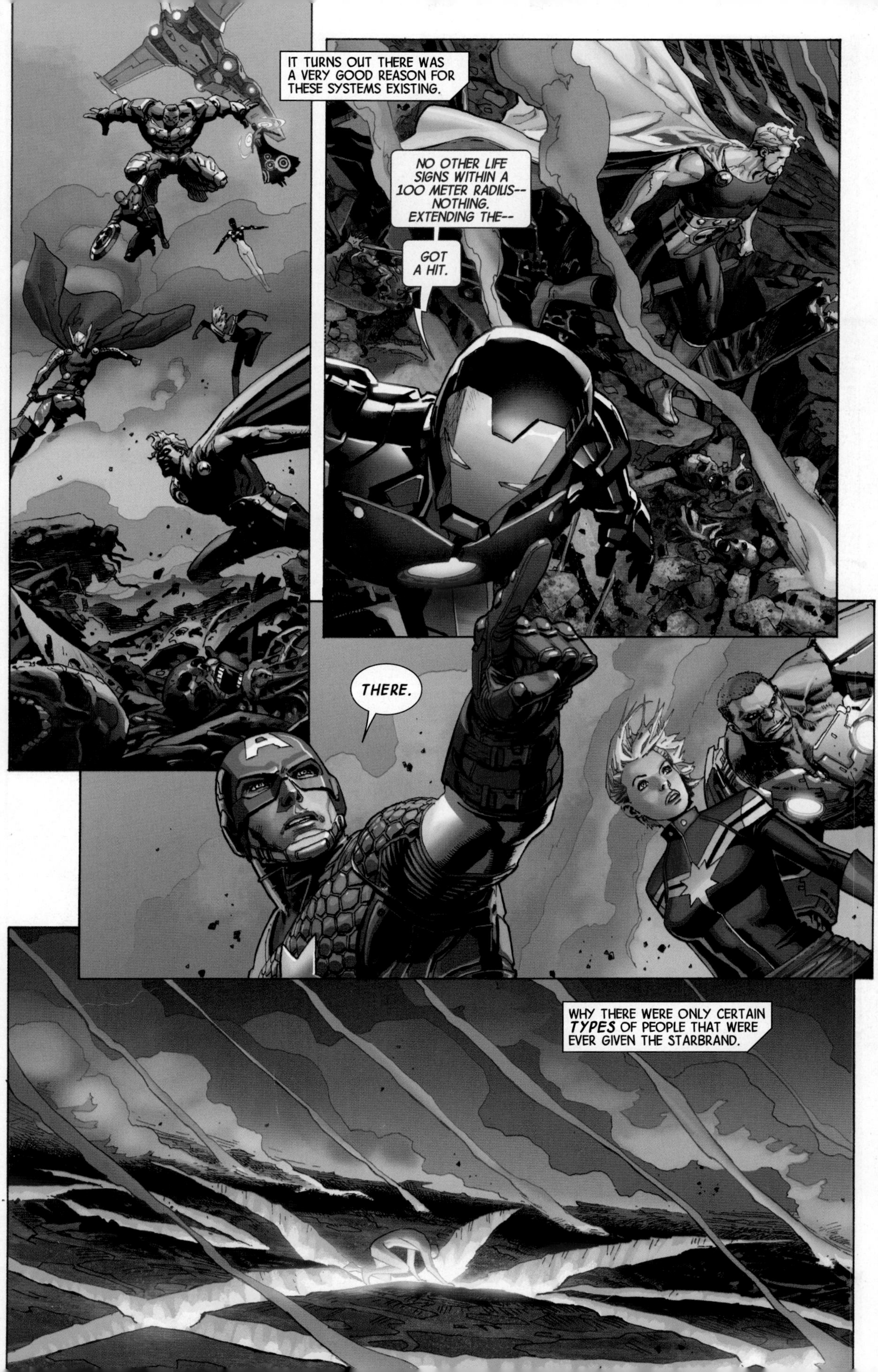
IT TURNS OUT THERE WAS A VERY GOOD REASON FOR THESE SYSTEMS EXISTING.
NO OTHER LIFE SIGNS WITHIN A 100 METER RADIUS-- NOTHING. EXTENDING THE--
GOT A HIT.
THERE.
WHY THERE WERE ONLY CERTAIN *TYPES* OF PEOPLE THAT WERE EVER GIVEN THE STARBRAND.

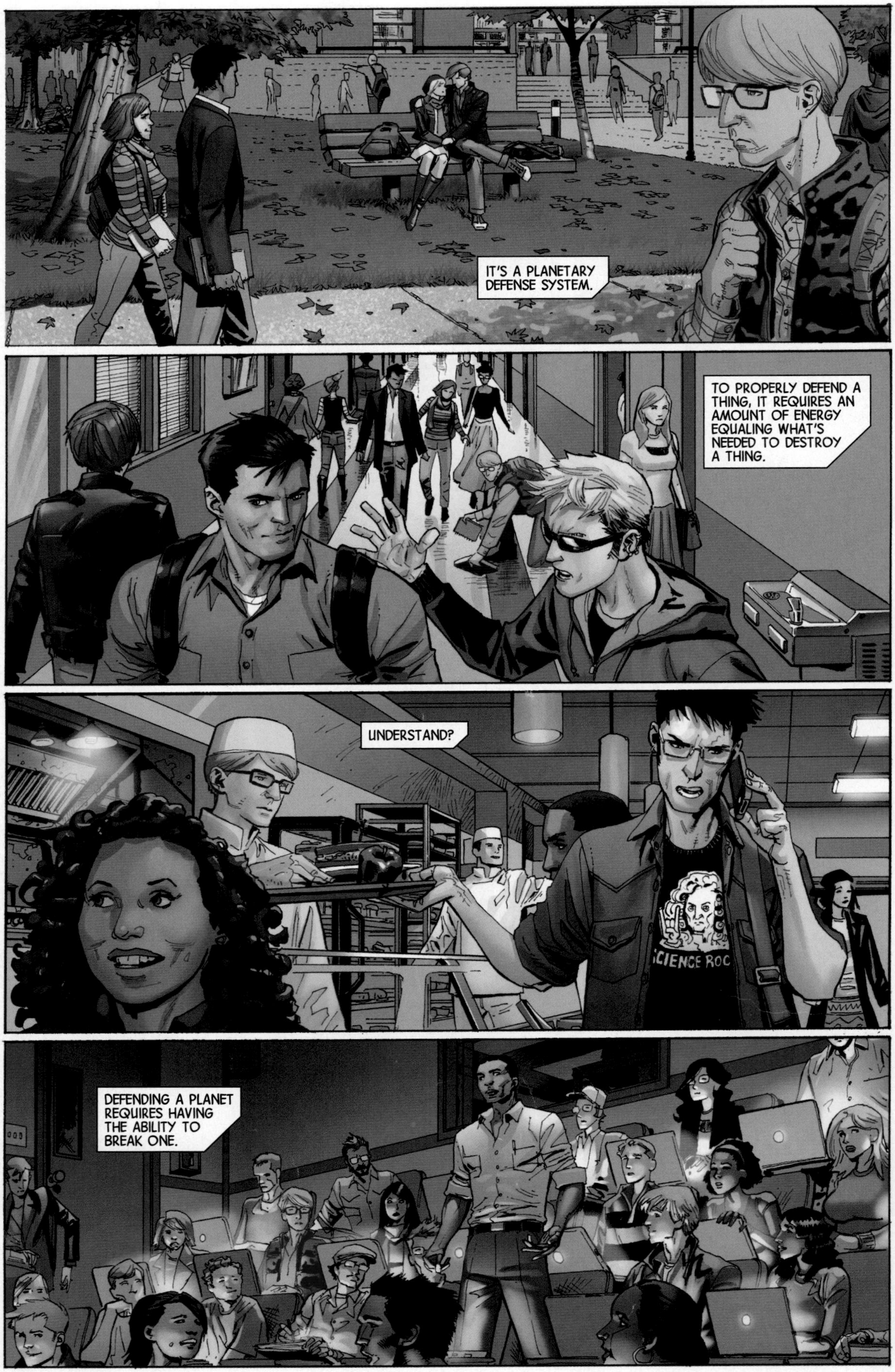
IT'S A PLANETARY DEFENSE SYSTEM.
TO PROPERLY DEFEND A THING, IT REQUIRES AN AMOUNT OF ENERGY EQUALING WHAT'S NEEDED TO DESTROY A THING.
UNDERSTAND?
SCIENCE ROC
DEFENDING A PLANET REQUIRES HAVING THE ABILITY TO BREAK ONE.

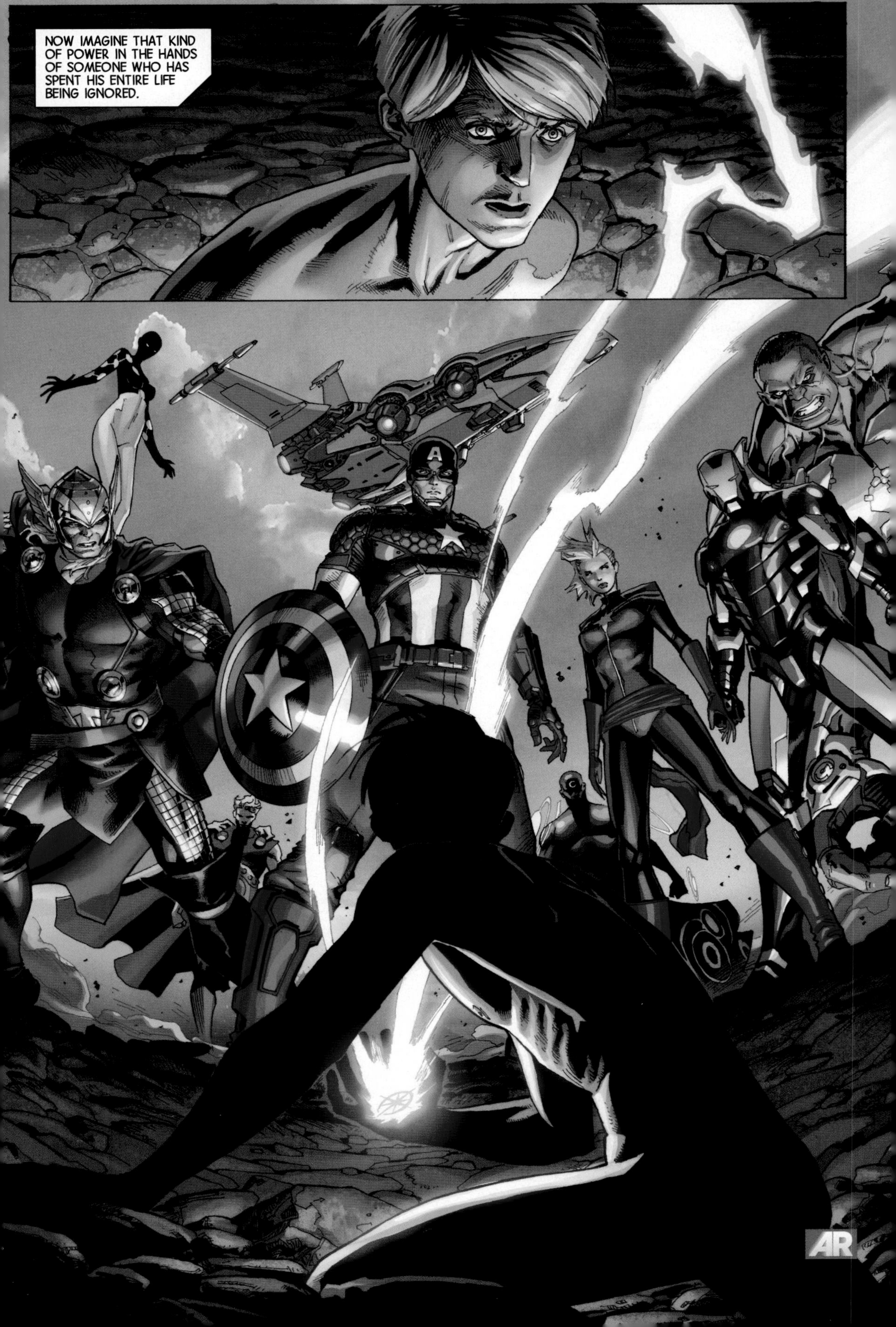
NOW IMAGINE THAT KIND OF POWER IN THE HANDS OF SOMEONE WHO HAS SPENT HIS ENTIRE LIFE BEING IGNORED.

"STARBRANDED"

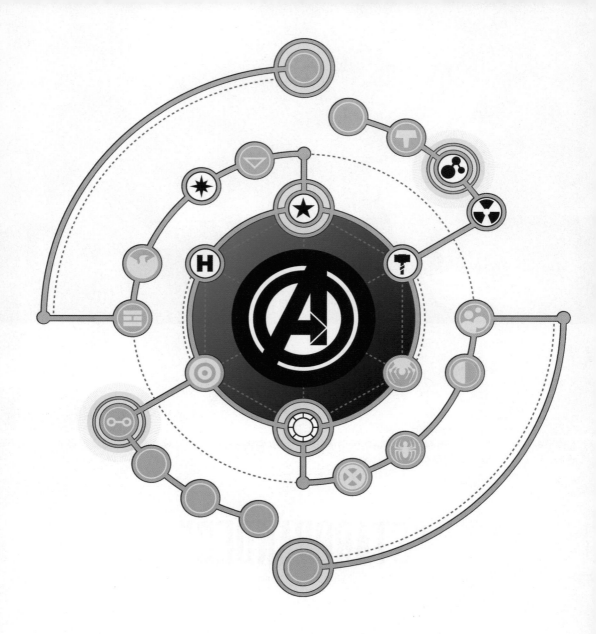

EARTH'S MIGHTIEST HEROES

CAPTAIN AMERICA · IRON MAN · THOR · HAWKEYE · BLACK WIDOW · HULK
WOLVERINE · SPIDER-MAN · CAPTAIN MARVEL · SPIDER-WOMAN
FALCON · SHANG-CHI · SUNSPOT · CANNONBALL · MANIFOLD
SMASHER · CAPTAIN UNIVERSE · HYPERION

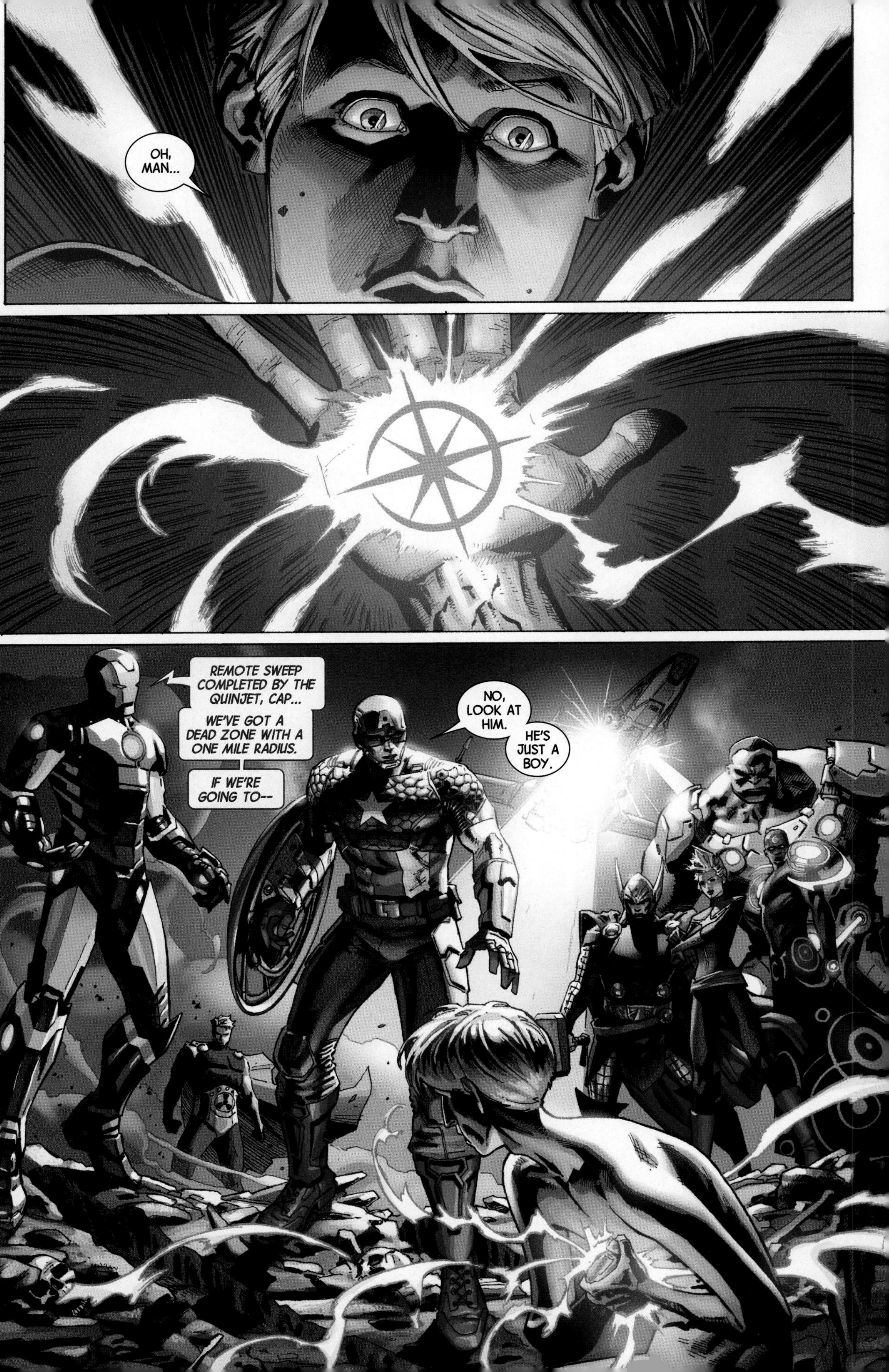
OH, MAN...
REMOTE SWEEP COMPLETED BY THE QUINJET, CAP...
WE'VE GOT A DEAD ZONE WITH A ONE MILE RADIUS.
IF WE'RE GOING TO--
NO, LOOK AT HIM.
HE'S JUST A BOY.

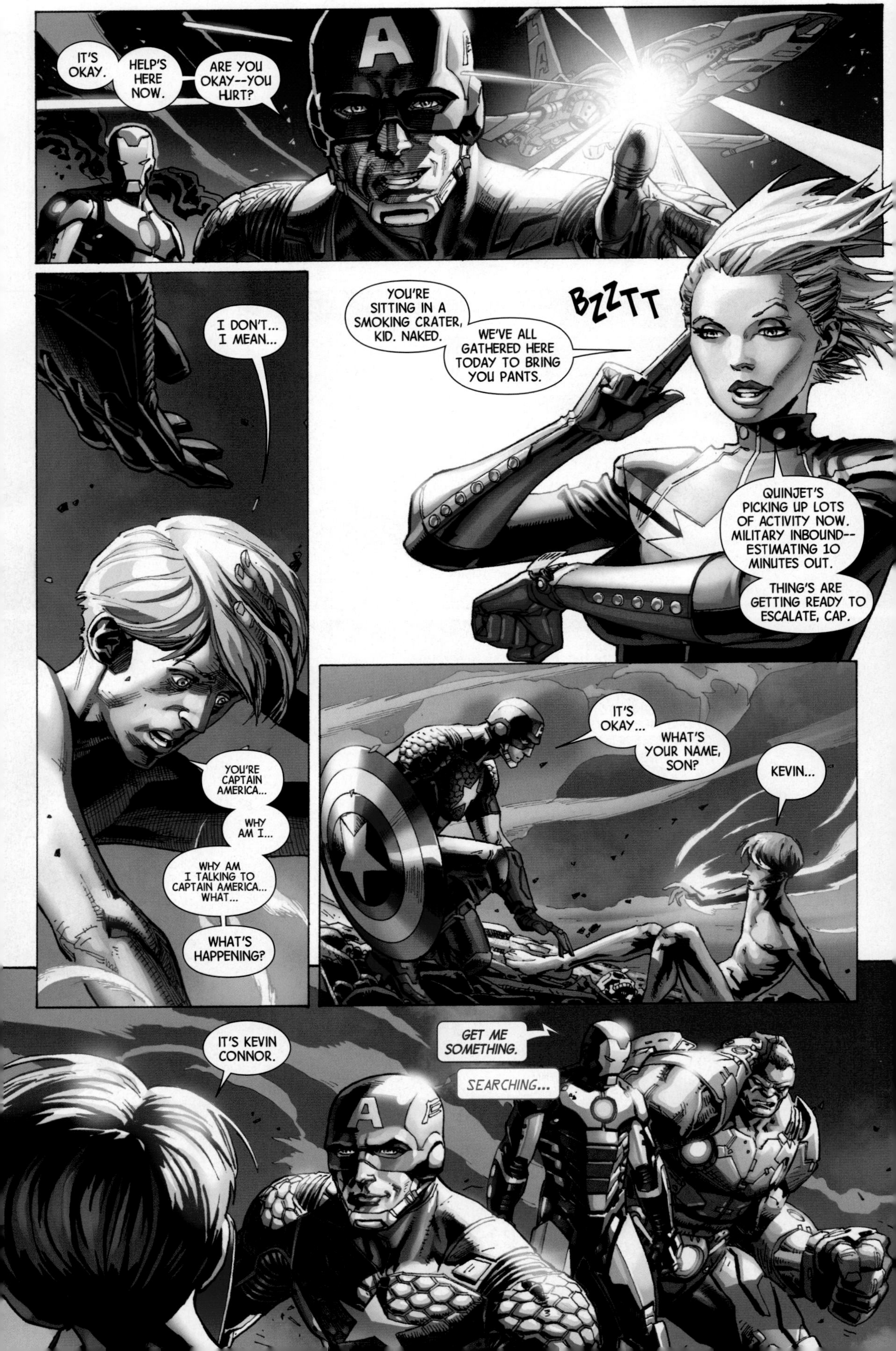
IT'S OKAY.
HELP'S HERE NOW.
ARE YOU OKAY--YOU HURT?
I DON'T... I MEAN...
YOU'RE SITTING IN A SMOKING CRATER, KID. NAKED.
WE'VE ALL GATHERED HERE TODAY TO BRING YOU PANTS.
BZZTT
QUINJET'S PICKING UP LOTS OF ACTIVITY NOW. MILITARY INBOUND--ESTIMATING 10 MINUTES OUT.
THING'S ARE GETTING READY TO ESCALATE, CAP.
YOU'RE CAPTAIN AMERICA...
WHY AM I...
WHY AM I TALKING TO CAPTAIN AMERICA... WHAT...
WHAT'S HAPPENING?
IT'S OKAY...
WHAT'S YOUR NAME, SON?
KEVIN...
IT'S KEVIN CONNOR.
GET ME SOMETHING.
SEARCHING...

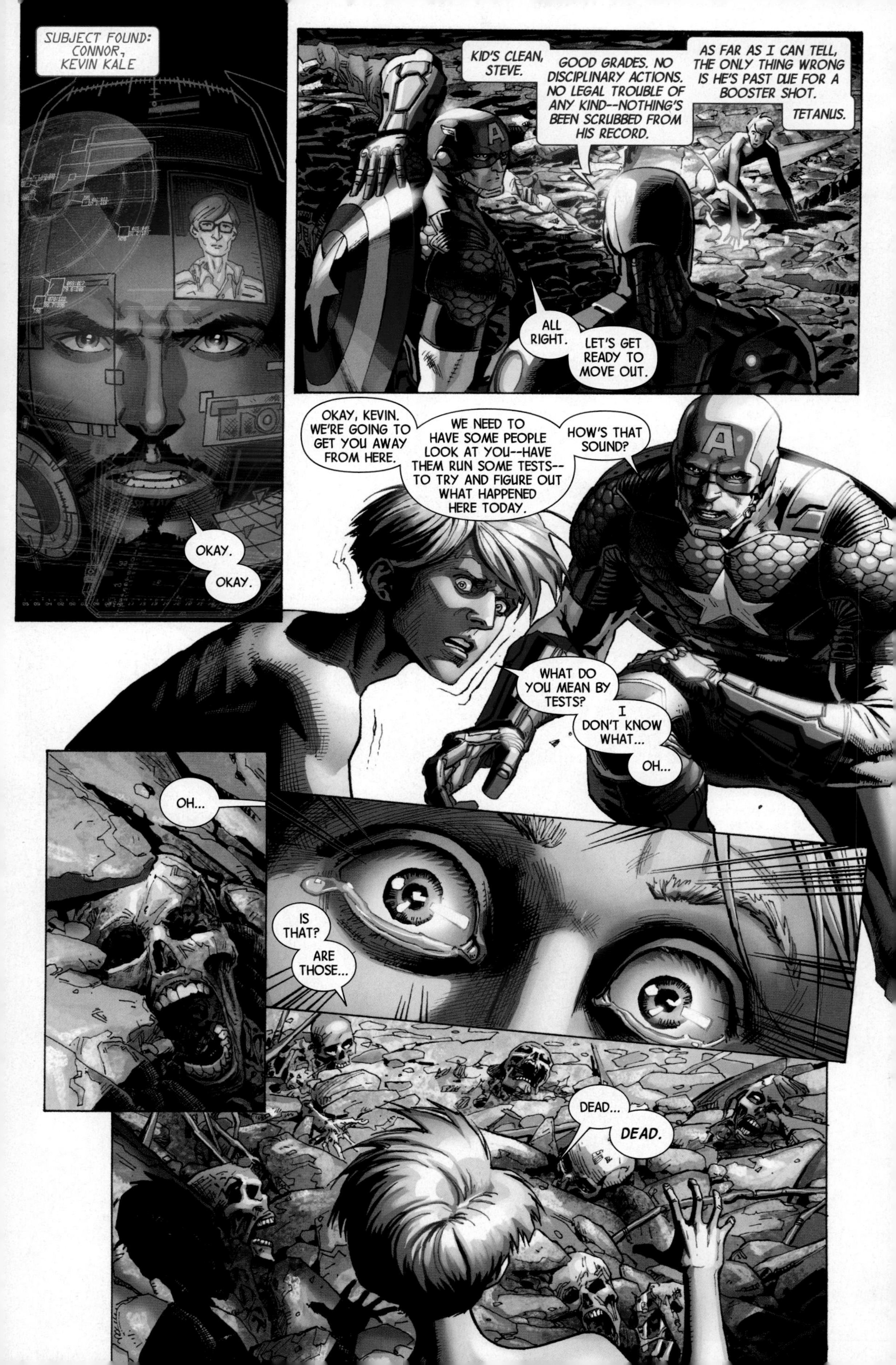

SUBJECT FOUND: CONNOR, KEVIN KALE
KID'S CLEAN, STEVE.
GOOD GRADES. NO DISCIPLINARY ACTIONS. NO LEGAL TROUBLE OF ANY KIND--NOTHING'S BEEN SCRUBBED FROM HIS RECORD.
AS FAR AS I CAN TELL, THE ONLY THING WRONG IS HE'S PAST DUE FOR A BOOSTER SHOT.
TETANUS.
ALL RIGHT.
LET'S GET READY TO MOVE OUT.
OKAY.
OKAY.
OKAY, KEVIN. WE'RE GOING TO GET YOU AWAY FROM HERE.
WE NEED TO HAVE SOME PEOPLE LOOK AT YOU--HAVE THEM RUN SOME TESTS--TO TRY AND FIGURE OUT WHAT HAPPENED HERE TODAY.
HOW'S THAT SOUND?
WHAT DO YOU MEAN BY TESTS?
I DON'T KNOW WHAT...
OH...
OH...
IS THAT?
ARE THOSE...
DEAD...
DEAD.

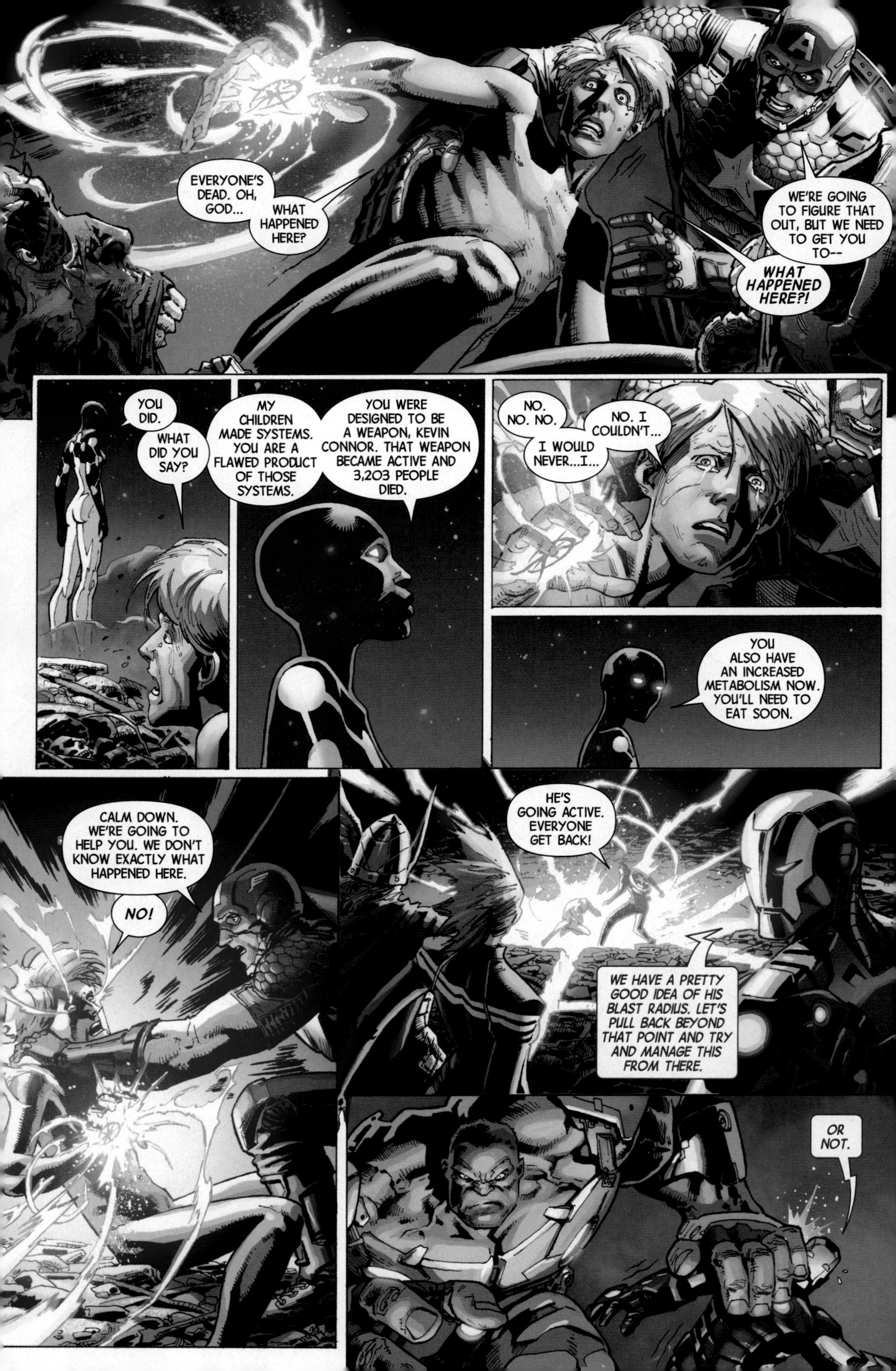

EVERYONE'S DEAD. OH, GOD...
WHAT HAPPENED HERE?
WE'RE GOING TO FIGURE THAT OUT, BUT WE NEED TO GET YOU TO--
WHAT HAPPENED HERE?!
YOU DID.
WHAT DID YOU SAY?
MY CHILDREN MADE SYSTEMS. YOU ARE A FLAWED PRODUCT OF THOSE SYSTEMS.
YOU WERE DESIGNED TO BE A WEAPON, KEVIN CONNOR. THAT WEAPON BECAME ACTIVE AND 3,203 PEOPLE DIED.
NO. NO. NO.
NO. I COULDN'T...
I WOULD NEVER...I...
YOU ALSO HAVE AN INCREASED METABOLISM NOW. YOU'LL NEED TO EAT SOON.
CALM DOWN. WE'RE GOING TO HELP YOU. WE DON'T KNOW EXACTLY WHAT HAPPENED HERE.
NO!
HE'S GOING ACTIVE. EVERYONE GET BACK!
WE HAVE A PRETTY GOOD IDEA OF HIS BLAST RADIUS. LET'S PULL BACK BEYOND THAT POINT AND TRY AND MANAGE THIS FROM THERE.
OR NOT.

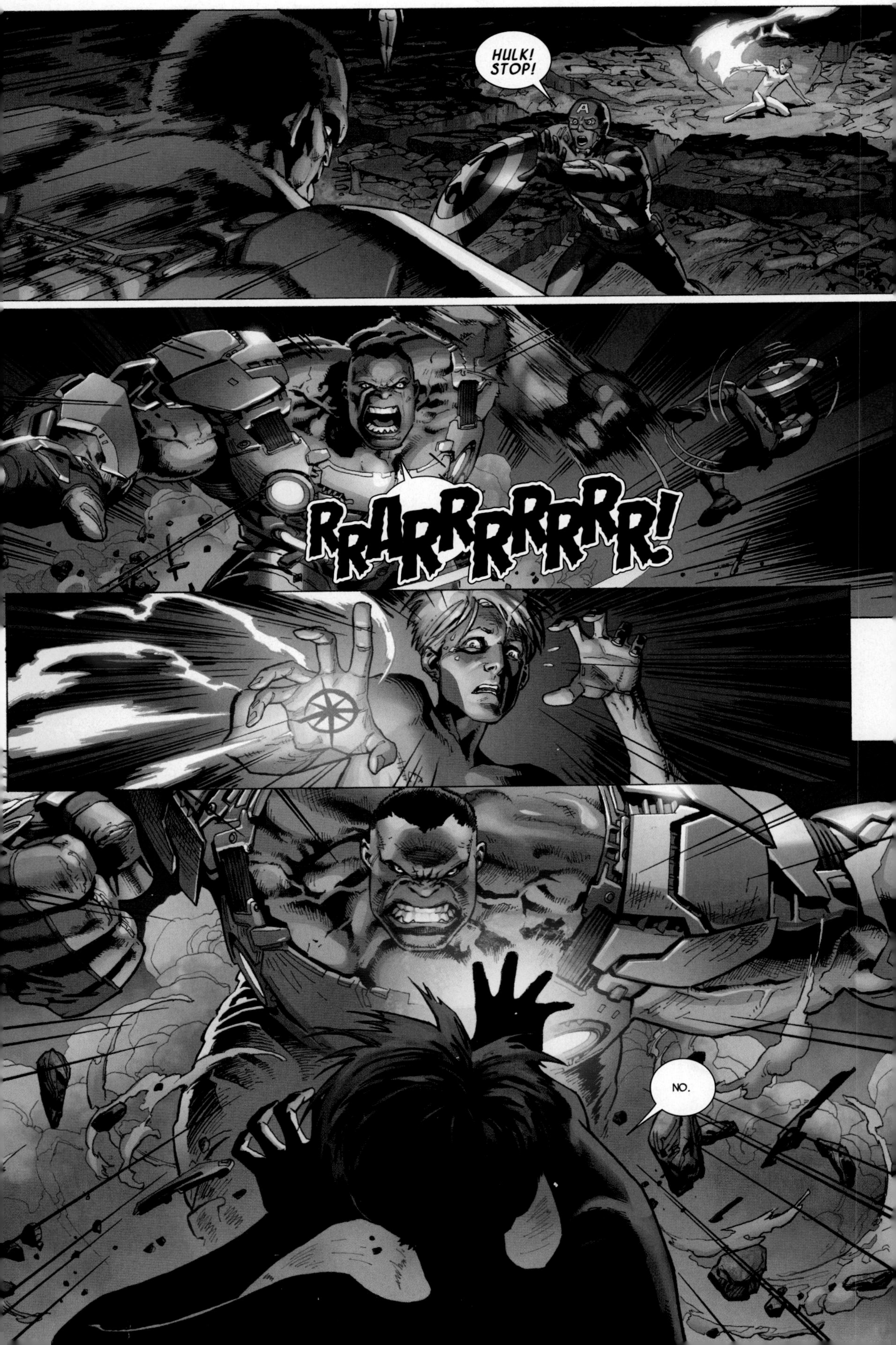
HULK! STOP!
RRARRRRRRR!
NO.

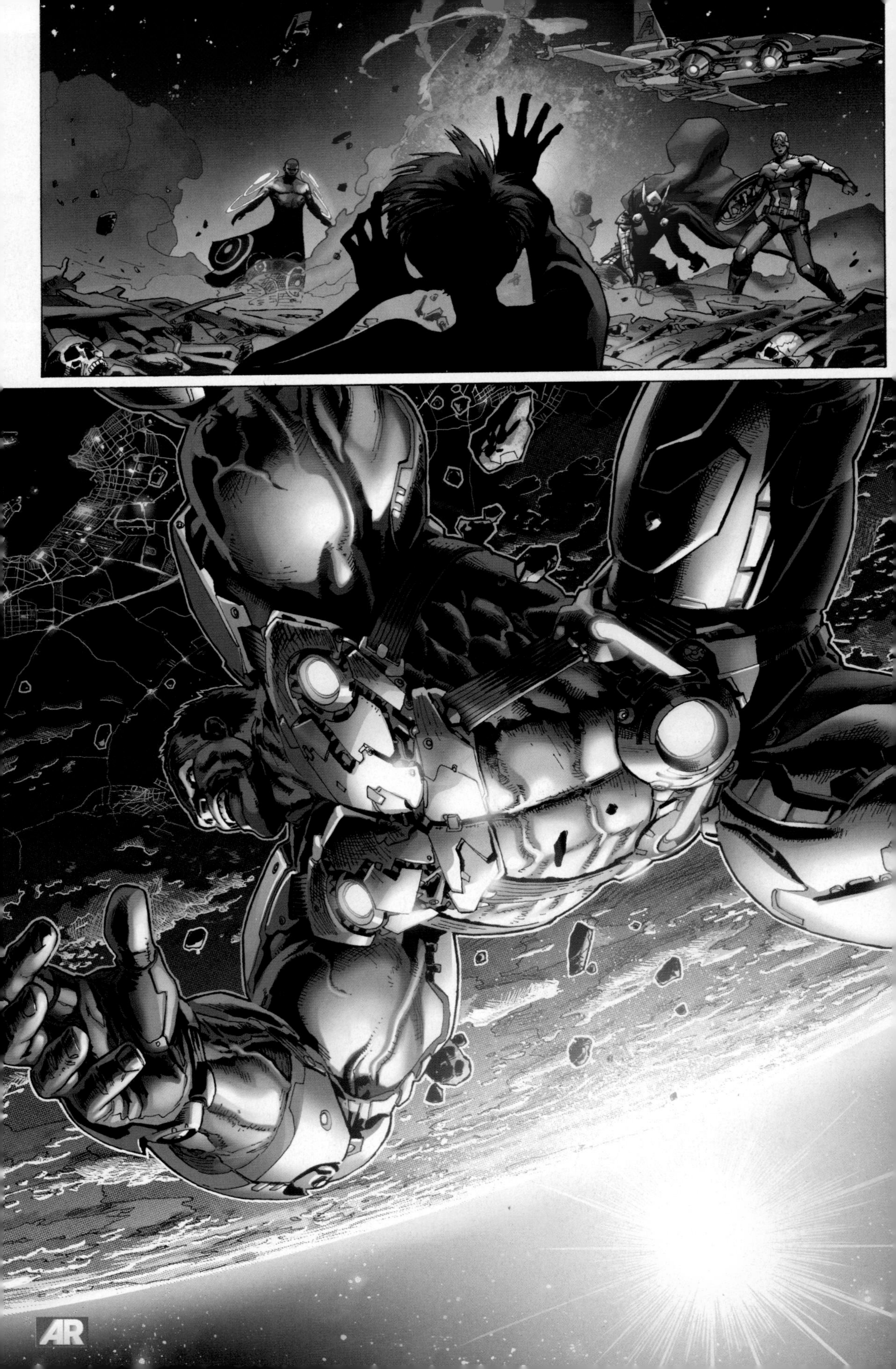

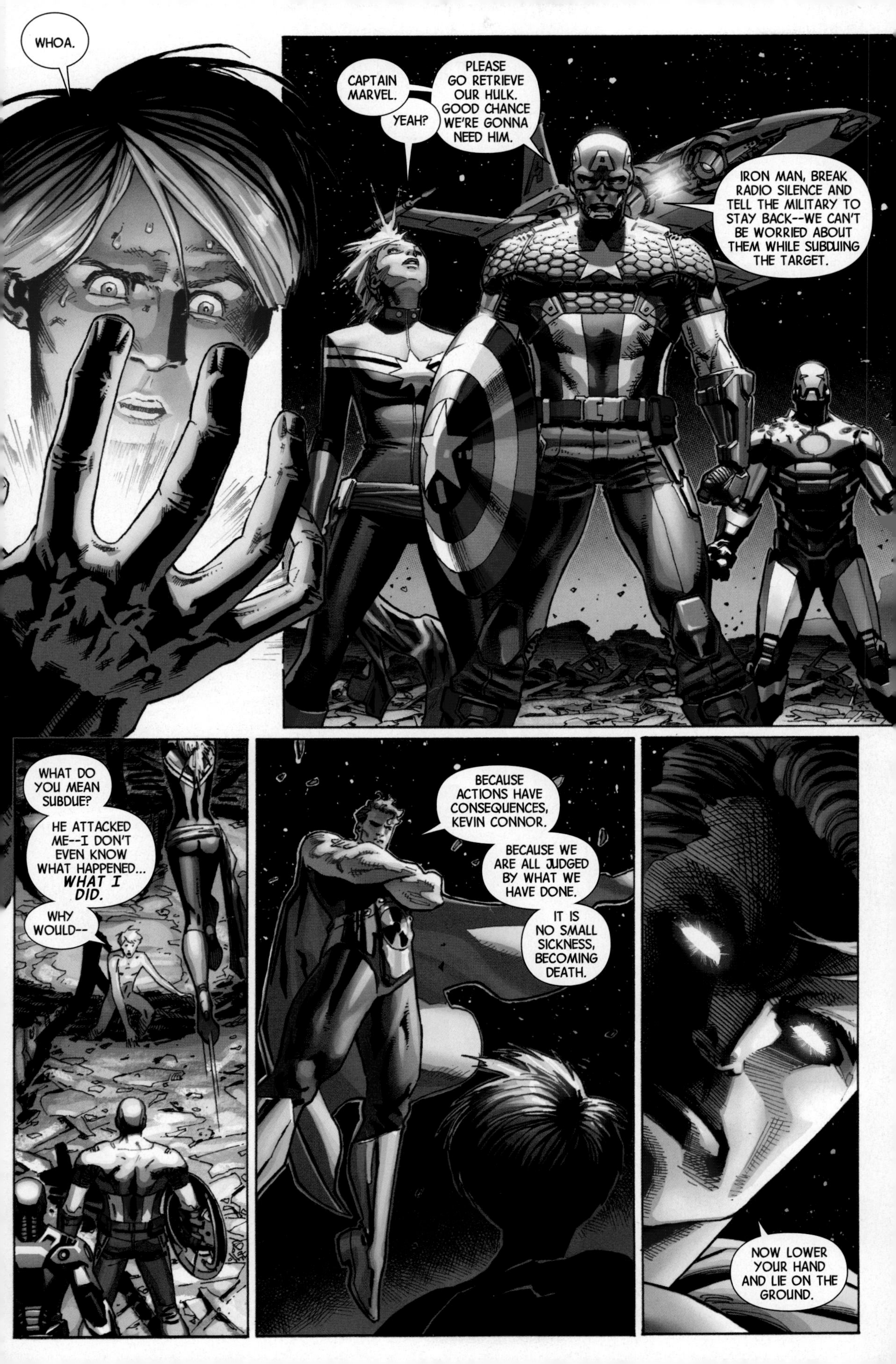
WHOA.
CAPTAIN MARVEL.
YEAH?
PLEASE GO RETRIEVE OUR HULK. GOOD CHANCE WE'RE GONNA NEED HIM.
IRON MAN, BREAK RADIO SILENCE AND TELL THE MILITARY TO STAY BACK--WE CAN'T BE WORRIED ABOUT THEM WHILE SUBDUING THE TARGET.
WHAT DO YOU MEAN SUBDUE?
HE ATTACKED ME--I DON'T EVEN KNOW WHAT HAPPENED... WHAT I DID.
WHY WOULD--
BECAUSE ACTIONS HAVE CONSEQUENCES, KEVIN CONNOR.
BECAUSE WE ARE ALL JUDGED BY WHAT WE HAVE DONE.
IT IS NO SMALL SICKNESS, BECOMING DEATH.
NOW LOWER YOUR HAND AND LIE ON THE GROUND.

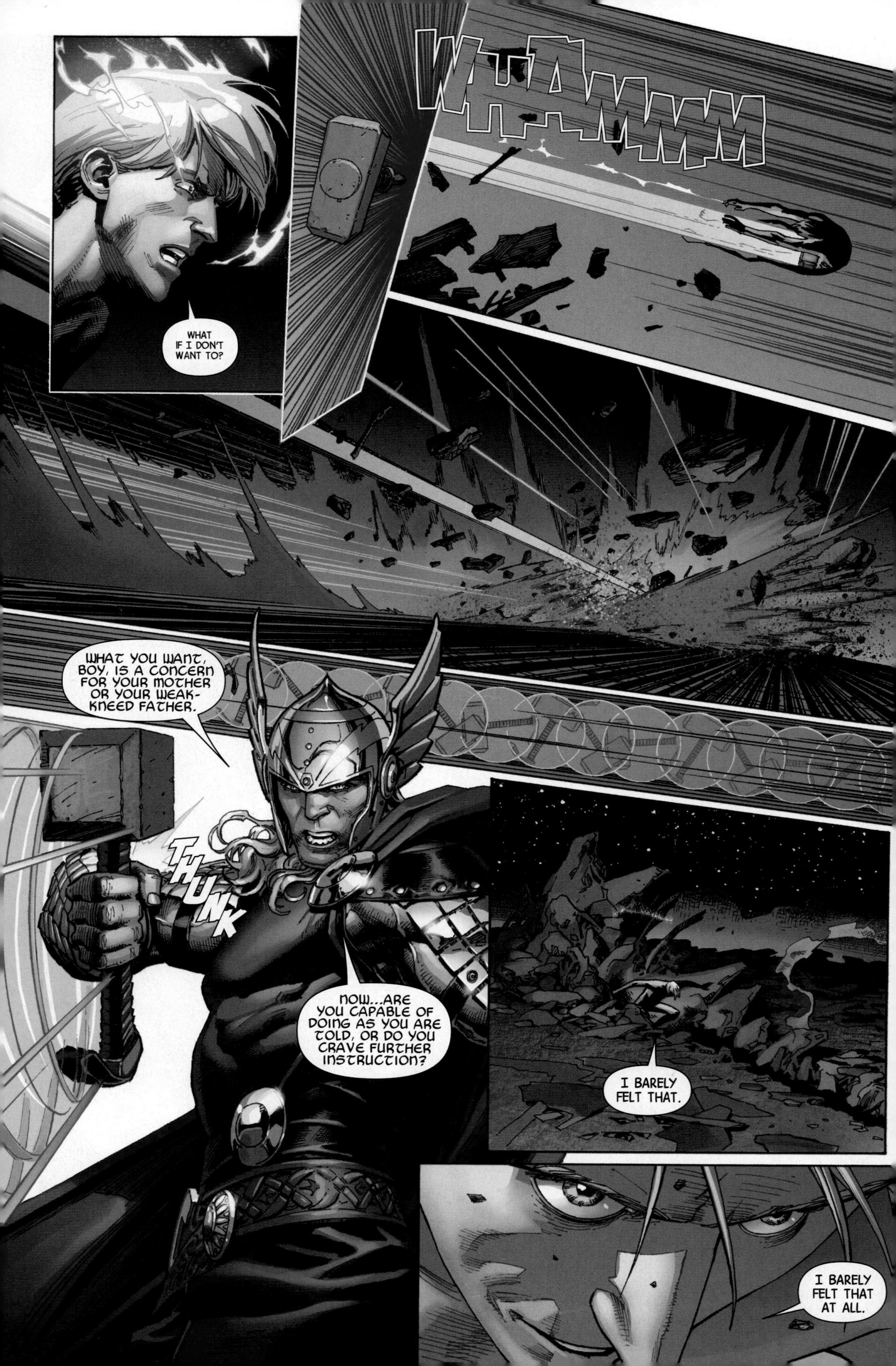
WHAT IF I DON'T WANT TO?
WHAMMM
WHAT YOU WANT, BOY, IS A CONCERN FOR YOUR MOTHER OR YOUR WEAK-KNEED FATHER.
THUNK
NOW...ARE YOU CAPABLE OF DOING AS YOU ARE TOLD, OR DO YOU CRAVE FURTHER INSTRUCTION?
I BARELY FELT THAT.
I BARELY FELT THAT AT ALL.

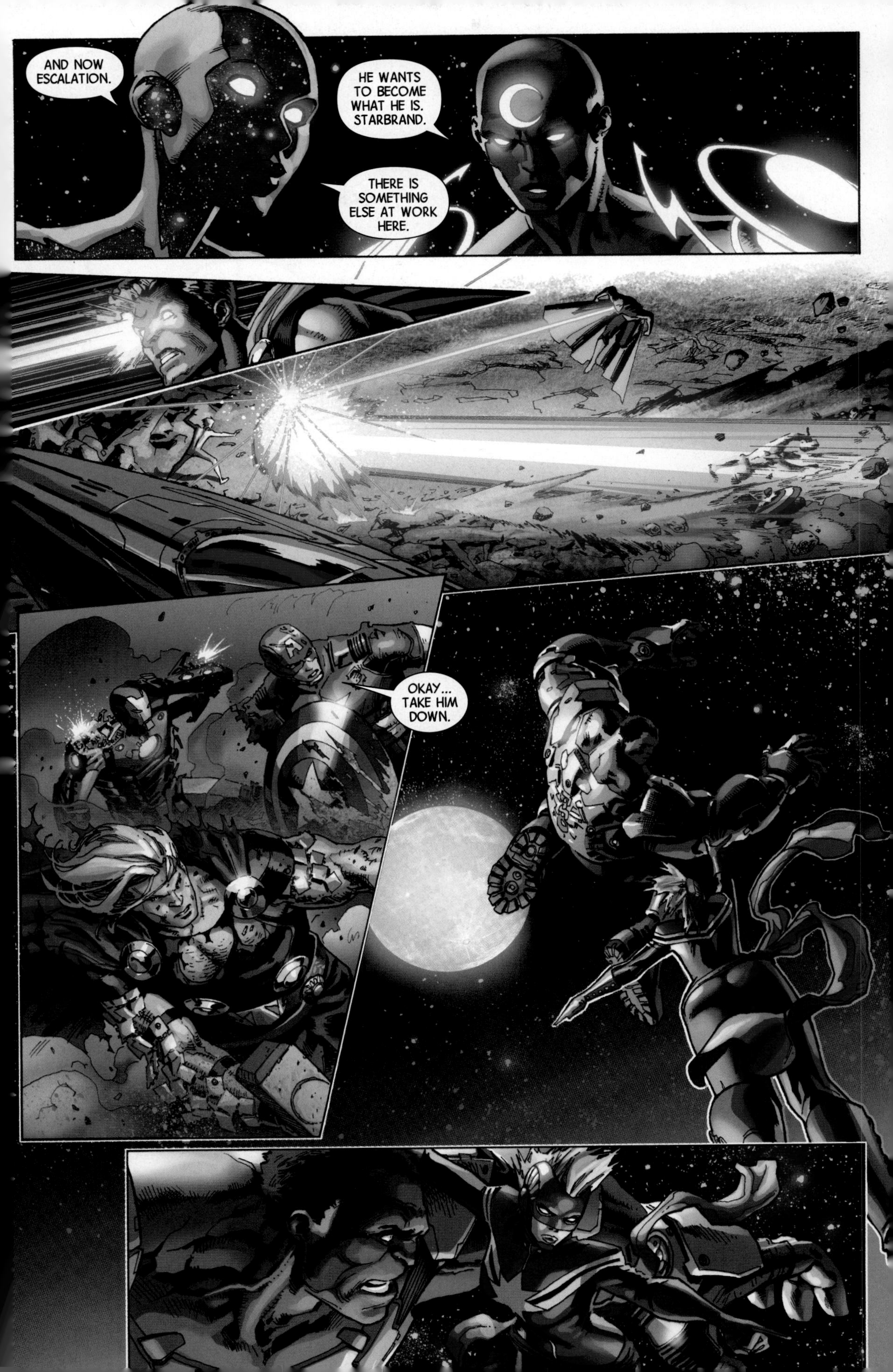
AND NOW ESCALATION.
HE WANTS TO BECOME WHAT HE IS. STARBRAND.
THERE IS SOMETHING ELSE AT WORK HERE.
OKAY... TAKE HIM DOWN.

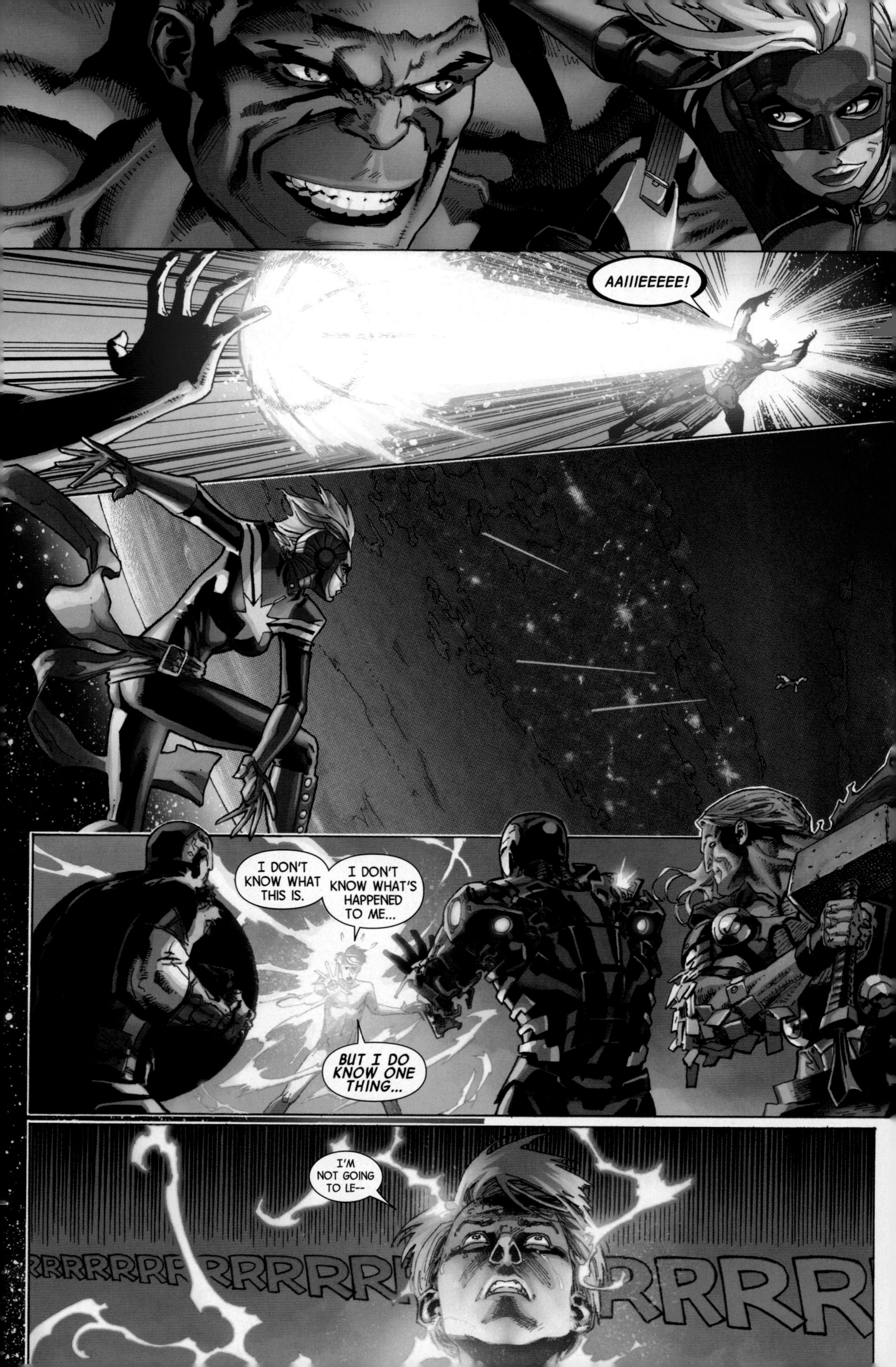
AAIIIEEEEE!
I DON'T KNOW WHAT THIS IS.
I DON'T KNOW WHAT'S HAPPENED TO ME...
BUT I DO KNOW ONE THING...
I'M NOT GOING TO LE--
RRRRRRRRRRRRRRRRRR

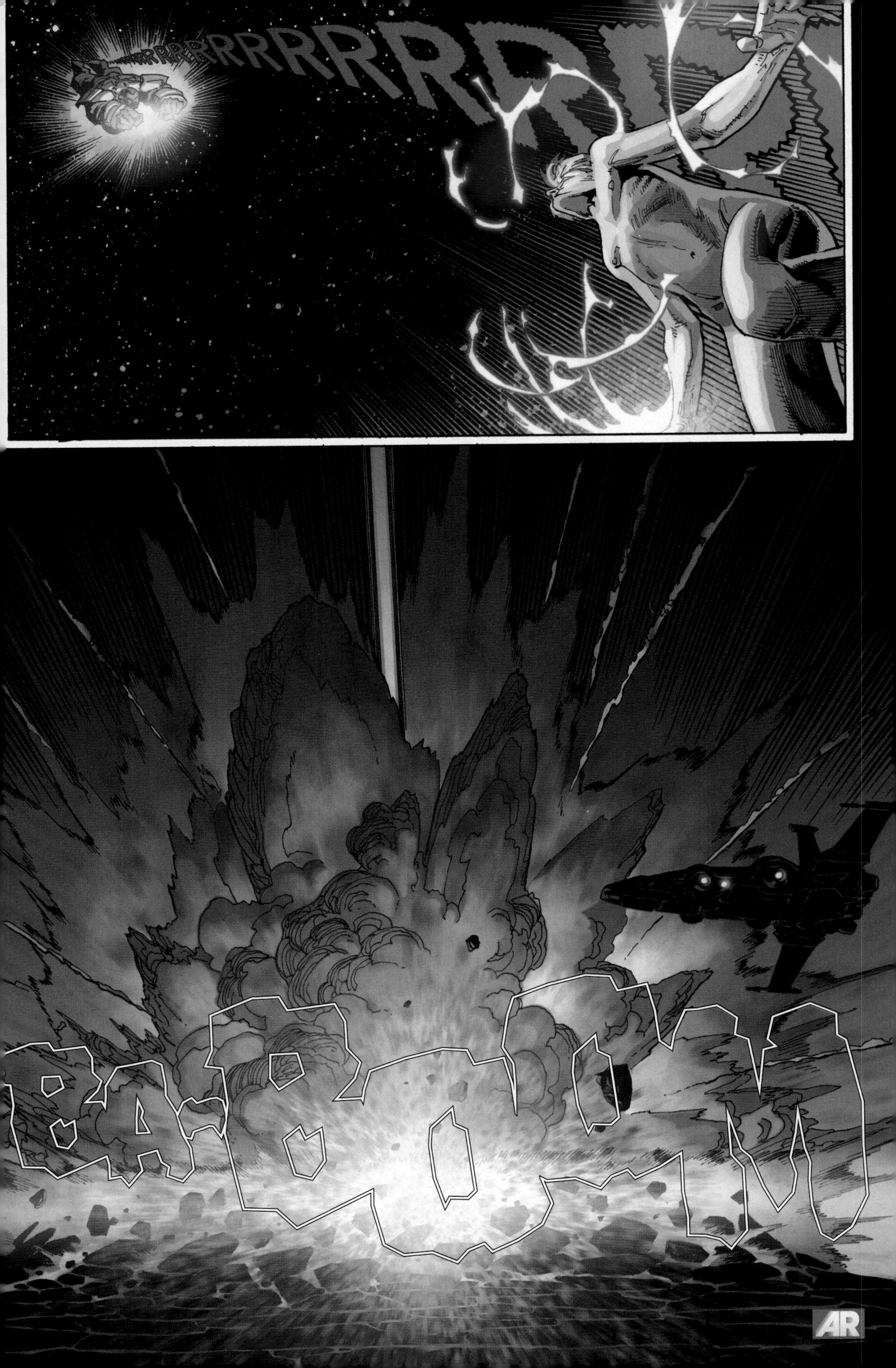
RRRRRRRRRRRRRRRRR
BA-BOOM

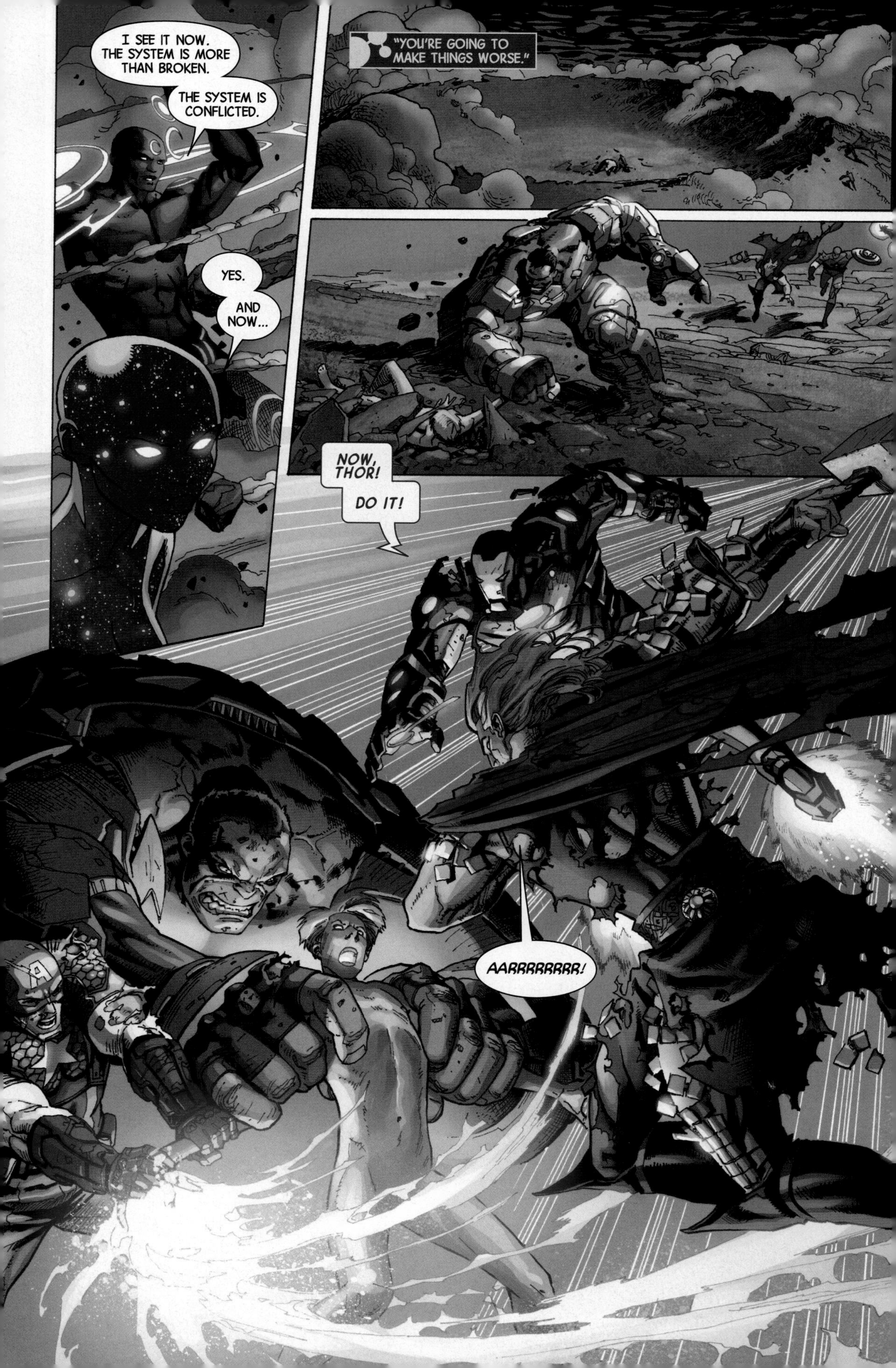
I SEE IT NOW. THE SYSTEM IS MORE THAN BROKEN.
THE SYSTEM IS CONFLICTED.
YES.
AND NOW...
"YOU'RE GOING TO MAKE THINGS WORSE."
NOW, THOR!
DO IT!
AARRRRRRRRR!

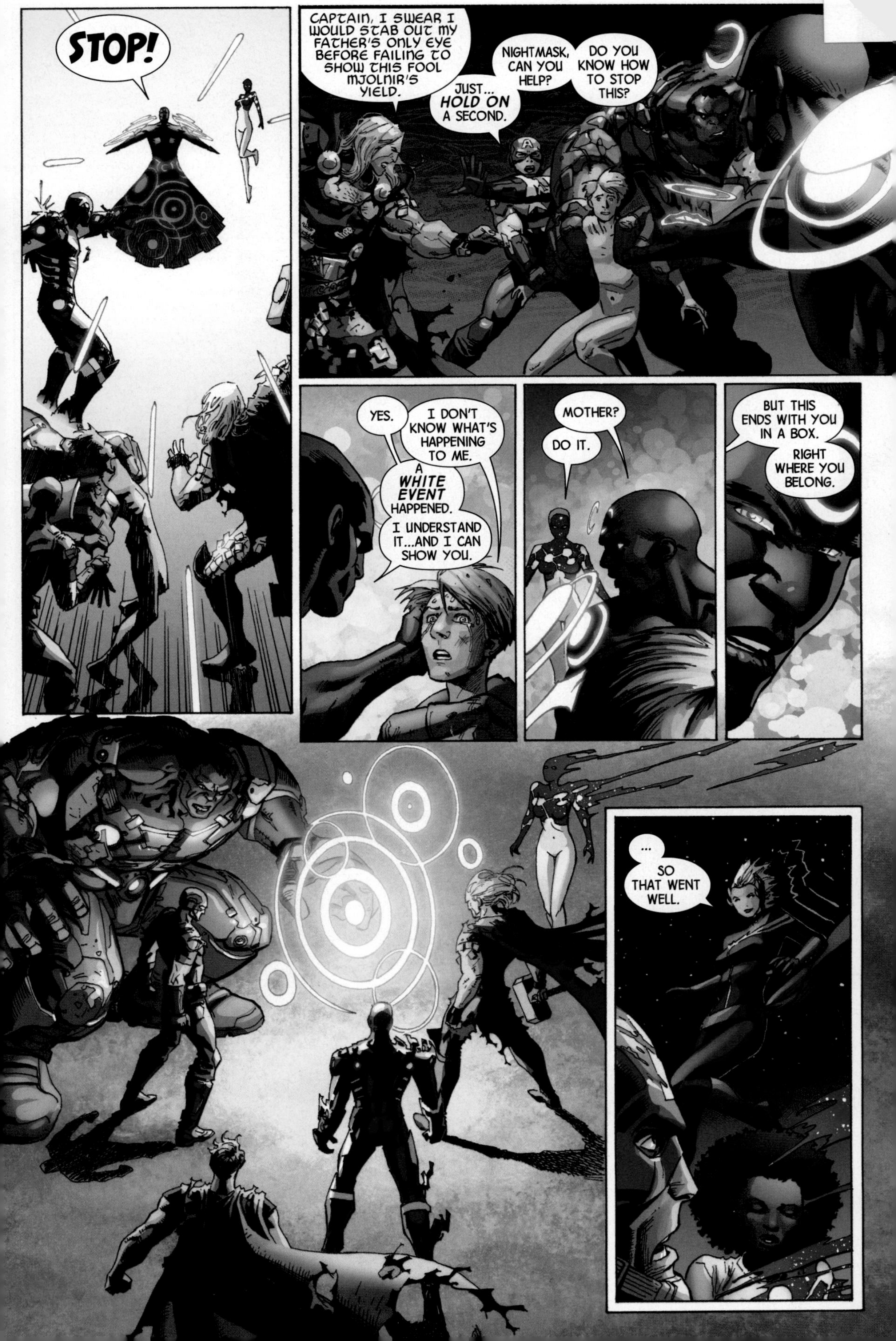
STOP!
CAPTAIN, I SWEAR I WOULD STAB OUT MY FATHER'S ONLY EYE BEFORE FAILING TO SHOW THIS FOOL MJOLNIR'S YIELD.
JUST... HOLD ON A SECOND.
NIGHTMASK, CAN YOU HELP?
DO YOU KNOW HOW TO STOP THIS?
YES.
I DON'T KNOW WHAT'S HAPPENING TO ME.
A WHITE EVENT HAPPENED.
I UNDERSTAND IT...AND I CAN SHOW YOU.
MOTHER?
DO IT.
BUT THIS ENDS WITH YOU IN A BOX.
RIGHT WHERE YOU BELONG.
...
SO THAT WENT WELL.

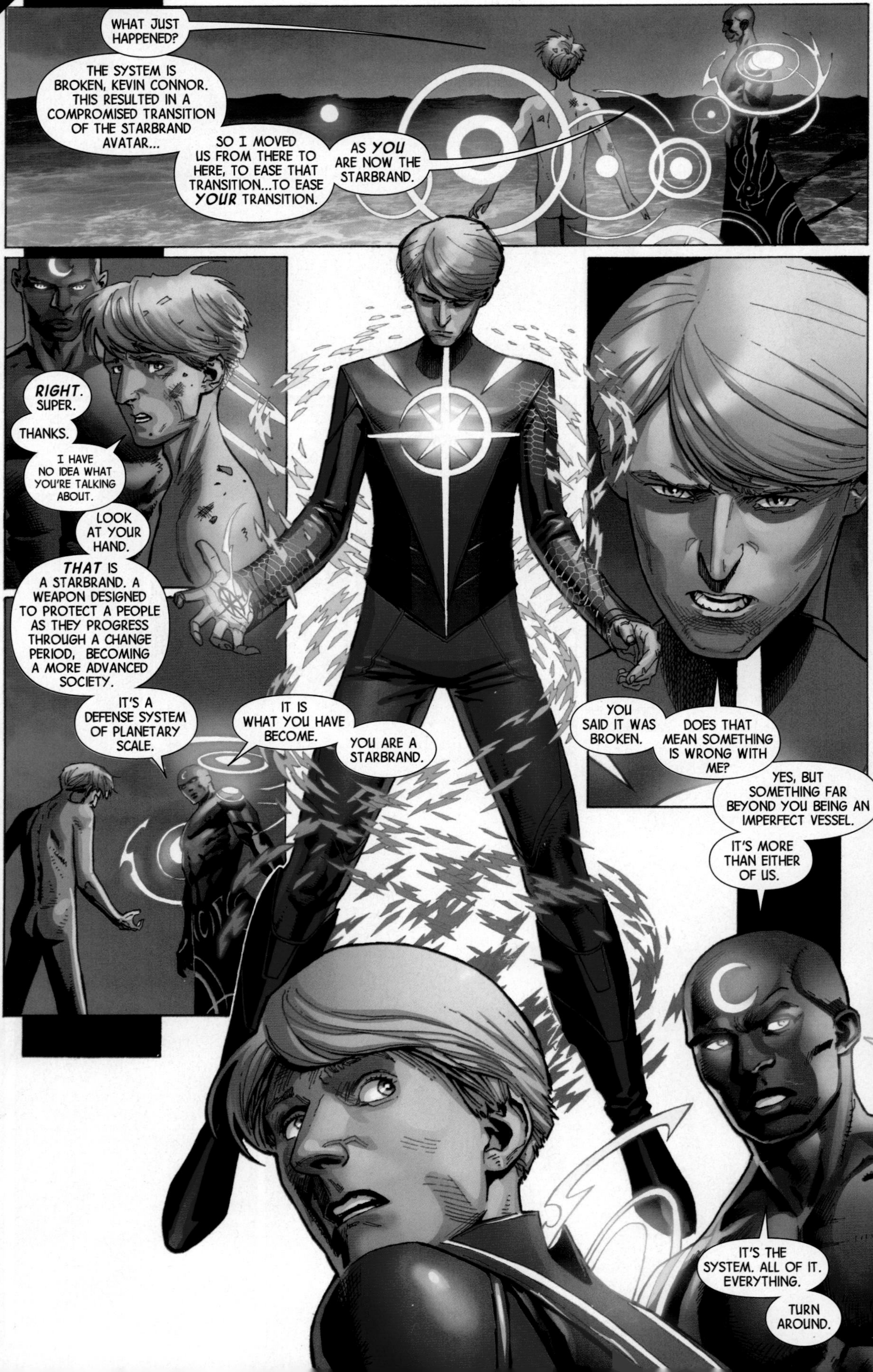

WHAT JUST HAPPENED?
THE SYSTEM IS BROKEN, KEVIN CONNOR. THIS RESULTED IN A COMPROMISED TRANSITION OF THE STARBRAND AVATAR...
SO I MOVED US FROM THERE TO HERE, TO EASE THAT TRANSITION...TO EASE *YOUR* TRANSITION.
AS *YOU* ARE NOW THE STARBRAND.
RIGHT. SUPER.
THANKS.
I HAVE NO IDEA WHAT YOU'RE TALKING ABOUT.
LOOK AT YOUR HAND.
THAT IS A STARBRAND. A WEAPON DESIGNED TO PROTECT A PEOPLE AS THEY PROGRESS THROUGH A CHANGE PERIOD, BECOMING A MORE ADVANCED SOCIETY.
IT'S A DEFENSE SYSTEM OF PLANETARY SCALE.
IT IS WHAT YOU HAVE BECOME.
YOU ARE A STARBRAND.
YOU SAID IT WAS BROKEN.
DOES THAT MEAN SOMETHING IS WRONG WITH ME?
YES, BUT SOMETHING FAR BEYOND YOU BEING AN IMPERFECT VESSEL.
IT'S MORE THAN EITHER OF US.
IT'S THE SYSTEM. ALL OF IT. EVERYTHING.
TURN AROUND.

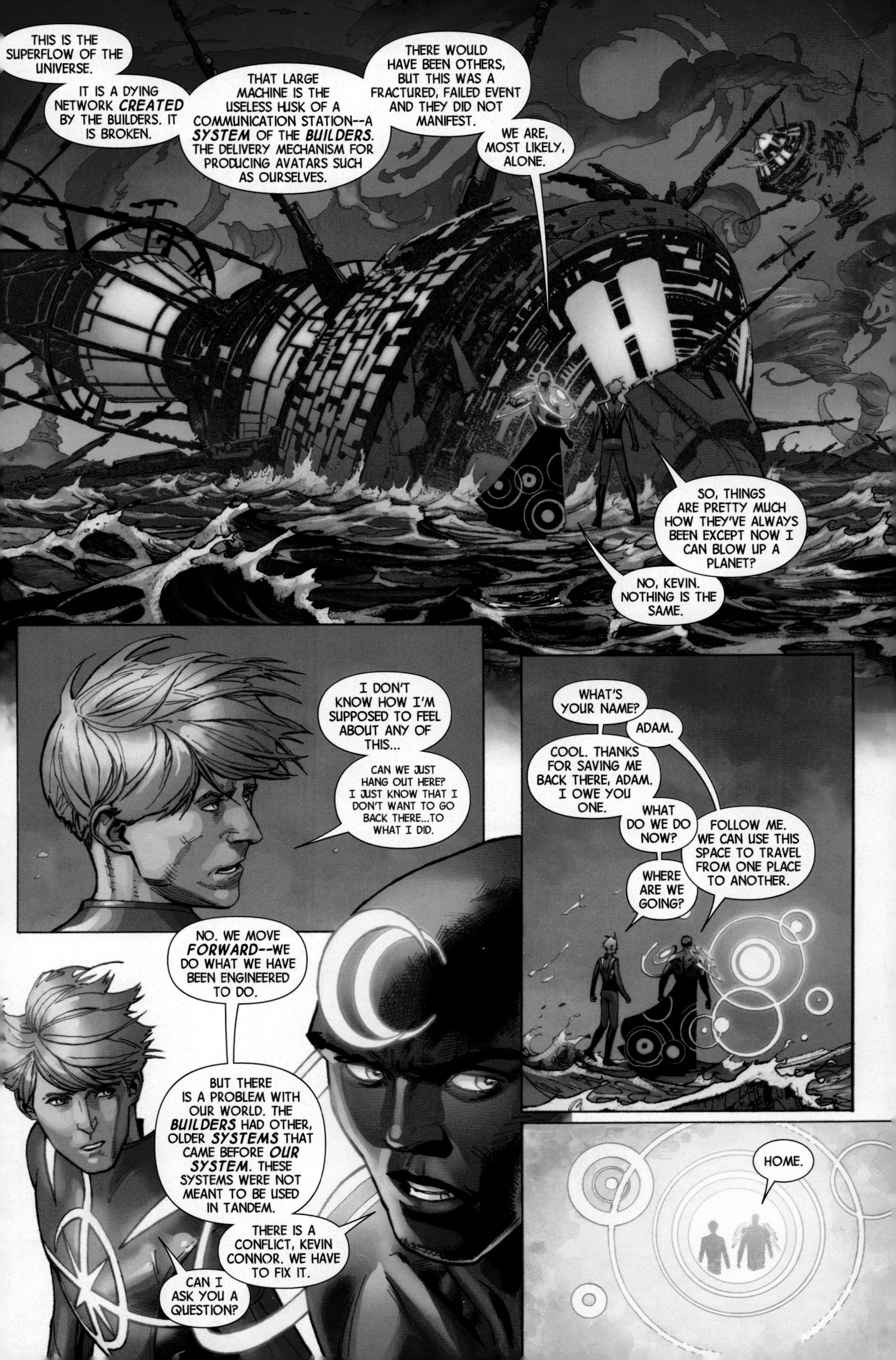
THIS IS THE SUPERFLOW OF THE UNIVERSE.
IT IS A DYING NETWORK CREATED BY THE BUILDERS. IT IS BROKEN.
THAT LARGE MACHINE IS THE USELESS HUSK OF A COMMUNICATION STATION--A SYSTEM OF THE BUILDERS. THE DELIVERY MECHANISM FOR PRODUCING AVATARS SUCH AS OURSELVES.
THERE WOULD HAVE BEEN OTHERS, BUT THIS WAS A FRACTURED, FAILED EVENT AND THEY DID NOT MANIFEST.
WE ARE, MOST LIKELY, ALONE.
SO, THINGS ARE PRETTY MUCH HOW THEY'VE ALWAYS BEEN EXCEPT NOW I CAN BLOW UP A PLANET?
NO, KEVIN. NOTHING IS THE SAME.
I DON'T KNOW HOW I'M SUPPOSED TO FEEL ABOUT ANY OF THIS...
CAN WE JUST HANG OUT HERE? I JUST KNOW THAT I DON'T WANT TO GO BACK THERE...TO WHAT I DID.
NO. WE MOVE FORWARD--WE DO WHAT WE HAVE BEEN ENGINEERED TO DO.
BUT THERE IS A PROBLEM WITH OUR WORLD. THE BUILDERS HAD OTHER, OLDER SYSTEMS THAT CAME BEFORE OUR SYSTEM. THESE SYSTEMS WERE NOT MEANT TO BE USED IN TANDEM.
THERE IS A CONFLICT, KEVIN CONNOR. WE HAVE TO FIX IT.
CAN I ASK YOU A QUESTION?
WHAT'S YOUR NAME?
ADAM.
COOL. THANKS FOR SAVING ME BACK THERE, ADAM. I OWE YOU ONE.
WHAT DO WE DO NOW?
FOLLOW ME. WE CAN USE THIS SPACE TO TRAVEL FROM ONE PLACE TO ANOTHER.
WHERE ARE WE GOING?
HOME.

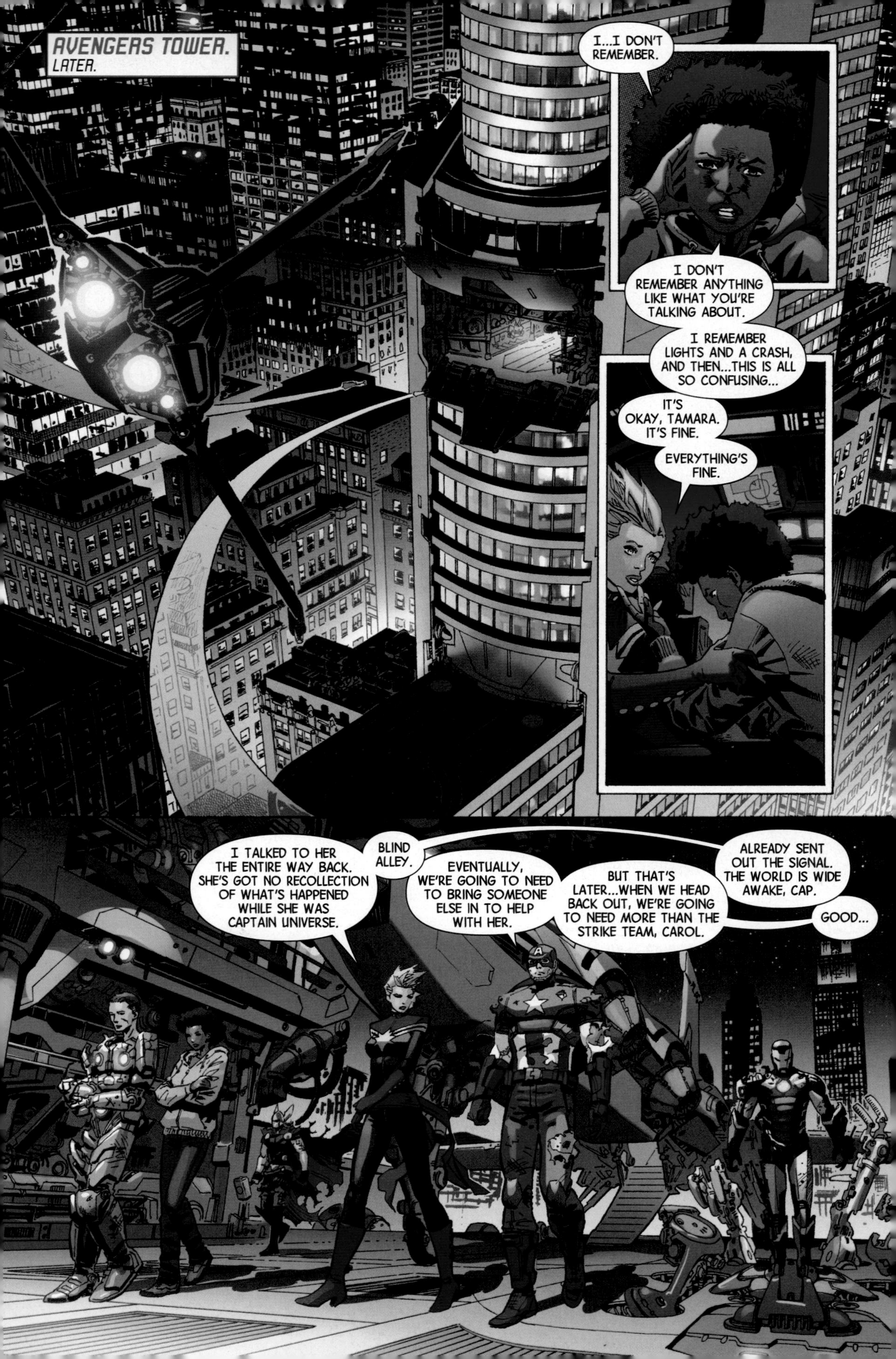
AVENGERS TOWER. LATER.
I...I DON'T REMEMBER.
I DON'T REMEMBER ANYTHING LIKE WHAT YOU'RE TALKING ABOUT.
I REMEMBER LIGHTS AND A CRASH, AND THEN...THIS IS ALL SO CONFUSING...
IT'S OKAY, TAMARA. IT'S FINE.
EVERYTHING'S FINE.
I TALKED TO HER THE ENTIRE WAY BACK. SHE'S GOT NO RECOLLECTION OF WHAT'S HAPPENED WHILE SHE WAS CAPTAIN UNIVERSE.
BLIND ALLEY.
EVENTUALLY, WE'RE GOING TO NEED TO BRING SOMEONE ELSE IN TO HELP WITH HER.
BUT THAT'S LATER...WHEN WE HEAD BACK OUT, WE'RE GOING TO NEED MORE THAN THE STRIKE TEAM, CAROL.
ALREADY SENT OUT THE SIGNAL. THE WORLD IS WIDE AWAKE, CAP.
GOOD...

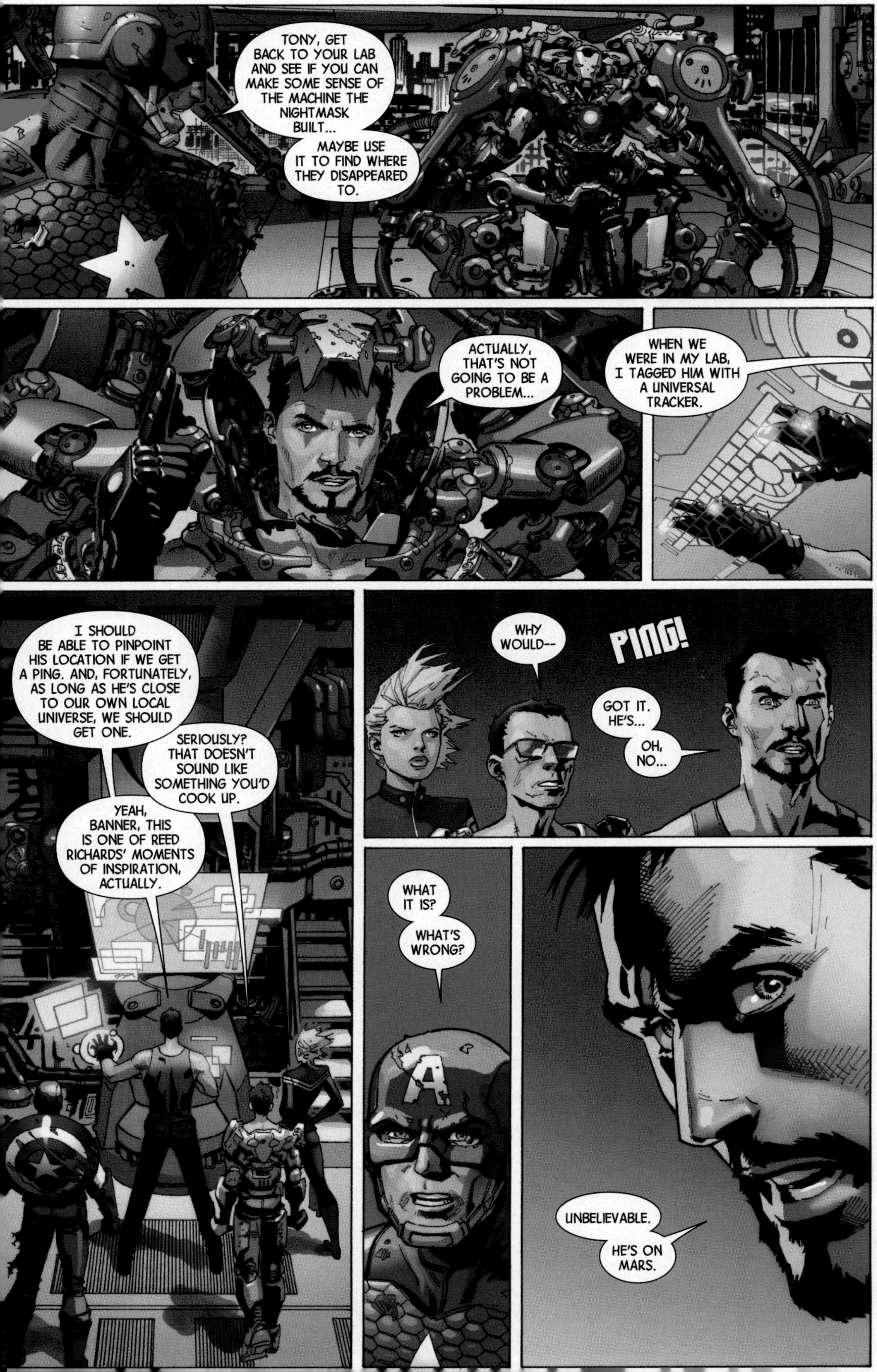

TONY, GET BACK TO YOUR LAB AND SEE IF YOU CAN MAKE SOME SENSE OF THE MACHINE THE NIGHTMASK BUILT...
MAYBE USE IT TO FIND WHERE THEY DISAPPEARED TO.
ACTUALLY, THAT'S NOT GOING TO BE A PROBLEM...
WHEN WE WERE IN MY LAB, I TAGGED HIM WITH A UNIVERSAL TRACKER.
I SHOULD BE ABLE TO PINPOINT HIS LOCATION IF WE GET A PING. AND, FORTUNATELY, AS LONG AS HE'S CLOSE TO OUR OWN LOCAL UNIVERSE, WE SHOULD GET ONE.
SERIOUSLY? THAT DOESN'T SOUND LIKE SOMETHING YOU'D COOK UP.
YEAH, BANNER, THIS IS ONE OF REED RICHARDS' MOMENTS OF INSPIRATION, ACTUALLY.
WHY WOULD--
PING!
GOT IT. HE'S...
OH, NO...
WHAT IT IS?
WHAT'S WRONG?
UNBELIEVABLE.
HE'S ON MARS.

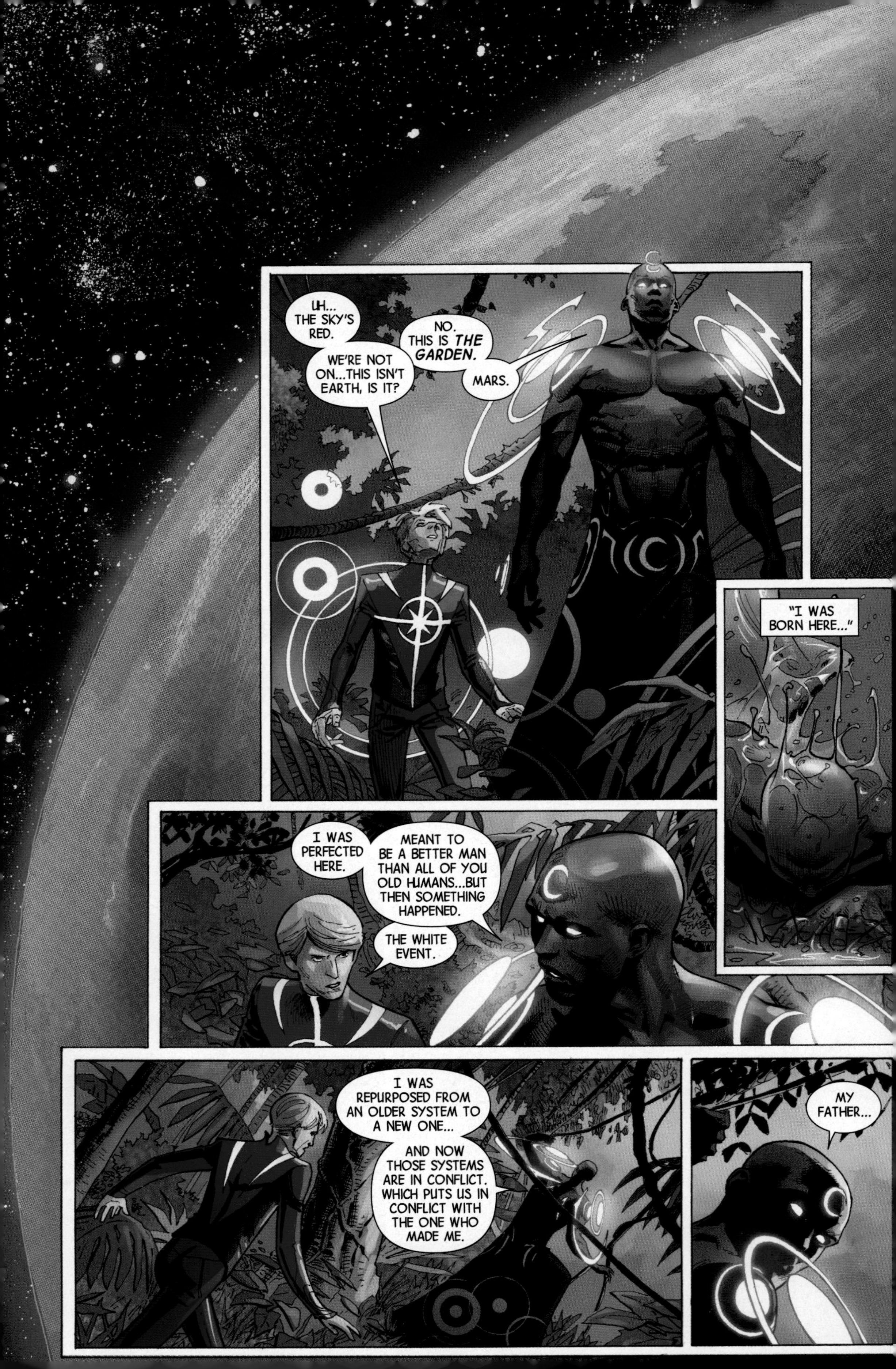

UH... THE SKY'S RED.
WE'RE NOT ON...THIS ISN'T EARTH, IS IT?
NO. THIS IS THE GARDEN.
MARS.
"I WAS BORN HERE..."
I WAS PERFECTED HERE.
MEANT TO BE A BETTER MAN THAN ALL OF YOU OLD HUMANS...BUT THEN SOMETHING HAPPENED.
THE WHITE EVENT.
I WAS REPURPOSED FROM AN OLDER SYSTEM TO A NEW ONE...
AND NOW THOSE SYSTEMS ARE IN CONFLICT. WHICH PUTS US IN CONFLICT WITH THE ONE WHO MADE ME.
MY FATHER...

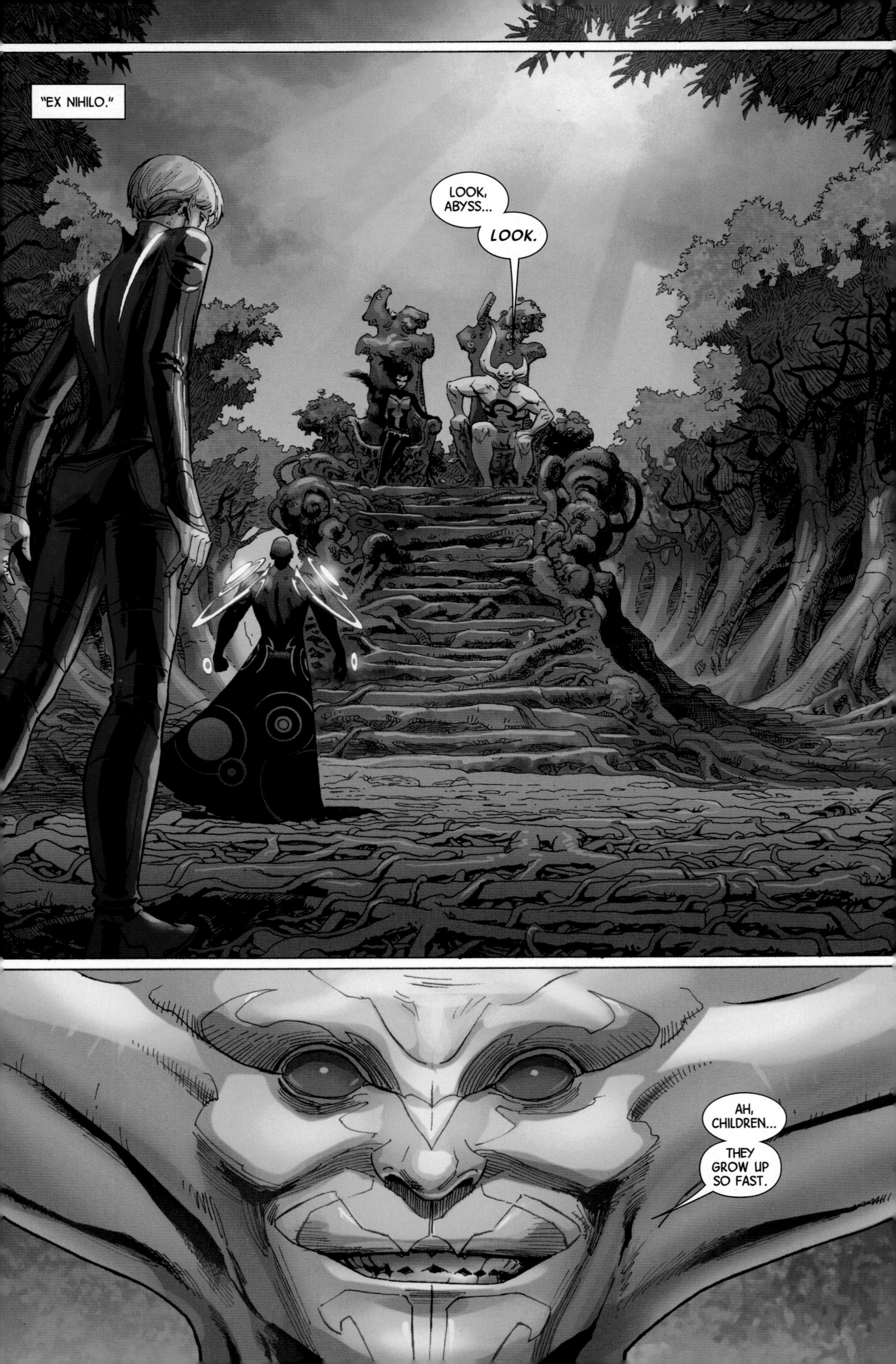
"EX NIHILO."
LOOK, ABYSS...
LOOK.
AH, CHILDREN...
THEY GROW UP SO FAST.

"STAR BOUND"

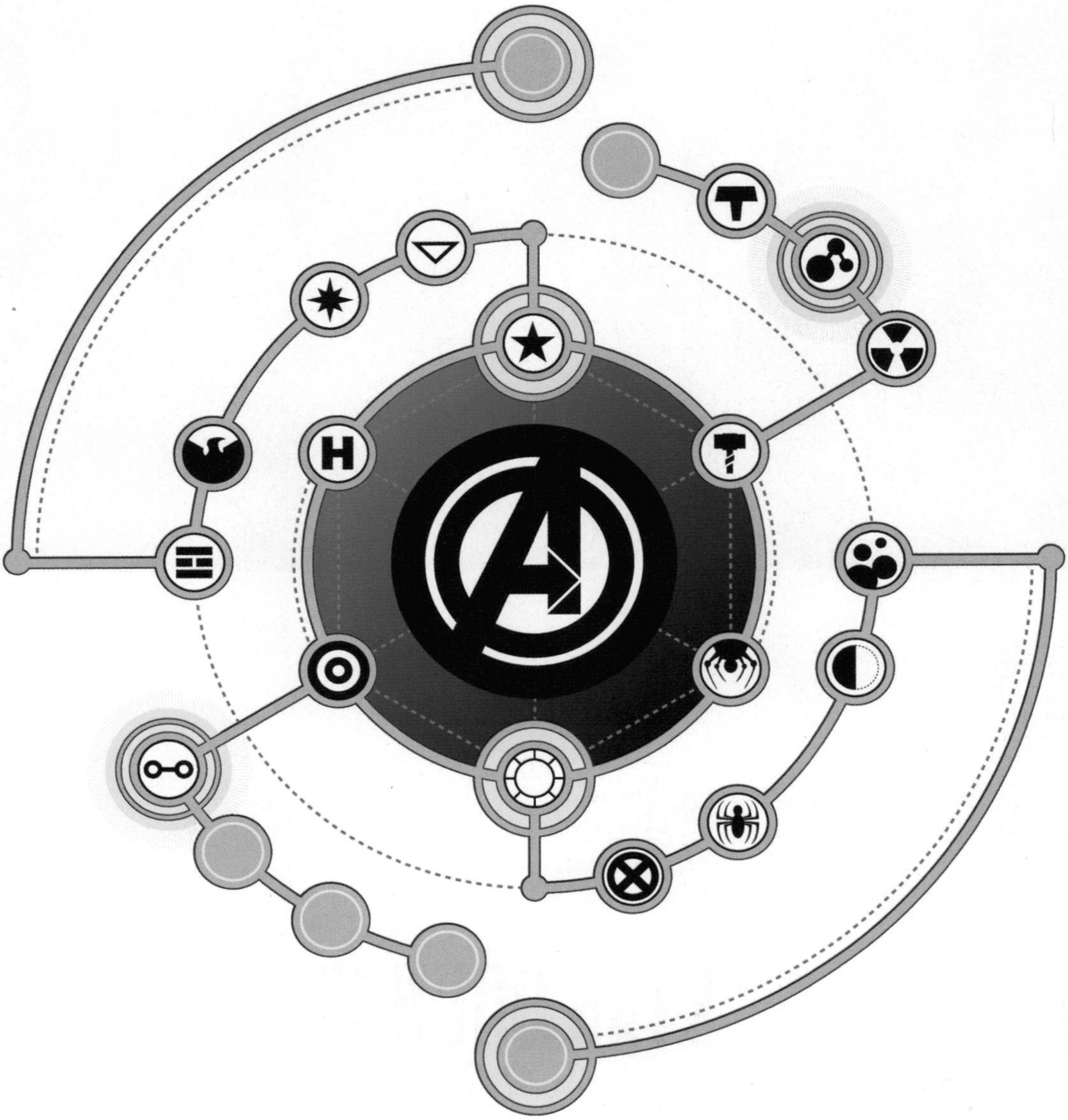

EARTH'S MIGHTIEST HEROES

CAPTAIN AMERICA · IRON MAN · THOR · HAWKEYE · BLACK WIDOW · HULK
WOLVERINE · SPIDER-MAN · CAPTAIN MARVEL · SPIDER-WOMAN
FALCON · SHANG-CHI · SUNSPOT · CANNONBALL · MANIFOLD
SMASHER · CAPTAIN UNIVERSE · HYPERION

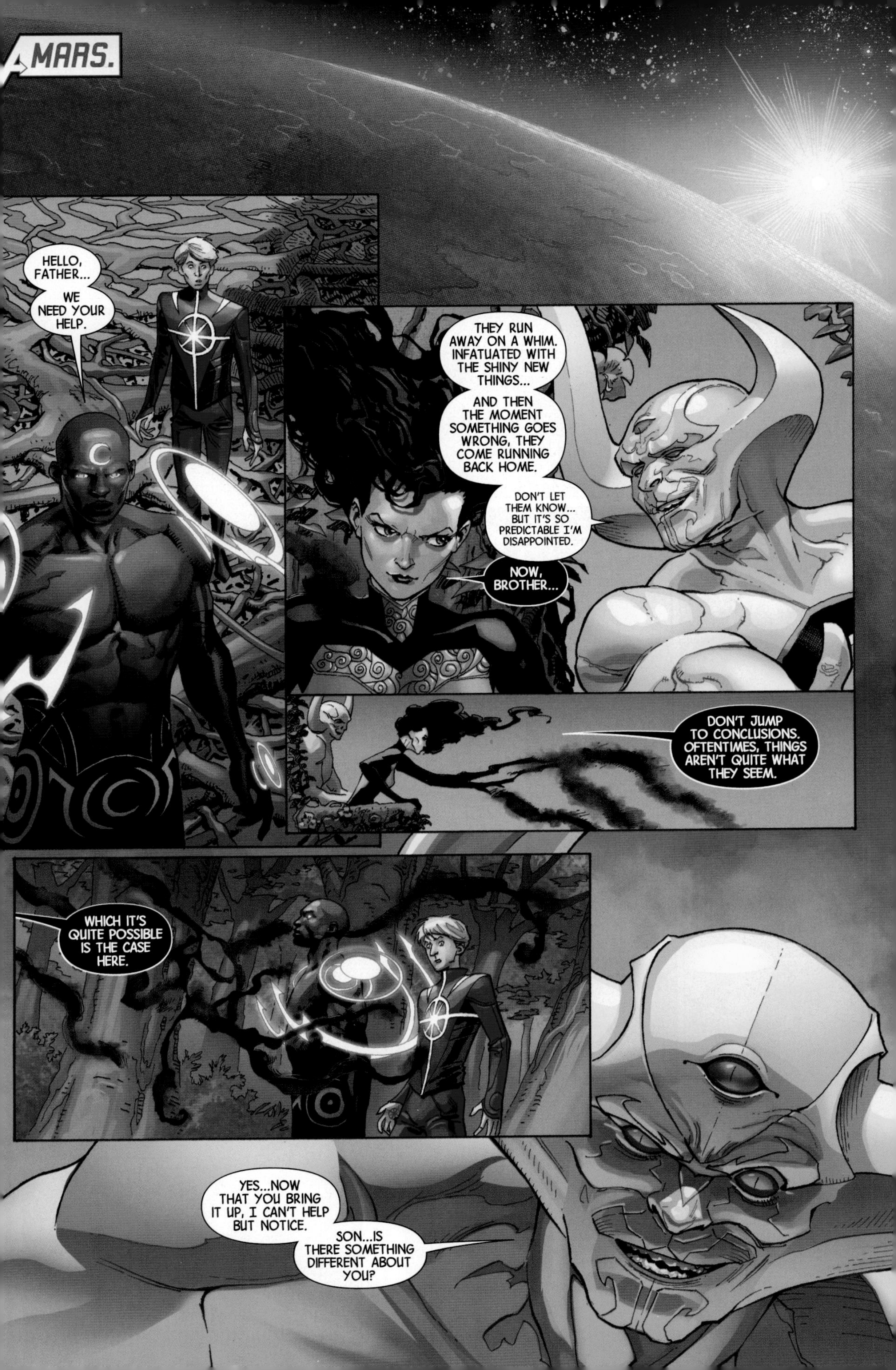

MARS.
HELLO, FATHER...
WE NEED YOUR HELP.
THEY RUN AWAY ON A WHIM. INFATUATED WITH THE SHINY NEW THINGS...
AND THEN THE MOMENT SOMETHING GOES WRONG, THEY COME RUNNING BACK HOME.
DON'T LET THEM KNOW... BUT IT'S SO PREDICTABLE I'M DISAPPOINTED.
NOW, BROTHER...
DON'T JUMP TO CONCLUSIONS. OFTENTIMES, THINGS AREN'T QUITE WHAT THEY SEEM.
WHICH IT'S QUITE POSSIBLE IS THE CASE HERE.
YES...NOW THAT YOU BRING IT UP, I CAN'T HELP BUT NOTICE.
SON...IS THERE SOMETHING DIFFERENT ABOUT YOU?

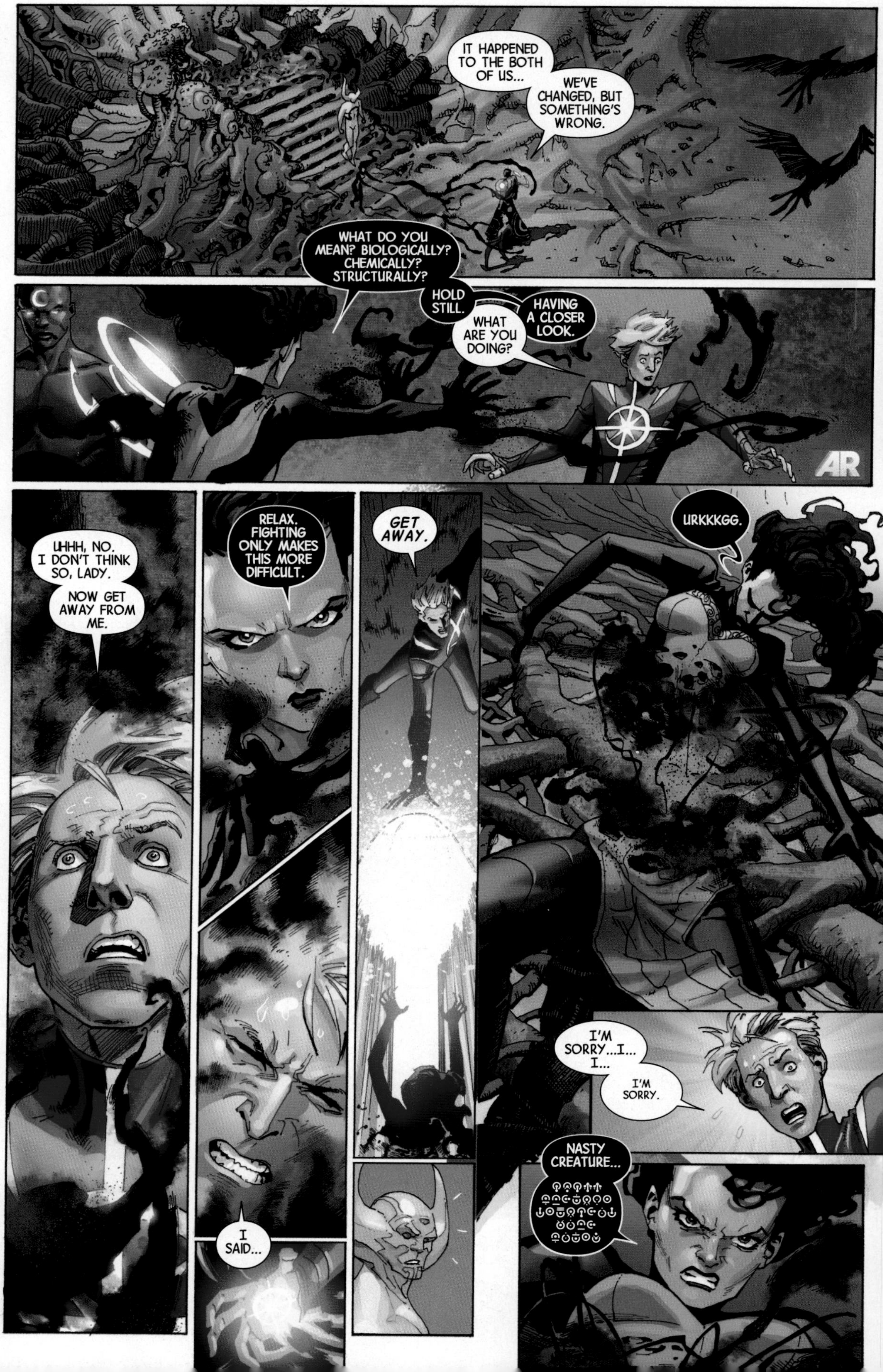
IT HAPPENED TO THE BOTH OF US...
WE'VE CHANGED, BUT SOMETHING'S WRONG.
WHAT DO YOU MEAN? BIOLOGICALLY? CHEMICALLY? STRUCTURALLY?
HOLD STILL.
WHAT ARE YOU DOING?
HAVING A CLOSER LOOK.
UHHH, NO. I DON'T THINK SO, LADY.
NOW GET AWAY FROM ME.
RELAX. FIGHTING ONLY MAKES THIS MORE DIFFICULT.
I SAID...
GET AWAY.
URKKKGG.
I'M SORRY...I... I...
I'M SORRY.
NASTY CREATURE...

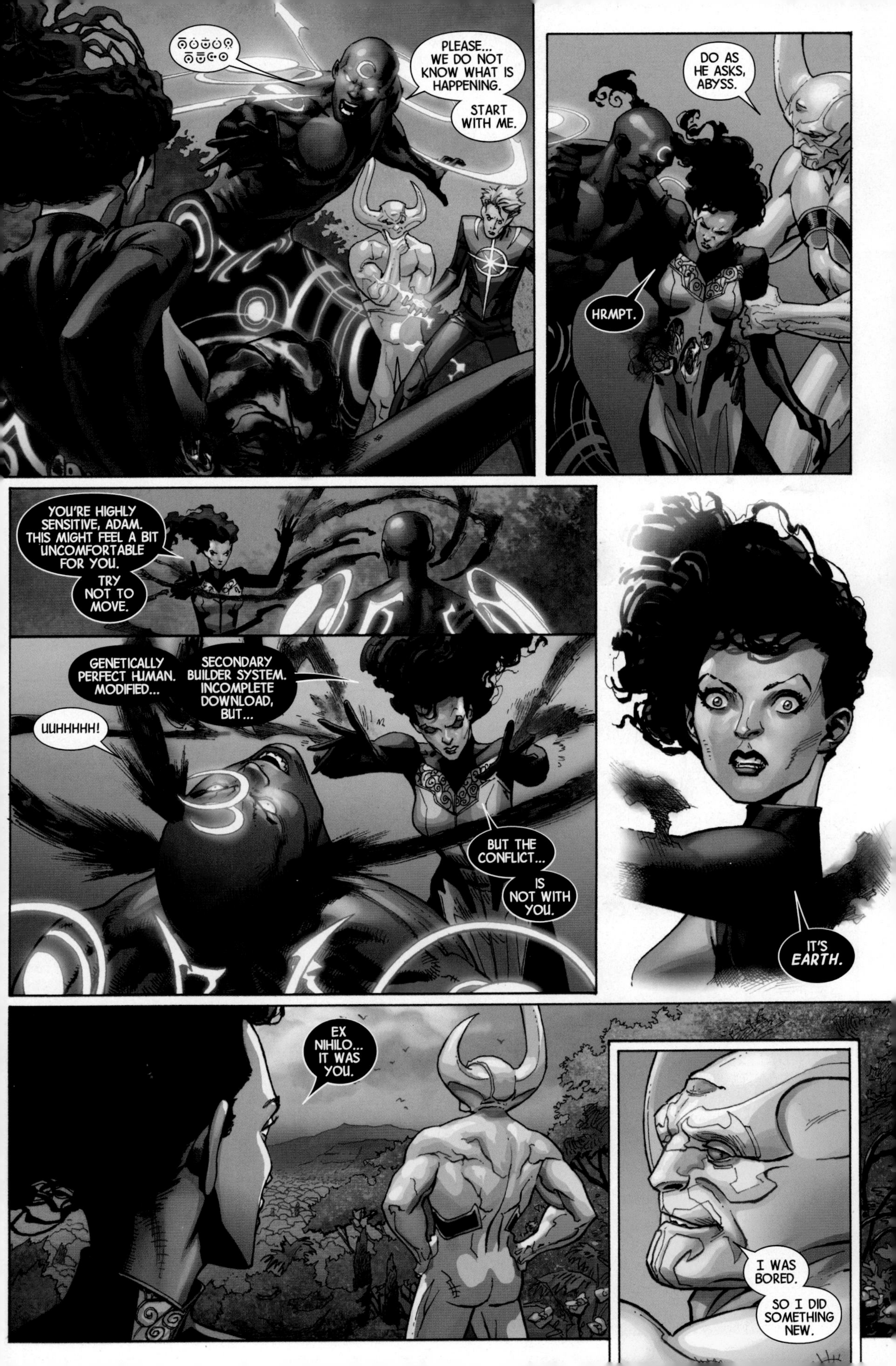
PLEASE... WE DO NOT KNOW WHAT IS HAPPENING.
START WITH ME.
DO AS HE ASKS, ABYSS.
HRMPT.
YOU'RE HIGHLY SENSITIVE, ADAM. THIS MIGHT FEEL A BIT UNCOMFORTABLE FOR YOU.
TRY NOT TO MOVE.
GENETICALLY PERFECT HUMAN. MODIFIED...
SECONDARY BUILDER SYSTEM. INCOMPLETE DOWNLOAD, BUT...
UUHHHHH!
BUT THE CONFLICT...
IS NOT WITH YOU.
IT'S *EARTH.*
EX NIHILO... IT WAS YOU.
I WAS BORED.
SO I DID SOMETHING NEW.

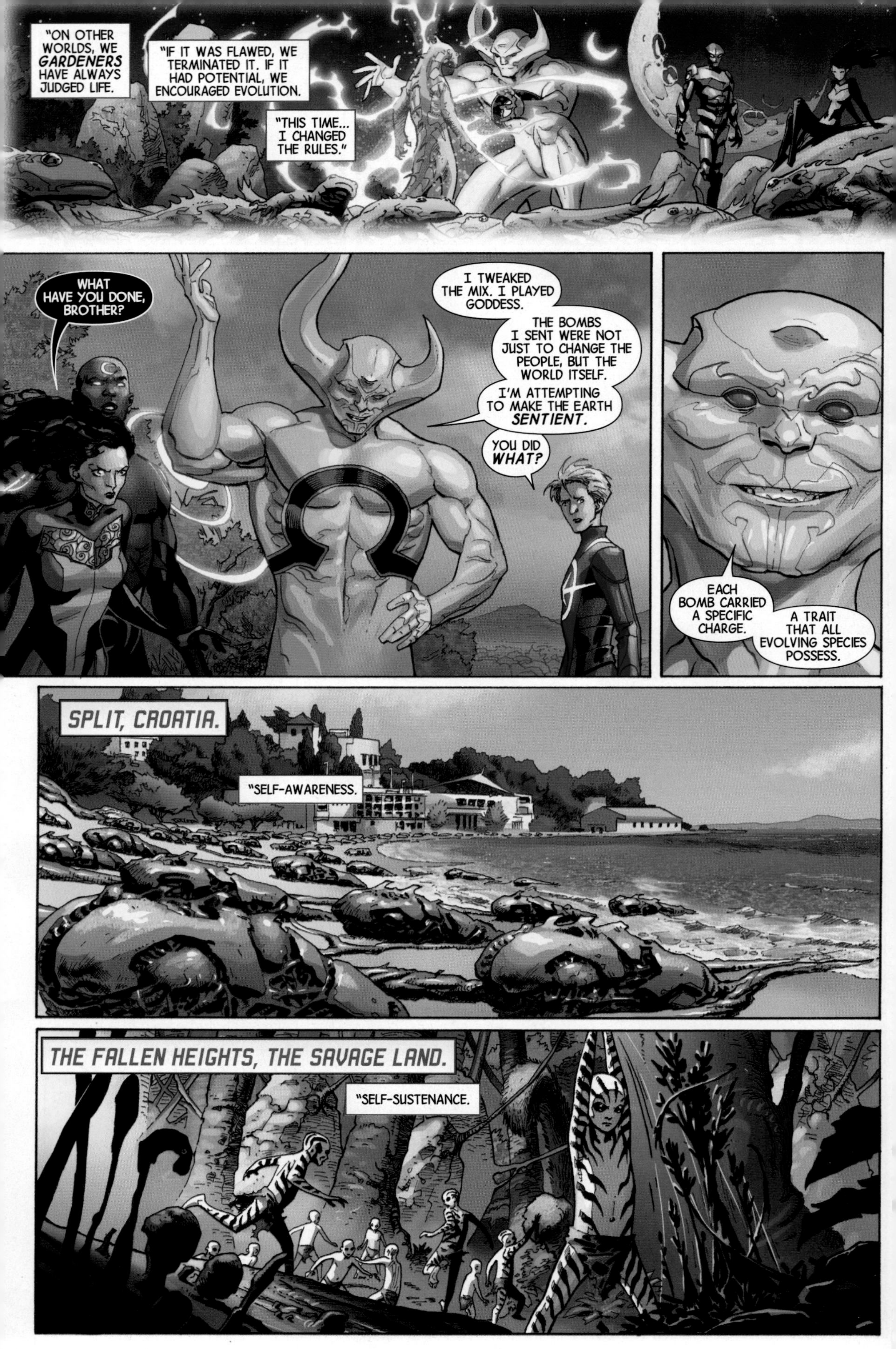
"ON OTHER WORLDS, WE *GARDENERS* HAVE ALWAYS JUDGED LIFE.
"IF IT WAS FLAWED, WE TERMINATED IT. IF IT HAD POTENTIAL, WE ENCOURAGED EVOLUTION.
"THIS TIME... I CHANGED THE RULES."
WHAT HAVE YOU DONE, BROTHER?
I TWEAKED THE MIX. I PLAYED GODDESS.
THE BOMBS I SENT WERE NOT JUST TO CHANGE THE PEOPLE, BUT THE WORLD ITSELF.
I'M ATTEMPTING TO MAKE THE EARTH *SENTIENT*.
YOU DID *WHAT?*
EACH BOMB CARRIED A SPECIFIC CHARGE.
A TRAIT THAT ALL EVOLVING SPECIES POSSESS.
SPLIT, CROATIA.
"SELF-AWARENESS.
THE FALLEN HEIGHTS, THE SAVAGE LAND.
"SELF-SUSTENANCE.

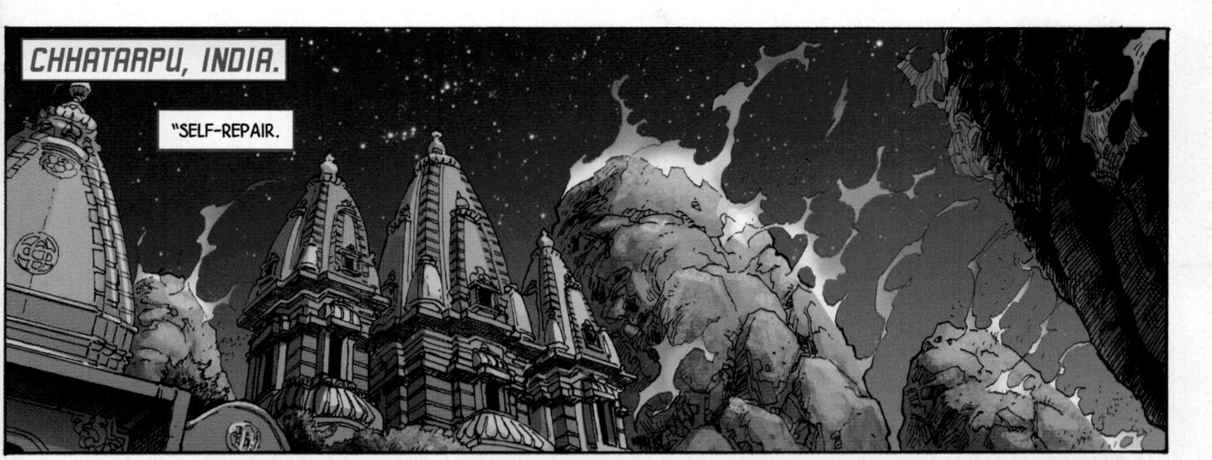
CHHATARPU, INDIA.
"SELF-REPAIR.

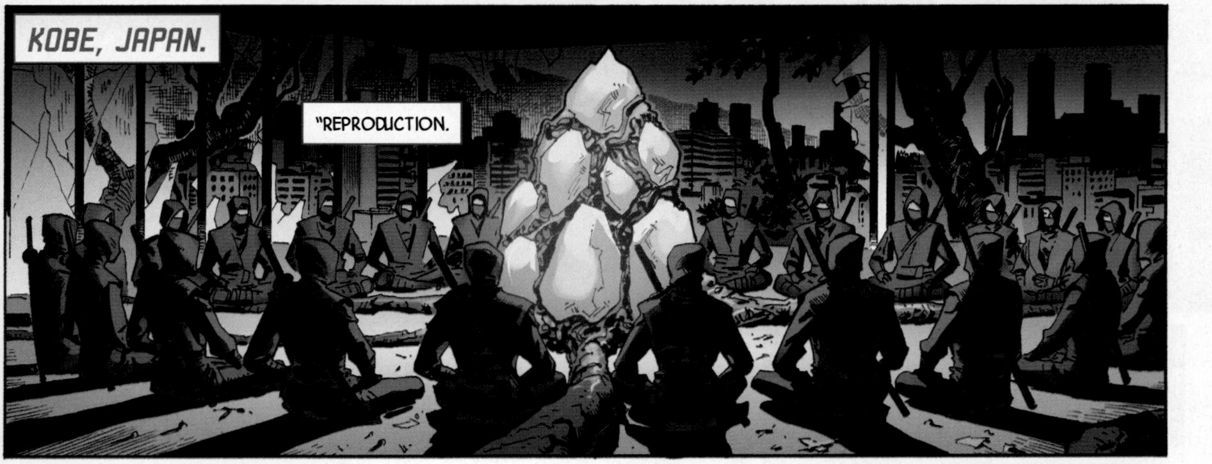
KOBE, JAPAN.
"REPRODUCTION.

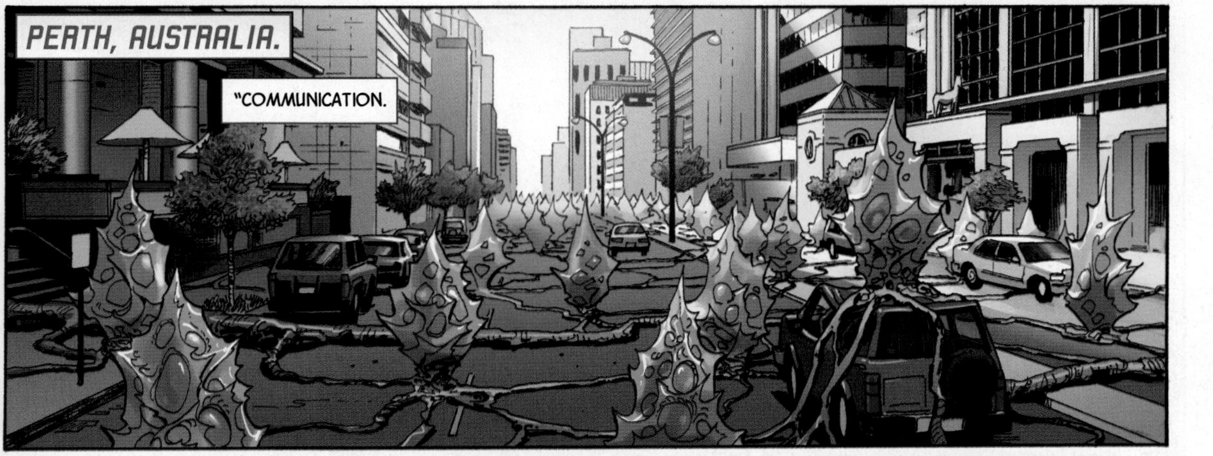
PERTH, AUSTRALIA.
"COMMUNICATION.

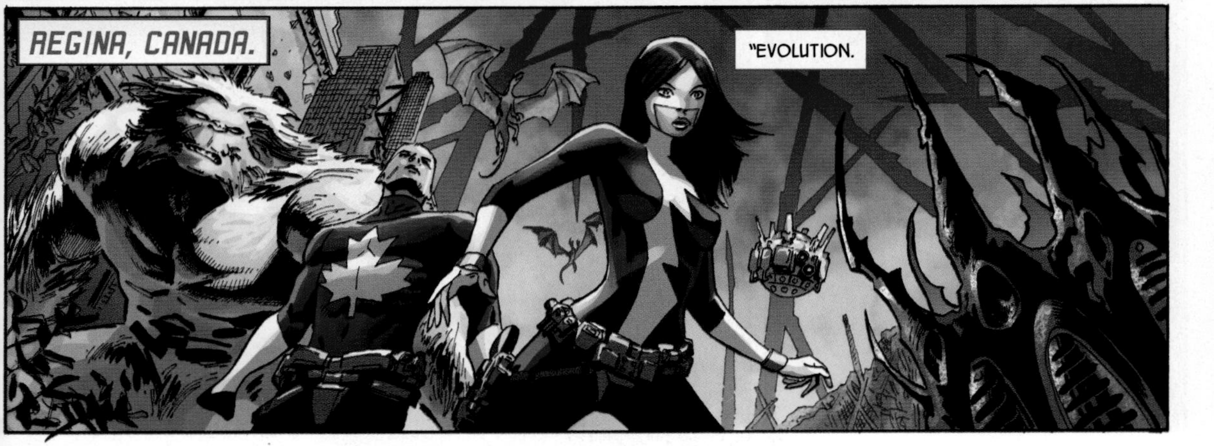
REGINA, CANADA.
"EVOLUTION.

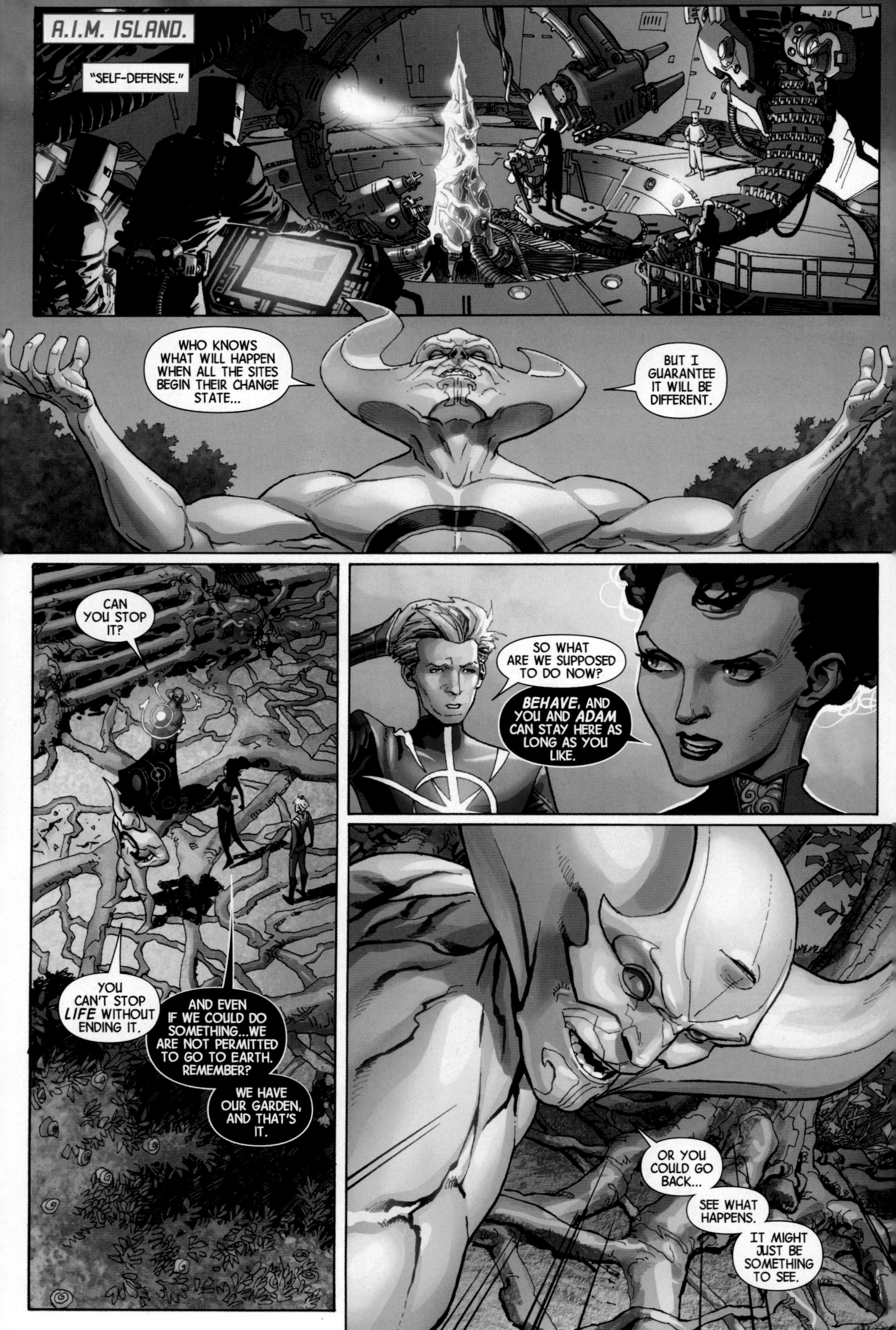
A.I.M. ISLAND.
"SELF-DEFENSE."
WHO KNOWS WHAT WILL HAPPEN WHEN ALL THE SITES BEGIN THEIR CHANGE STATE...
BUT I GUARANTEE IT WILL BE DIFFERENT.
CAN YOU STOP IT?
YOU CAN'T STOP LIFE WITHOUT ENDING IT.
AND EVEN IF WE COULD DO SOMETHING...WE ARE NOT PERMITTED TO GO TO EARTH. REMEMBER?
WE HAVE OUR GARDEN, AND THAT'S IT.
SO WHAT ARE WE SUPPOSED TO DO NOW?
BEHAVE, AND YOU AND ADAM CAN STAY HERE AS LONG AS YOU LIKE.
OR YOU COULD GO BACK...
SEE WHAT HAPPENS.
IT MIGHT JUST BE SOMETHING TO SEE.

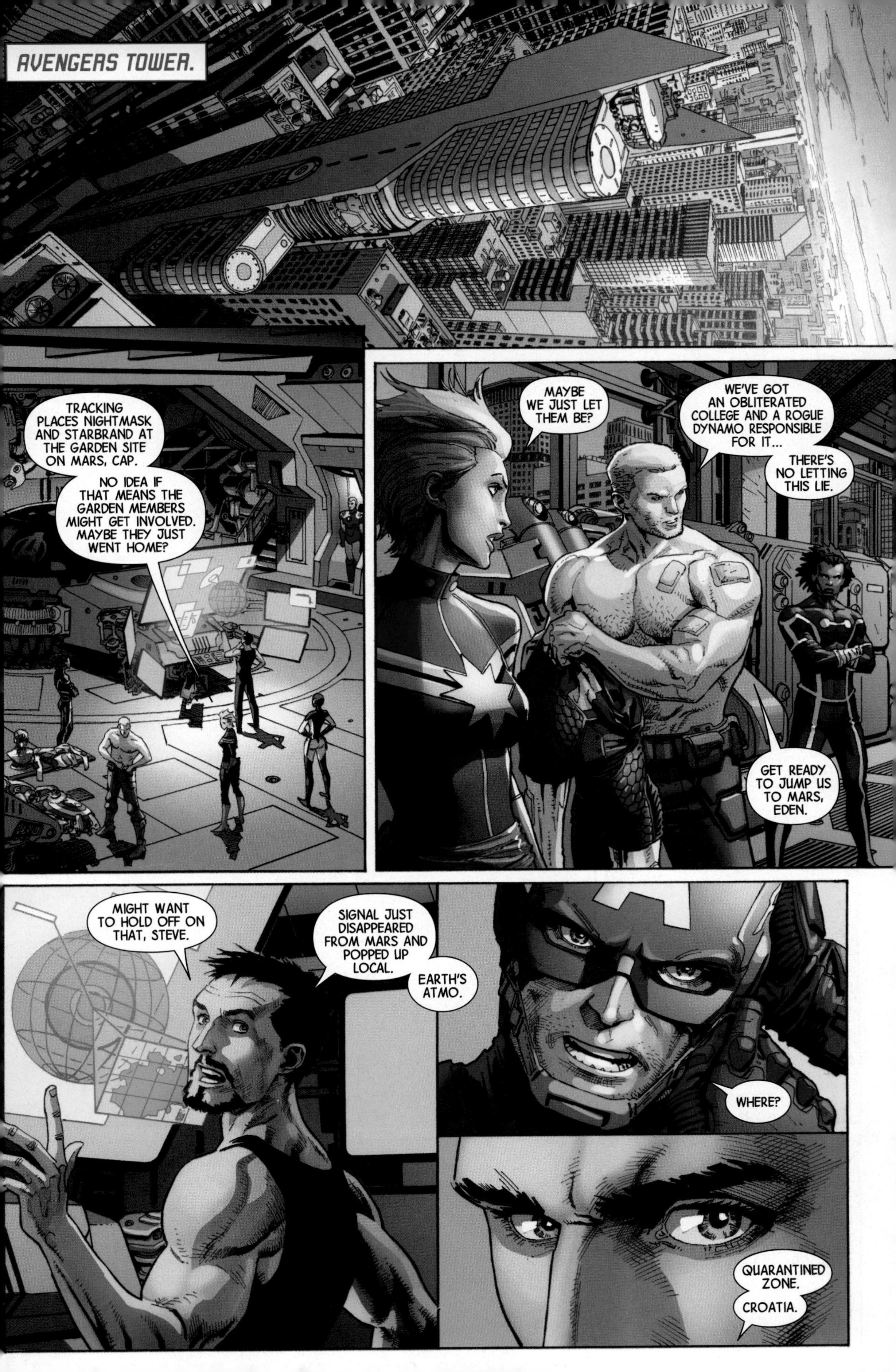
AVENGERS TOWER.
TRACKING PLACES NIGHTMASK AND STARBRAND AT THE GARDEN SITE ON MARS, CAP.
NO IDEA IF THAT MEANS THE GARDEN MEMBERS MIGHT GET INVOLVED. MAYBE THEY JUST WENT HOME?
MAYBE WE JUST LET THEM BE?
WE'VE GOT AN OBLITERATED COLLEGE AND A ROGUE DYNAMO RESPONSIBLE FOR IT...
THERE'S NO LETTING THIS LIE.
GET READY TO JUMP US TO MARS, EDEN.
MIGHT WANT TO HOLD OFF ON THAT, STEVE.
SIGNAL JUST DISAPPEARED FROM MARS AND POPPED UP LOCAL.
EARTH'S ATMO.
WHERE?
QUARANTINED ZONE.
CROATIA.

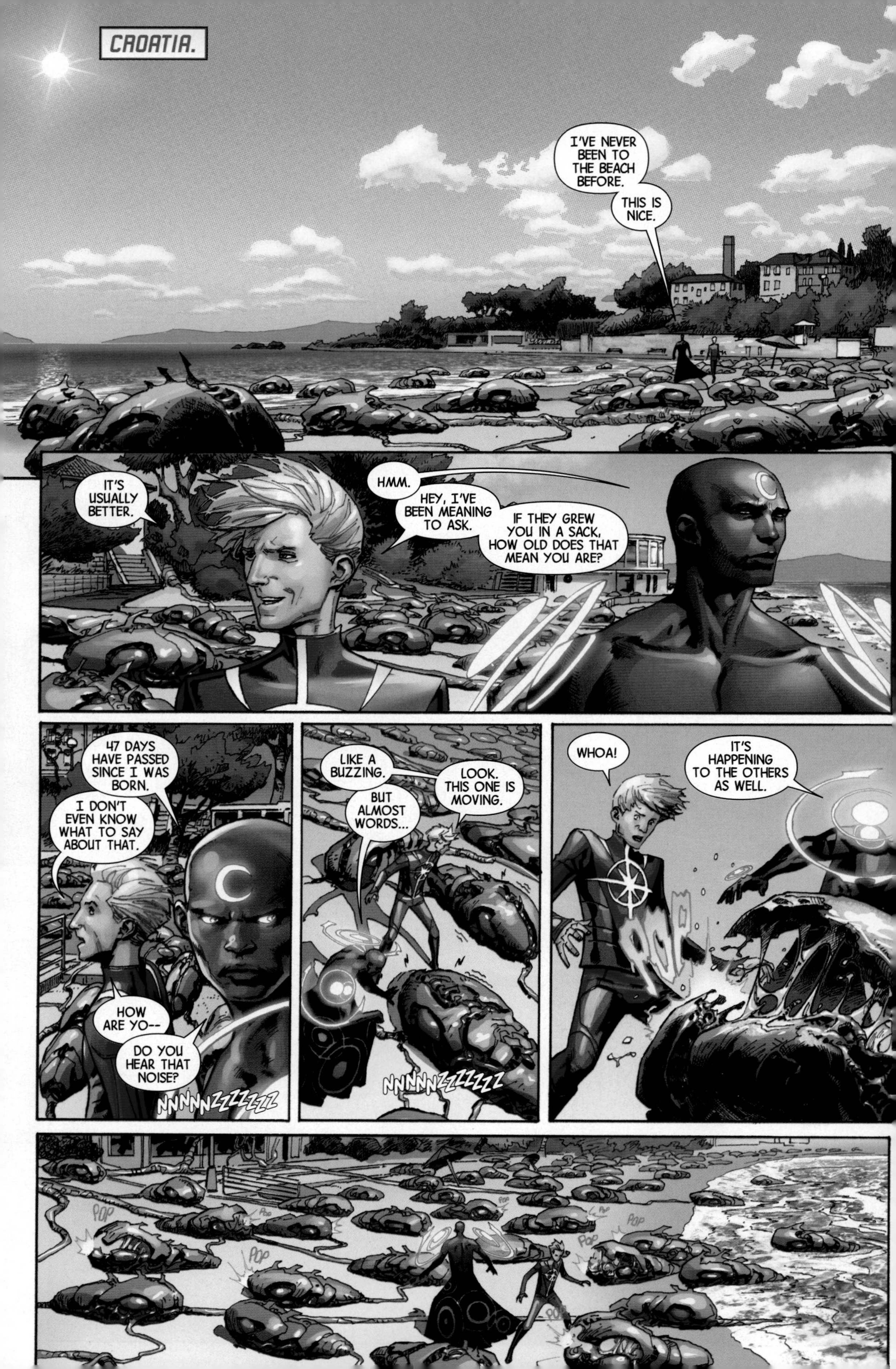
CROATIA.
I'VE NEVER BEEN TO THE BEACH BEFORE.
THIS IS NICE.
IT'S USUALLY BETTER.
HMM.
HEY, I'VE BEEN MEANING TO ASK.
IF THEY GREW YOU IN A SACK, HOW OLD DOES THAT MEAN YOU ARE?
47 DAYS HAVE PASSED SINCE I WAS BORN.
I DON'T EVEN KNOW WHAT TO SAY ABOUT THAT.
HOW ARE YO--
DO YOU HEAR THAT NOISE?
NNNNNZZZZZZZ
LIKE A BUZZING.
BUT ALMOST WORDS...
LOOK. THIS ONE IS MOVING.
NNNNNZZZZZZZ
WHOA!
IT'S HAPPENING TO THE OTHERS AS WELL.
POP
POP
POP
POP
POP
POP
POP
POP

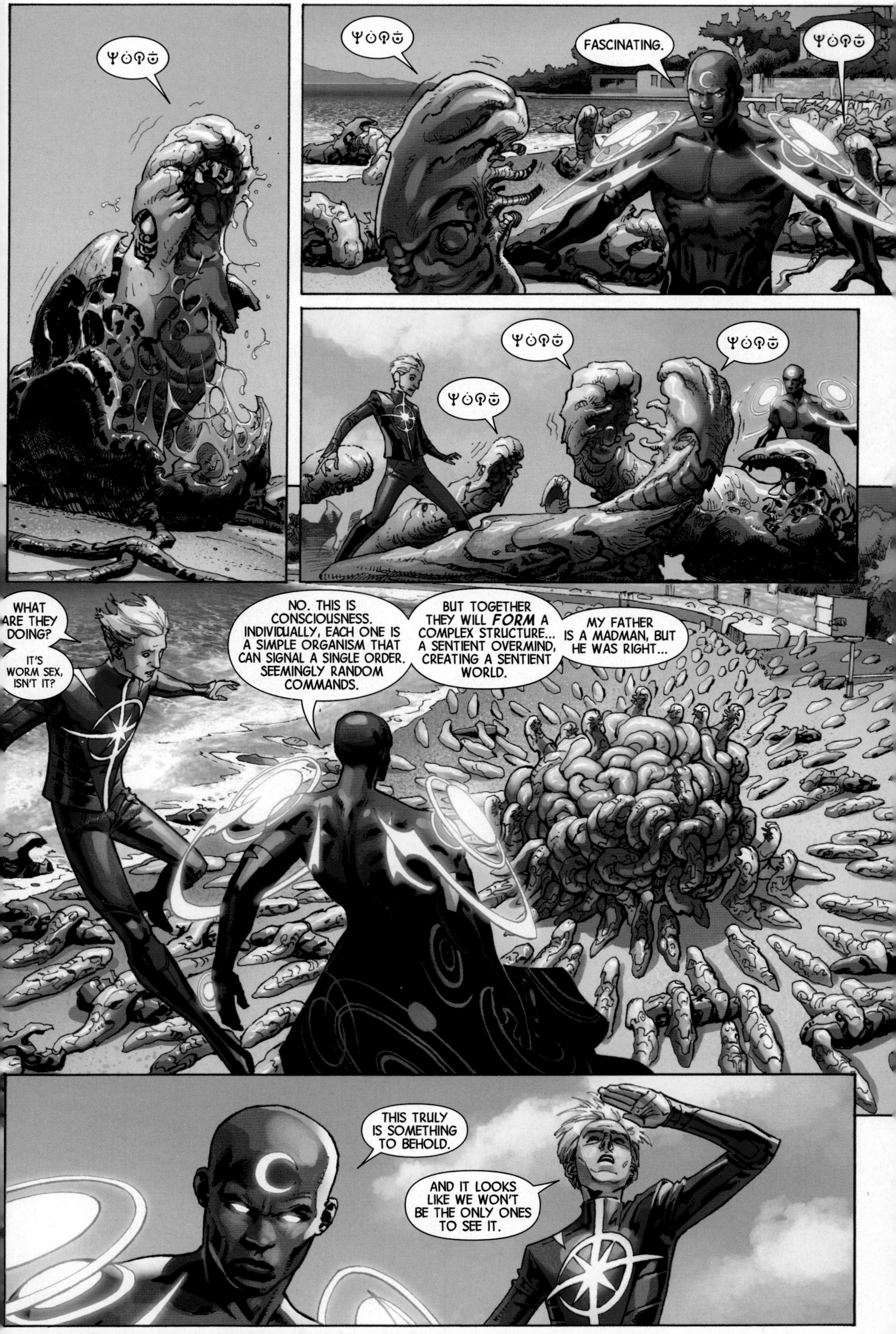

ΨÖΦÕ
ΨÖΦÕ
FASCINATING.
ΨÖΦÕ
ΨÖΦÕ
ΨÖΦÕ
ΨÖΦÕ
WHAT ARE THEY DOING?
IT'S WORM SEX, ISN'T IT?
NO. THIS IS CONSCIOUSNESS. INDIVIDUALLY, EACH ONE IS A SIMPLE ORGANISM THAT CAN SIGNAL A SINGLE ORDER. SEEMINGLY RANDOM COMMANDS.
BUT TOGETHER THEY WILL *FORM* A COMPLEX STRUCTURE... A SENTIENT OVERMIND, CREATING A SENTIENT WORLD.
MY FATHER IS A MADMAN, BUT HE WAS RIGHT...
THIS TRULY IS SOMETHING TO BEHOLD.
AND IT LOOKS LIKE WE WON'T BE THE ONLY ONES TO SEE IT.

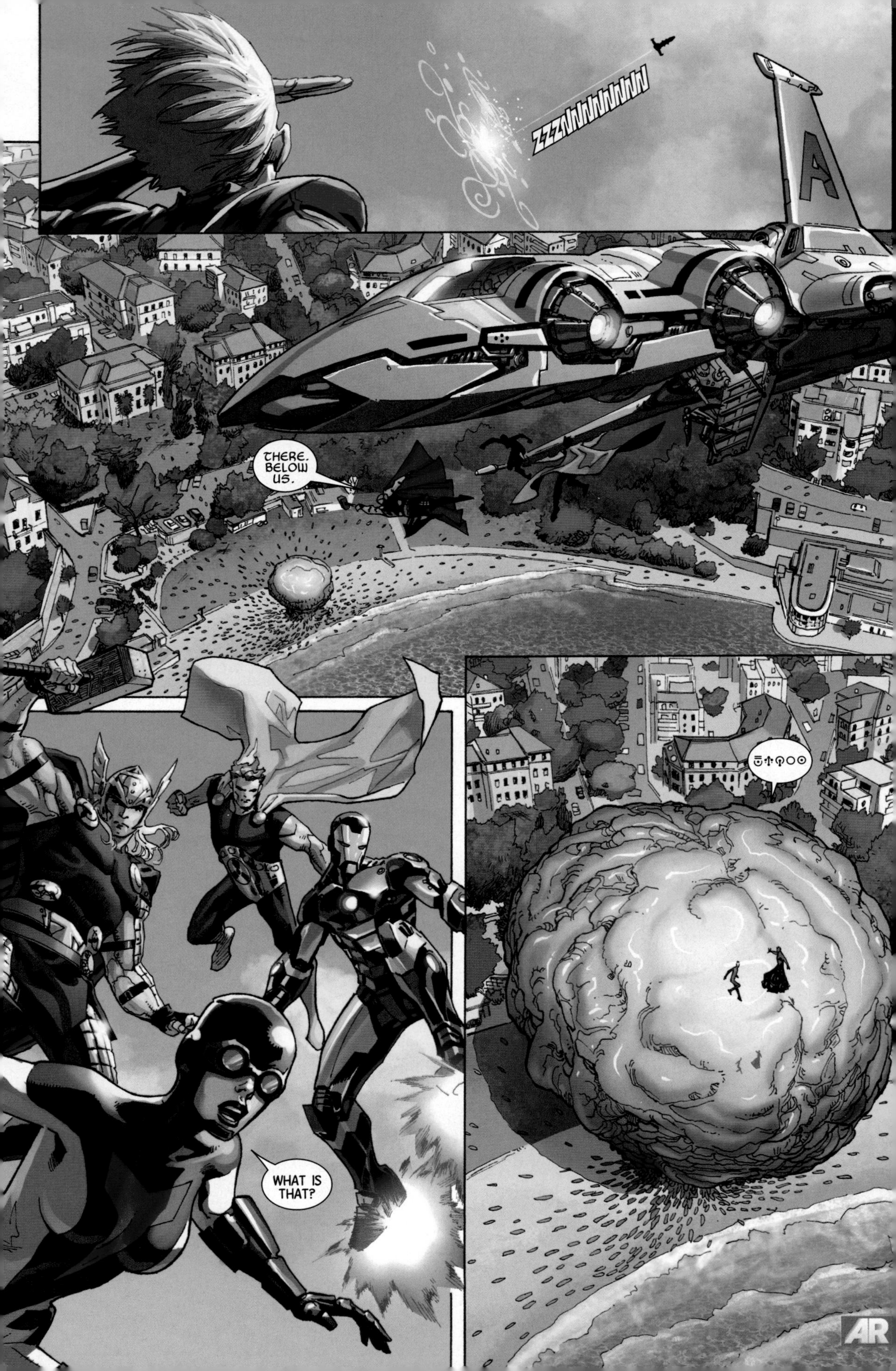
ZZZNNNNNNNN
THERE. BELOW US.
WHAT IS THAT?
AR

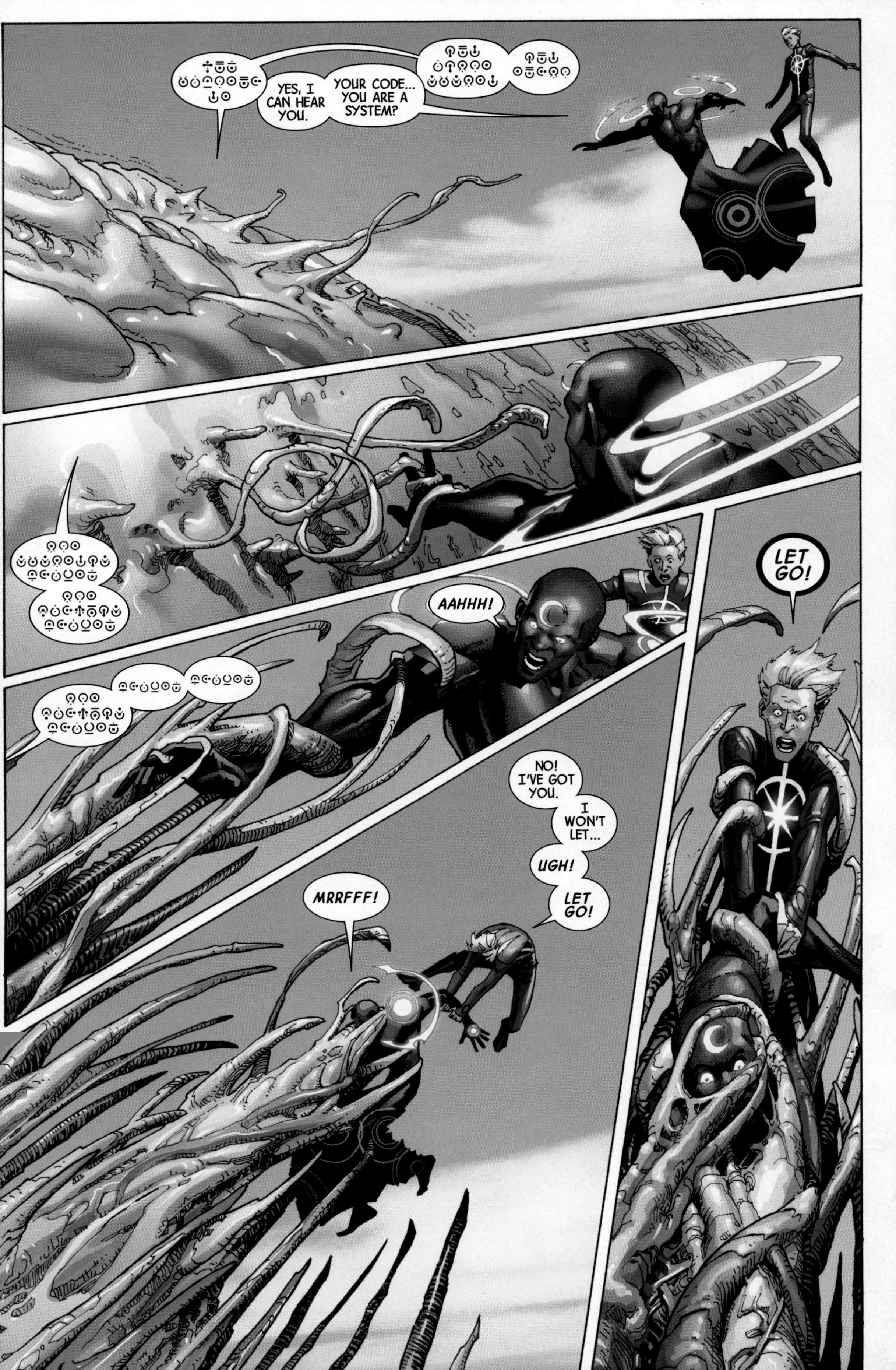
YES, I CAN HEAR YOU.
YOUR CODE... YOU ARE A SYSTEM?
AAHHH!
LET GO!
NO! I'VE GOT YOU.
I WON'T LET...
UGH!
LET GO!
MRRFFF!

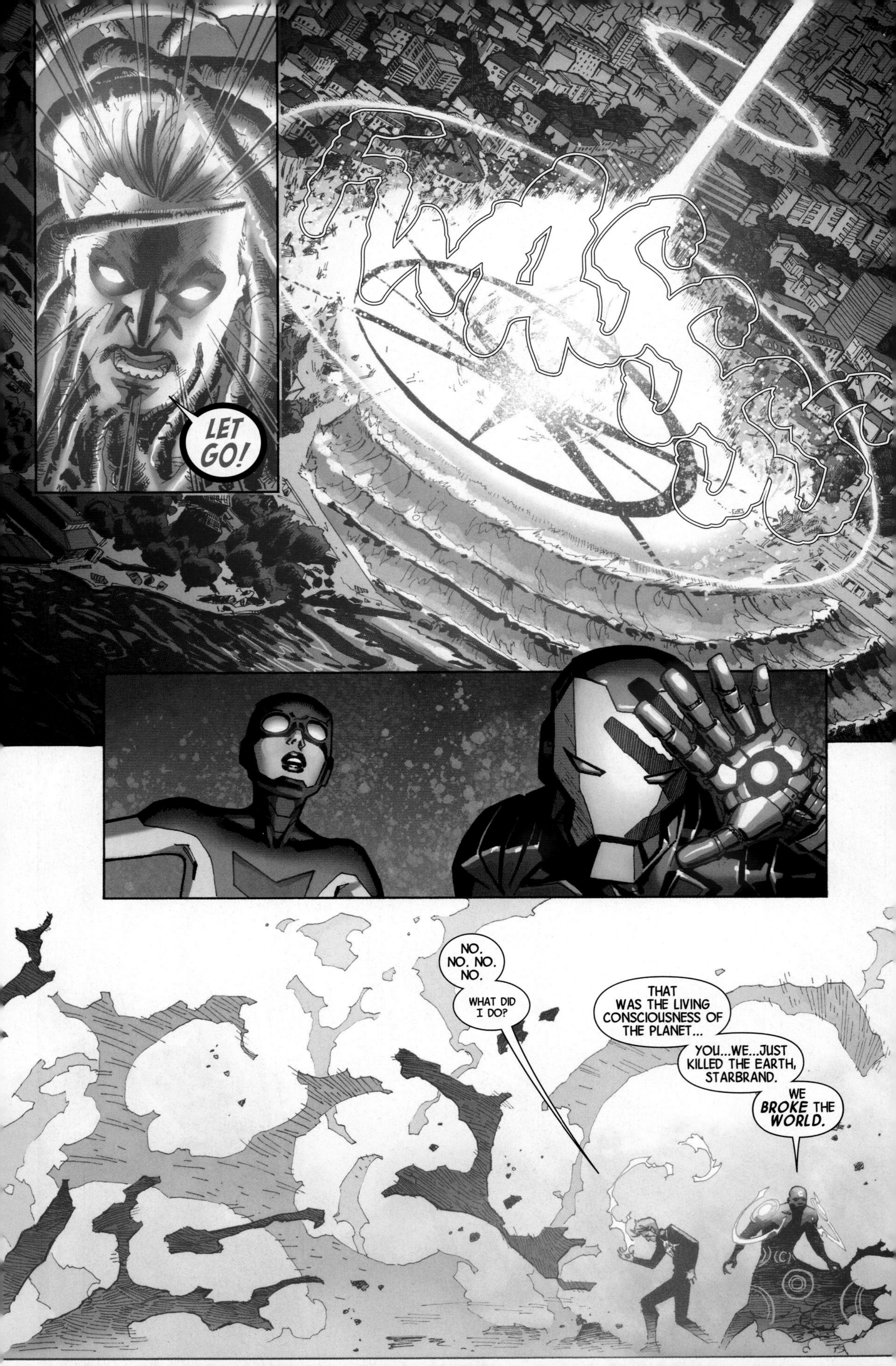
LET GO!
NO. NO. NO. NO.
WHAT DID I DO?
THAT WAS THE LIVING CONSCIOUSNESS OF THE PLANET...
YOU...WE...JUST KILLED THE EARTH, STARBRAND.
WE BROKE THE WORLD.

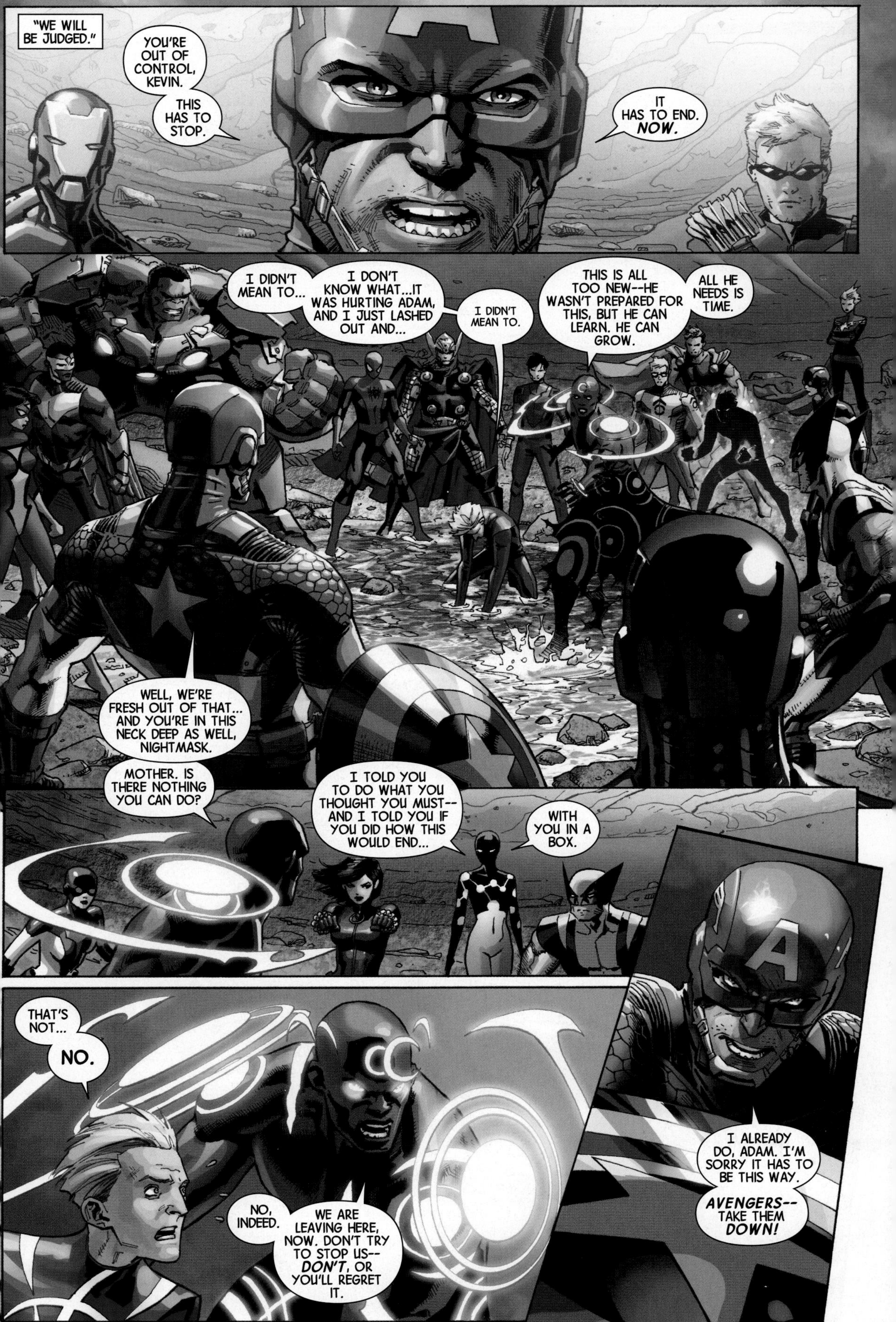
"WE WILL BE JUDGED."
YOU'RE OUT OF CONTROL, KEVIN.
THIS HAS TO STOP.
IT HAS TO END. NOW.
I DIDN'T MEAN TO...
I DON'T KNOW WHAT...IT WAS HURTING ADAM, AND I JUST LASHED OUT AND...
I DIDN'T MEAN TO.
THIS IS ALL TOO NEW--HE WASN'T PREPARED FOR THIS, BUT HE CAN LEARN. HE CAN GROW.
ALL HE NEEDS IS TIME.
WELL, WE'RE FRESH OUT OF THAT... AND YOU'RE IN THIS NECK DEEP AS WELL, NIGHTMASK.
MOTHER. IS THERE NOTHING YOU CAN DO?
I TOLD YOU TO DO WHAT YOU THOUGHT YOU MUST--AND I TOLD YOU IF YOU DID HOW THIS WOULD END...
WITH YOU IN A BOX.
THAT'S NOT...
NO.
NO, INDEED.
WE ARE LEAVING HERE, NOW. DON'T TRY TO STOP US--DON'T, OR YOU'LL REGRET IT.
I ALREADY DO, ADAM. I'M SORRY IT HAS TO BE THIS WAY.
AVENGERS--TAKE THEM DOWN!

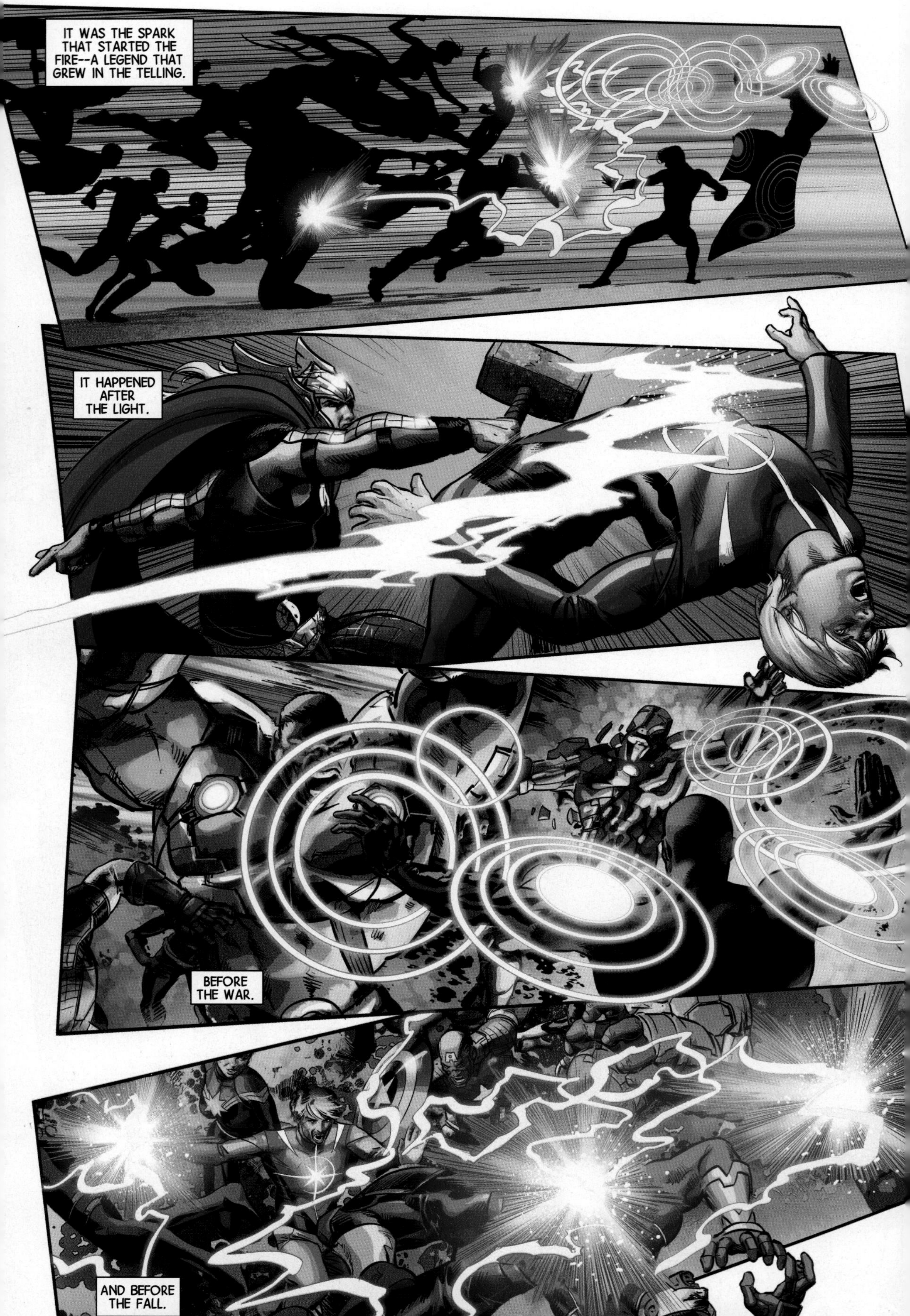
IT WAS THE SPARK THAT STARTED THE FIRE--A LEGEND THAT GREW IN THE TELLING.
IT HAPPENED AFTER THE LIGHT.
BEFORE THE WAR.
AND BEFORE THE FALL.

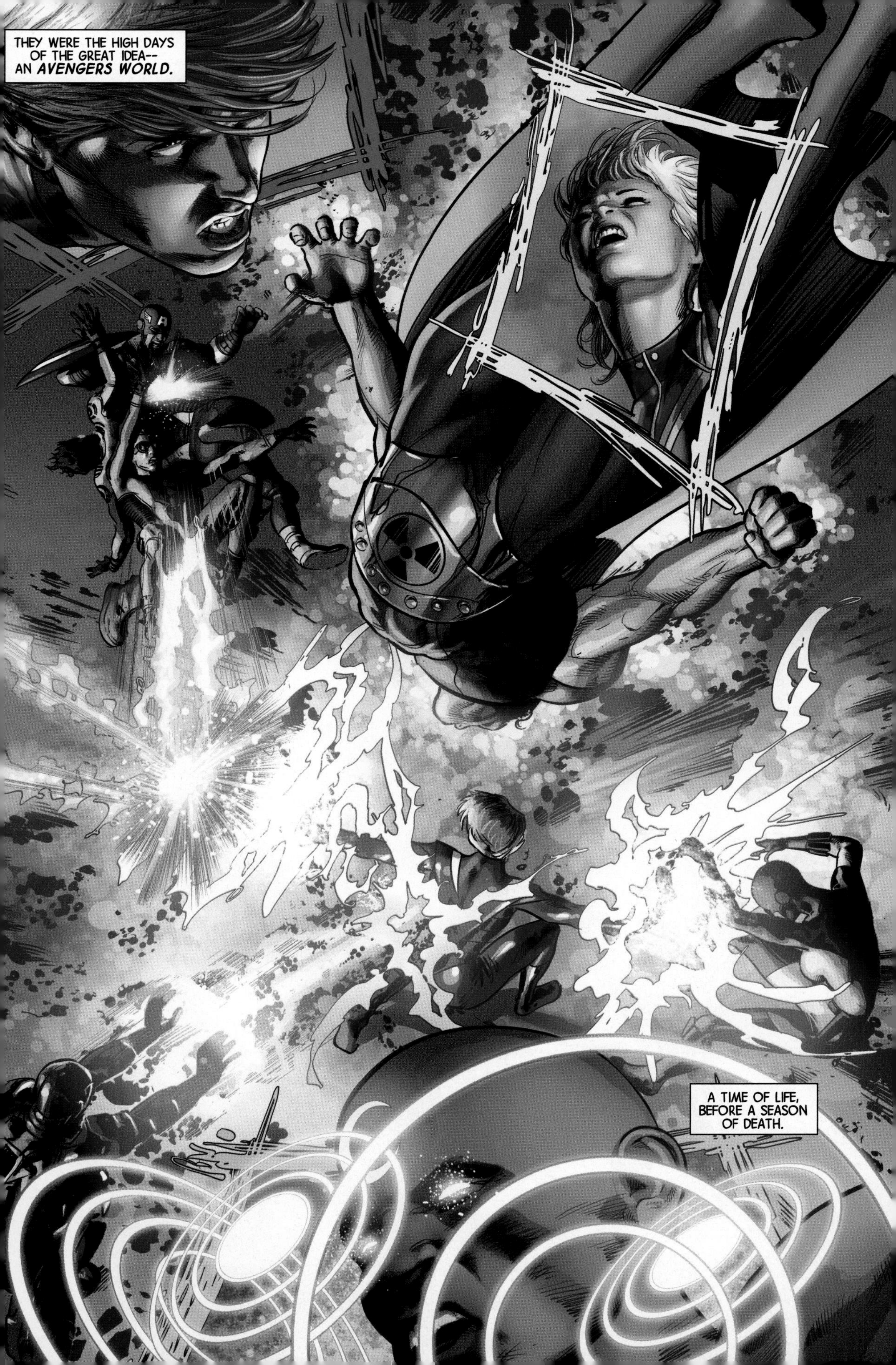
THEY WERE THE HIGH DAYS OF THE GREAT IDEA-- AN *AVENGERS WORLD.*
A TIME OF LIFE, BEFORE A SEASON OF DEATH.

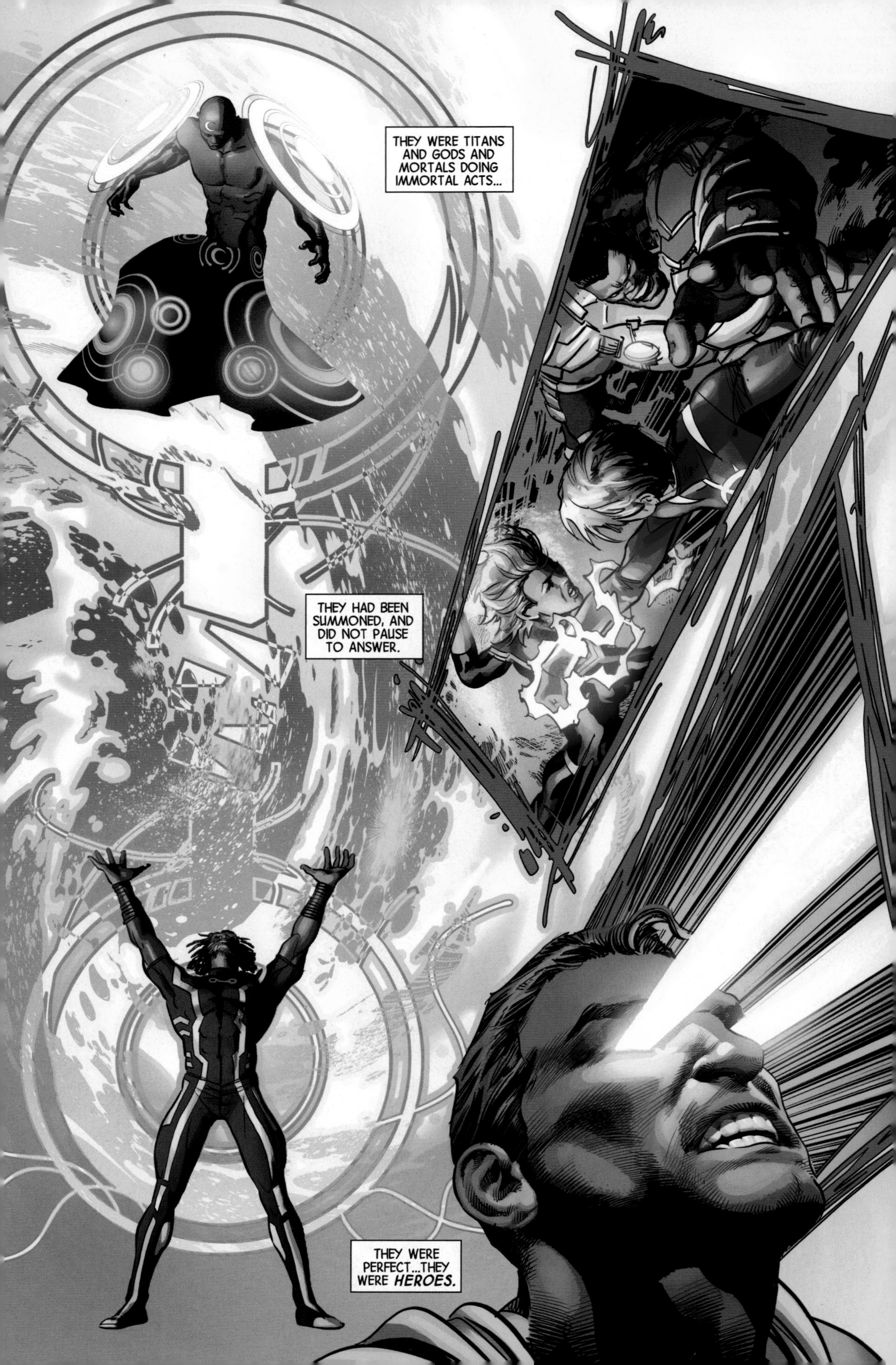
THEY WERE TITANS AND GODS AND MORTALS DOING IMMORTAL ACTS...
THEY HAD BEEN SUMMONED, AND DID NOT PAUSE TO ANSWER.
THEY WERE PERFECT...THEY WERE *HEROES.*

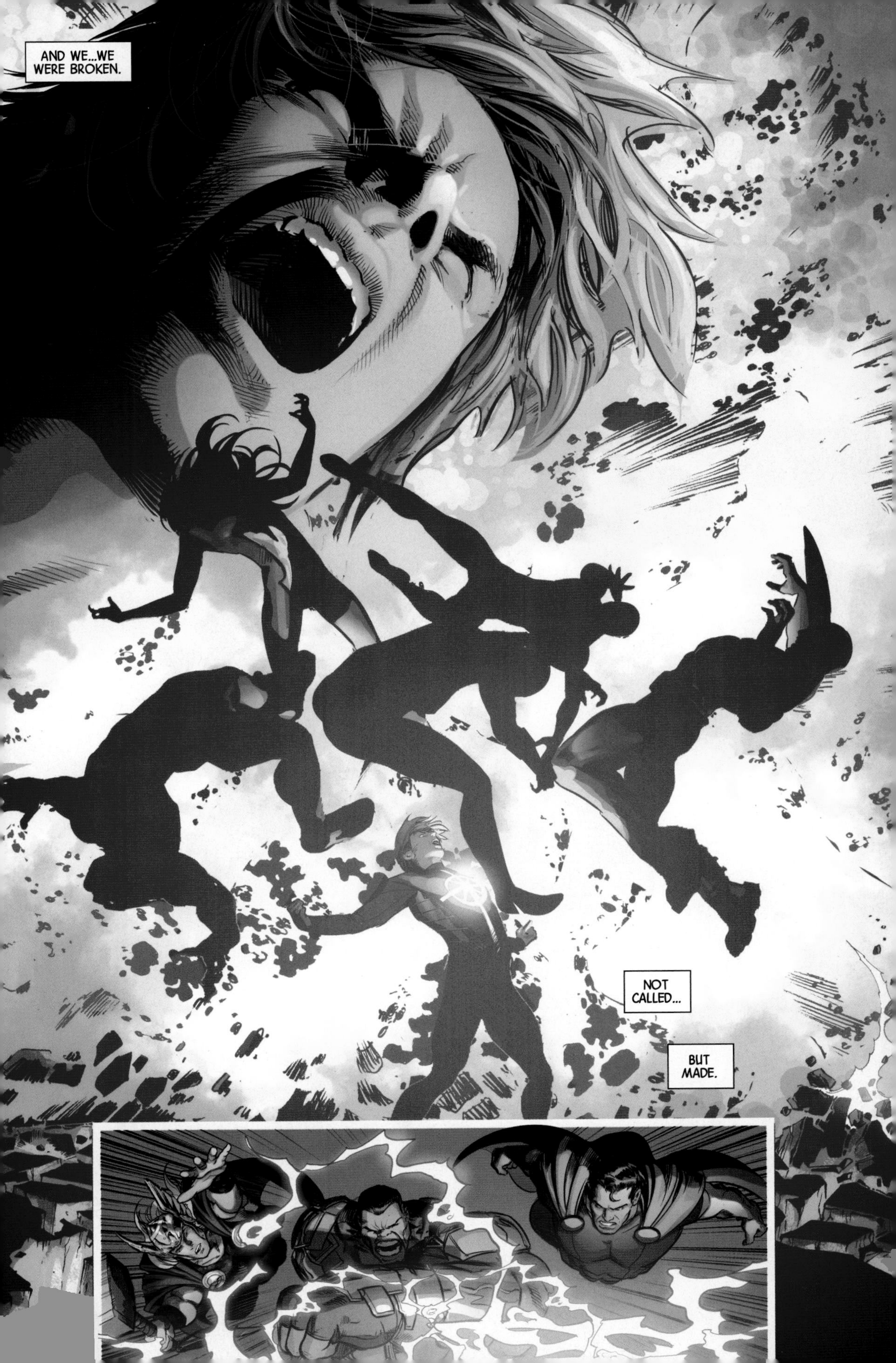
AND WE...WE WERE BROKEN.
NOT CALLED...
BUT MADE.

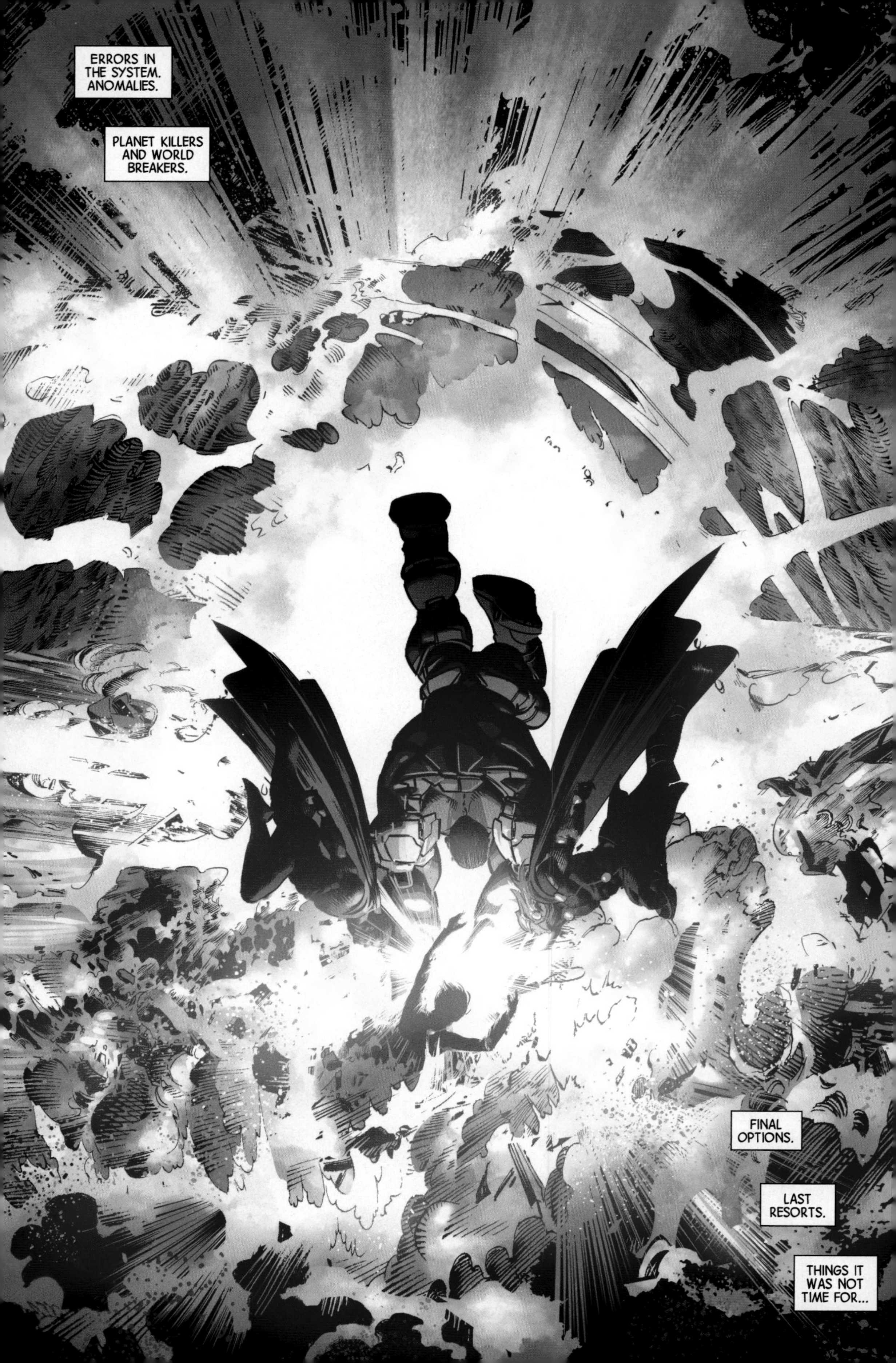
ERRORS IN THE SYSTEM. ANOMALIES.
PLANET KILLERS AND WORLD BREAKERS.
FINAL OPTIONS.
LAST RESORTS.
THINGS IT WAS NOT TIME FOR...

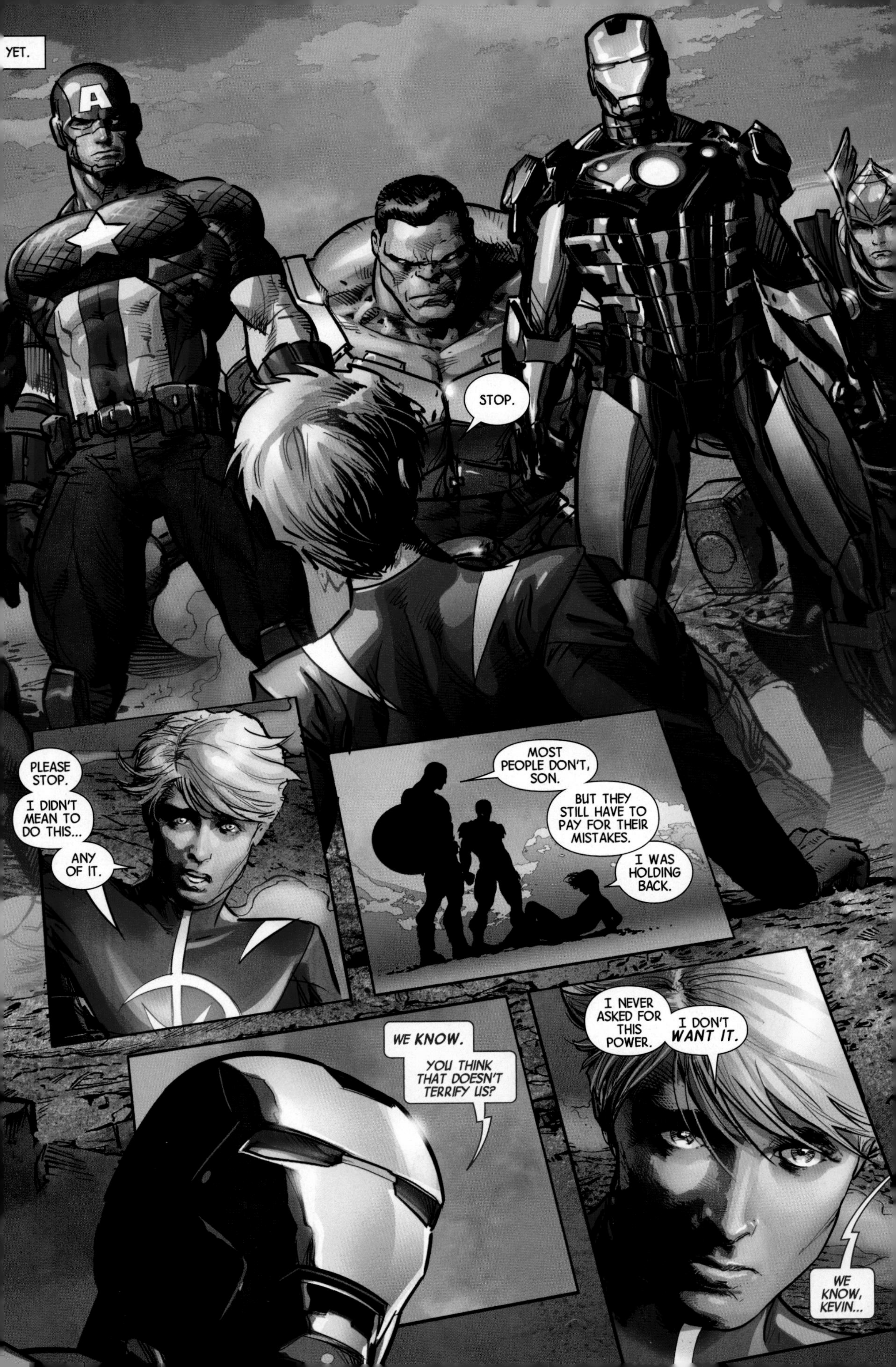

YET.
STOP.
PLEASE STOP.
I DIDN'T MEAN TO DO THIS...
ANY OF IT.
MOST PEOPLE DON'T, SON.
BUT THEY STILL HAVE TO PAY FOR THEIR MISTAKES.
I WAS HOLDING BACK.
WE KNOW.
YOU THINK THAT DOESN'T TERRIFY US?
I NEVER ASKED FOR THIS POWER.
I DON'T WANT IT.
WE KNOW, KEVIN...

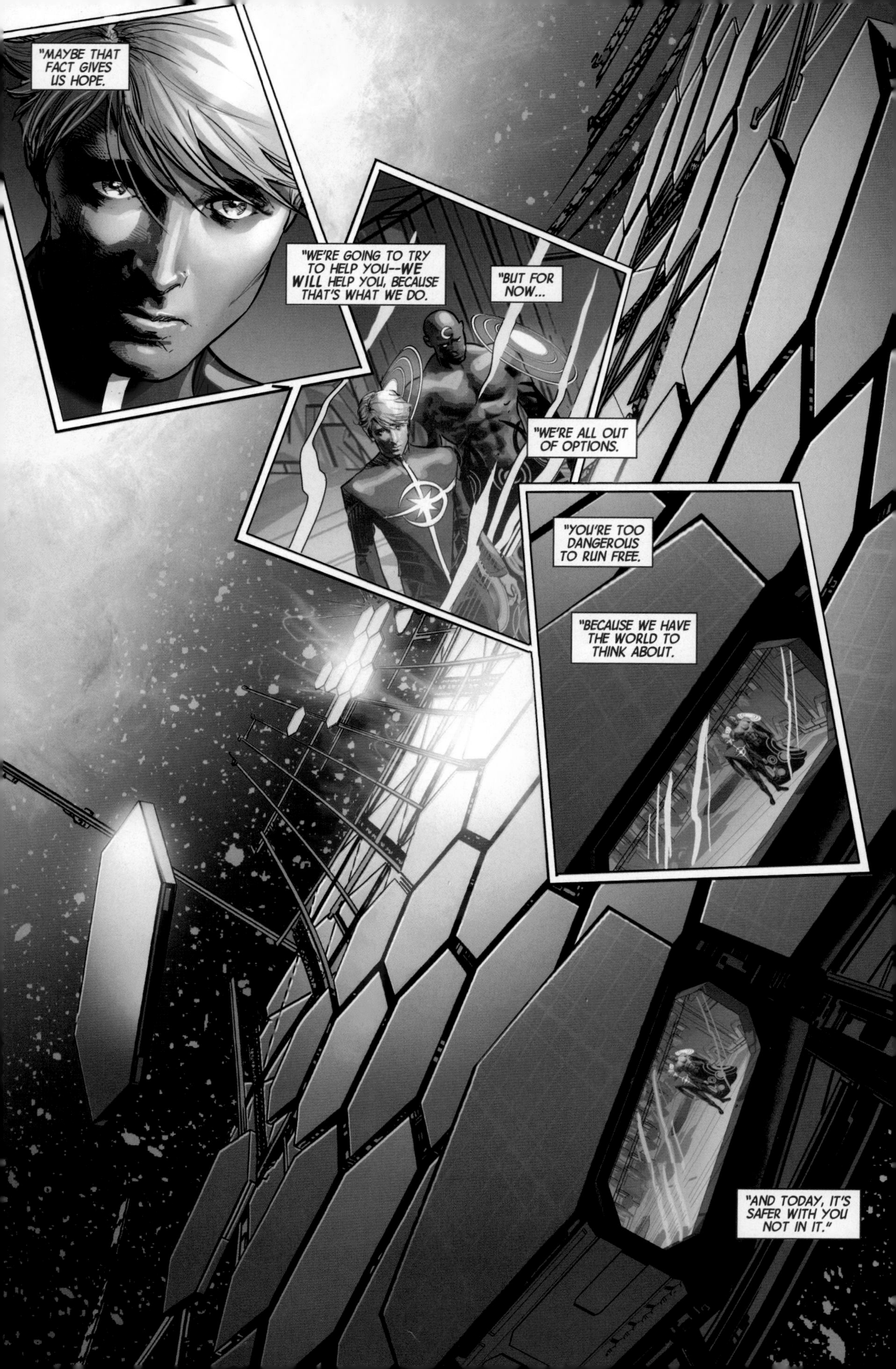
"MAYBE THAT FACT GIVES US HOPE.
"WE'RE GOING TO TRY TO HELP YOU--WE WILL HELP YOU, BECAUSE THAT'S WHAT WE DO.
"BUT FOR NOW...
"WE'RE ALL OUT OF OPTIONS.
"YOU'RE TOO DANGEROUS TO RUN FREE.
"BECAUSE WE HAVE THE WORLD TO THINK ABOUT.
"AND TODAY, IT'S SAFER WITH YOU NOT IN IT."

"VALIDATOR"

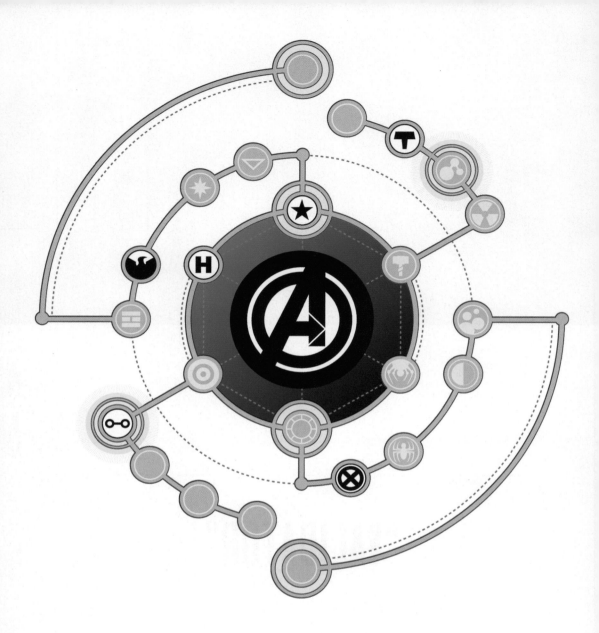

EARTH'S MIGHTIEST HEROES

CAPTAIN AMERICA · IRON MAN · THOR · HAWKEYE · BLACK WIDOW · HULK
WOLVERINE · SPIDER-MAN · CAPTAIN MARVEL · SPIDER-WOMAN
FALCON · SHANG-CHI · SUNSPOT · CANNONBALL · MANIFOLD
SMASHER · CAPTAIN UNIVERSE · HYPERION

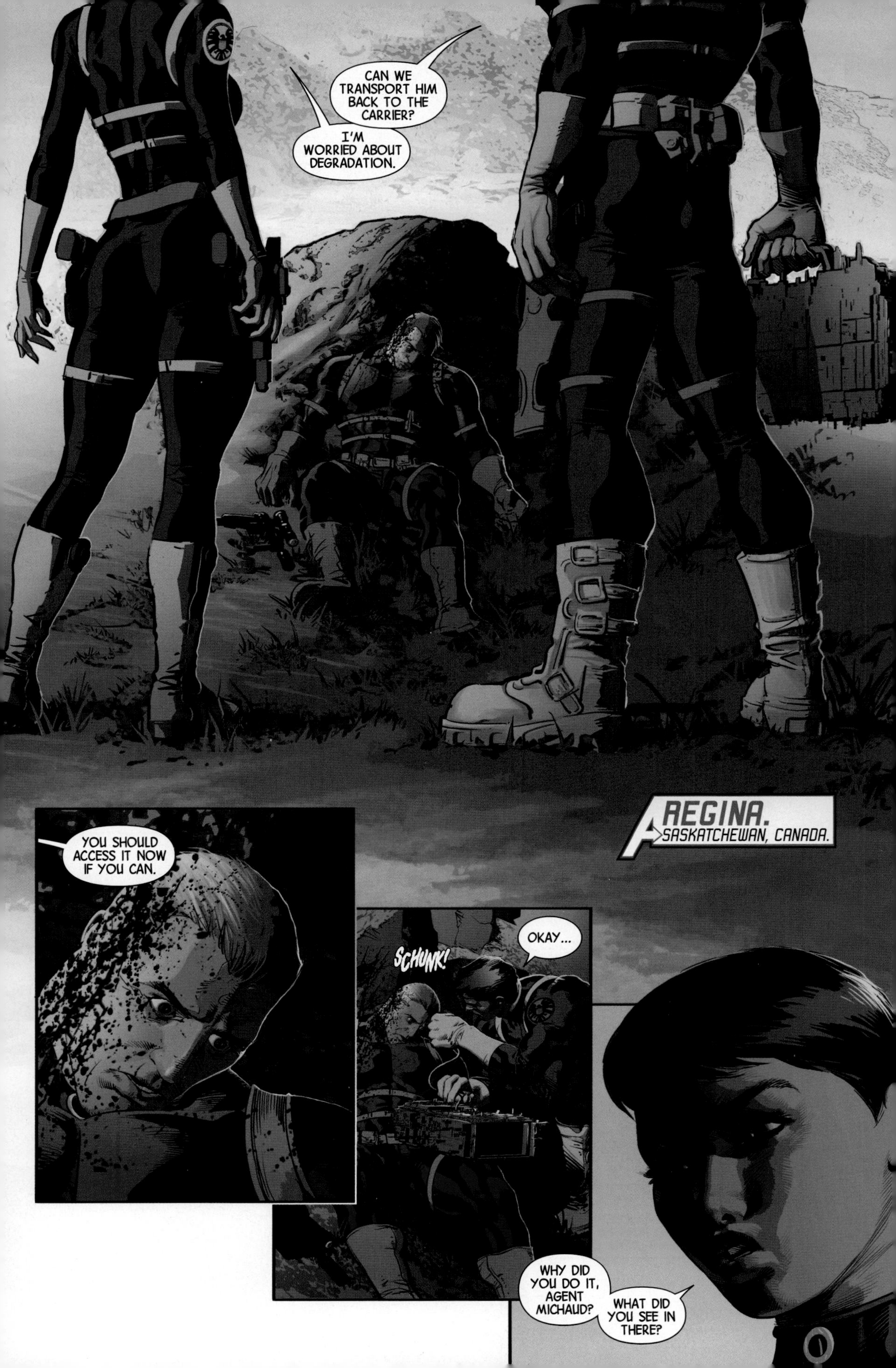
CAN WE TRANSPORT HIM BACK TO THE CARRIER?
I'M WORRIED ABOUT DEGRADATION.
REGINA. SASKATCHEWAN, CANADA.
YOU SHOULD ACCESS IT NOW IF YOU CAN.
OKAY...
SCHUNK!
WHY DID YOU DO IT, AGENT MICHAUD?
WHAT DID YOU SEE IN THERE?

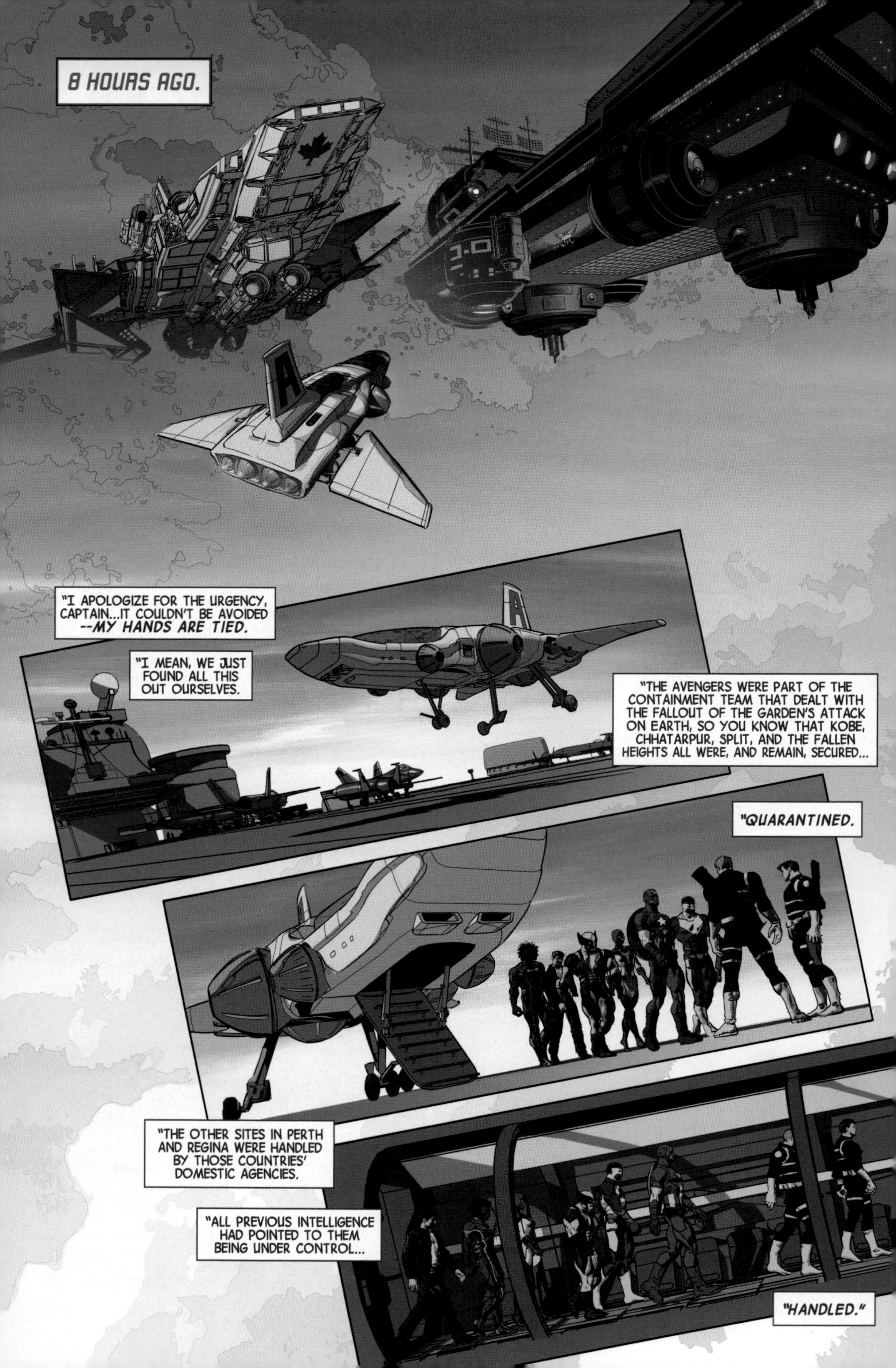
8 HOURS AGO.
"I APOLOGIZE FOR THE URGENCY, CAPTAIN...IT COULDN'T BE AVOIDED --MY HANDS ARE TIED.
"I MEAN, WE JUST FOUND ALL THIS OUT OURSELVES.
"THE AVENGERS WERE PART OF THE CONTAINMENT TEAM THAT DEALT WITH THE FALLOUT OF THE GARDEN'S ATTACK ON EARTH, SO YOU KNOW THAT KOBE, CHHATARPUR, SPLIT, AND THE FALLEN HEIGHTS ALL WERE, AND REMAIN, SECURED...
"QUARANTINED.
"THE OTHER SITES IN PERTH AND REGINA WERE HANDLED BY THOSE COUNTRIES' DOMESTIC AGENCIES.
"ALL PREVIOUS INTELLIGENCE HAD POINTED TO THEM BEING UNDER CONTROL...
"HANDLED."

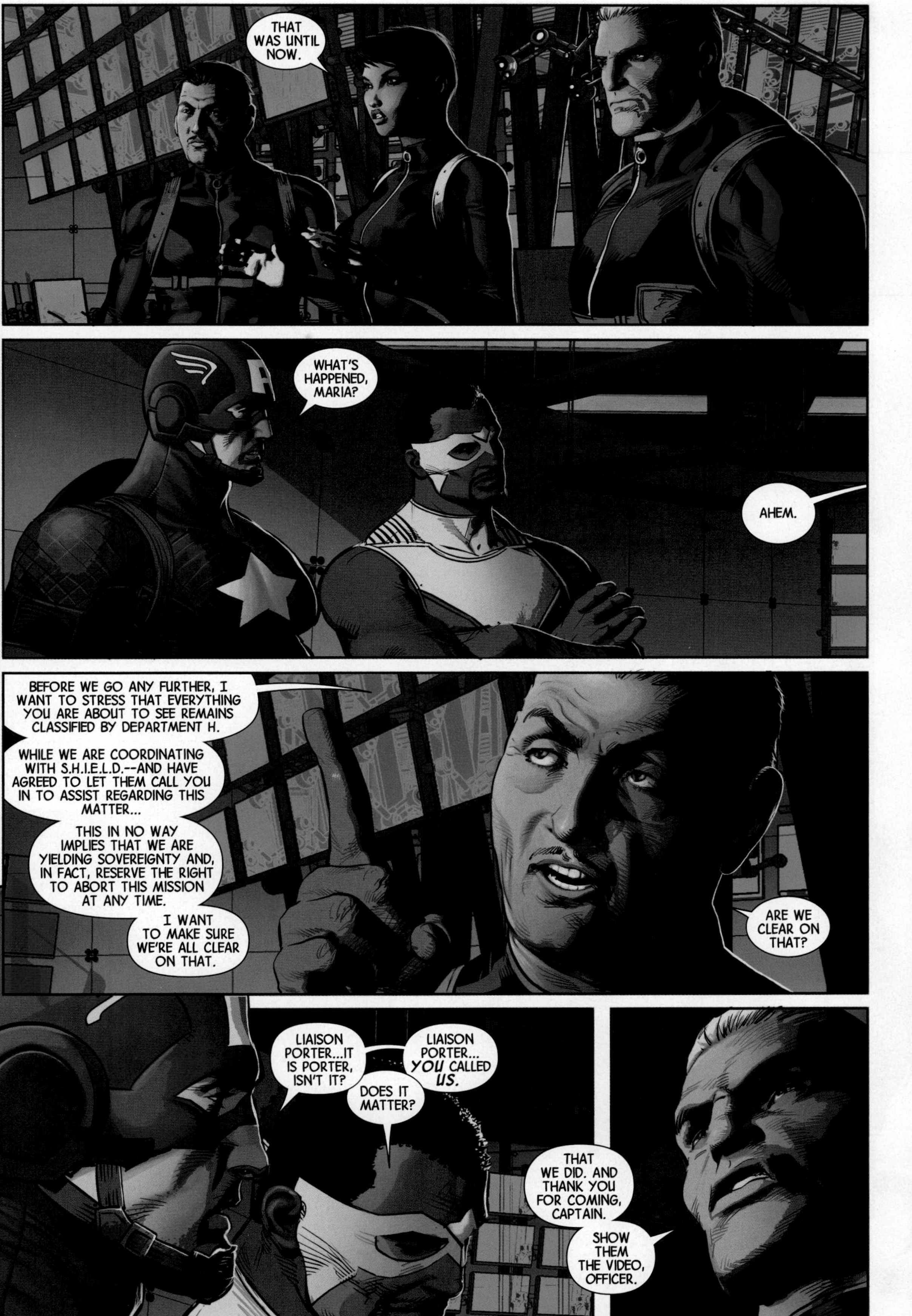

THAT WAS UNTIL NOW.
WHAT'S HAPPENED, MARIA?
AHEM.
BEFORE WE GO ANY FURTHER, I WANT TO STRESS THAT EVERYTHING YOU ARE ABOUT TO SEE REMAINS CLASSIFIED BY DEPARTMENT H.
WHILE WE ARE COORDINATING WITH S.H.I.E.L.D.--AND HAVE AGREED TO LET THEM CALL YOU IN TO ASSIST REGARDING THIS MATTER...
THIS IN NO WAY IMPLIES THAT WE ARE YIELDING SOVEREIGNTY AND, IN FACT, RESERVE THE RIGHT TO ABORT THIS MISSION AT ANY TIME.
I WANT TO MAKE SURE WE'RE ALL CLEAR ON THAT.
ARE WE CLEAR ON THAT?
LIAISON PORTER...IT IS PORTER, ISN'T IT?
DOES IT MATTER?
LIAISON PORTER... YOU CALLED US.
THAT WE DID. AND THANK YOU FOR COMING, CAPTAIN.
SHOW THEM THE VIDEO, OFFICER.

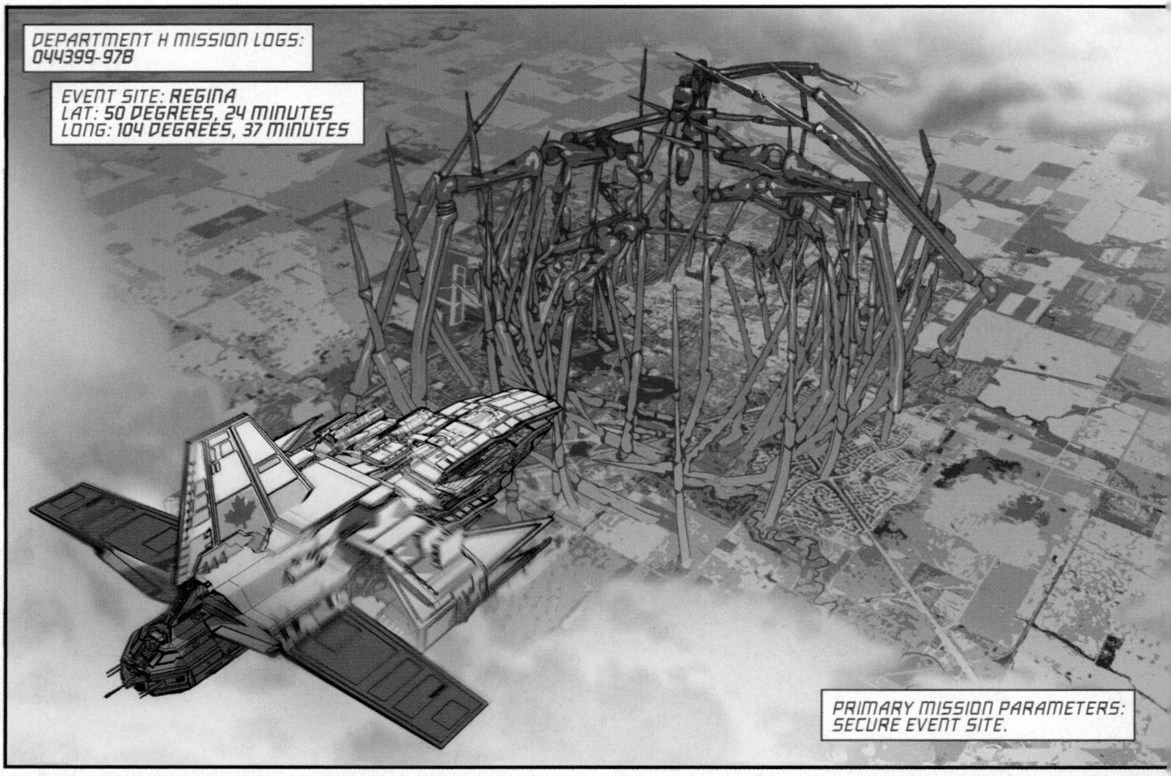
DEPARTMENT H MISSION LOGS:
044399-97B
EVENT SITE: REGINA
LAT: 50 DEGREES, 24 MINUTES
LONG: 104 DEGREES, 37 MINUTES
PRIMARY MISSION PARAMETERS:
SECURE EVENT SITE.

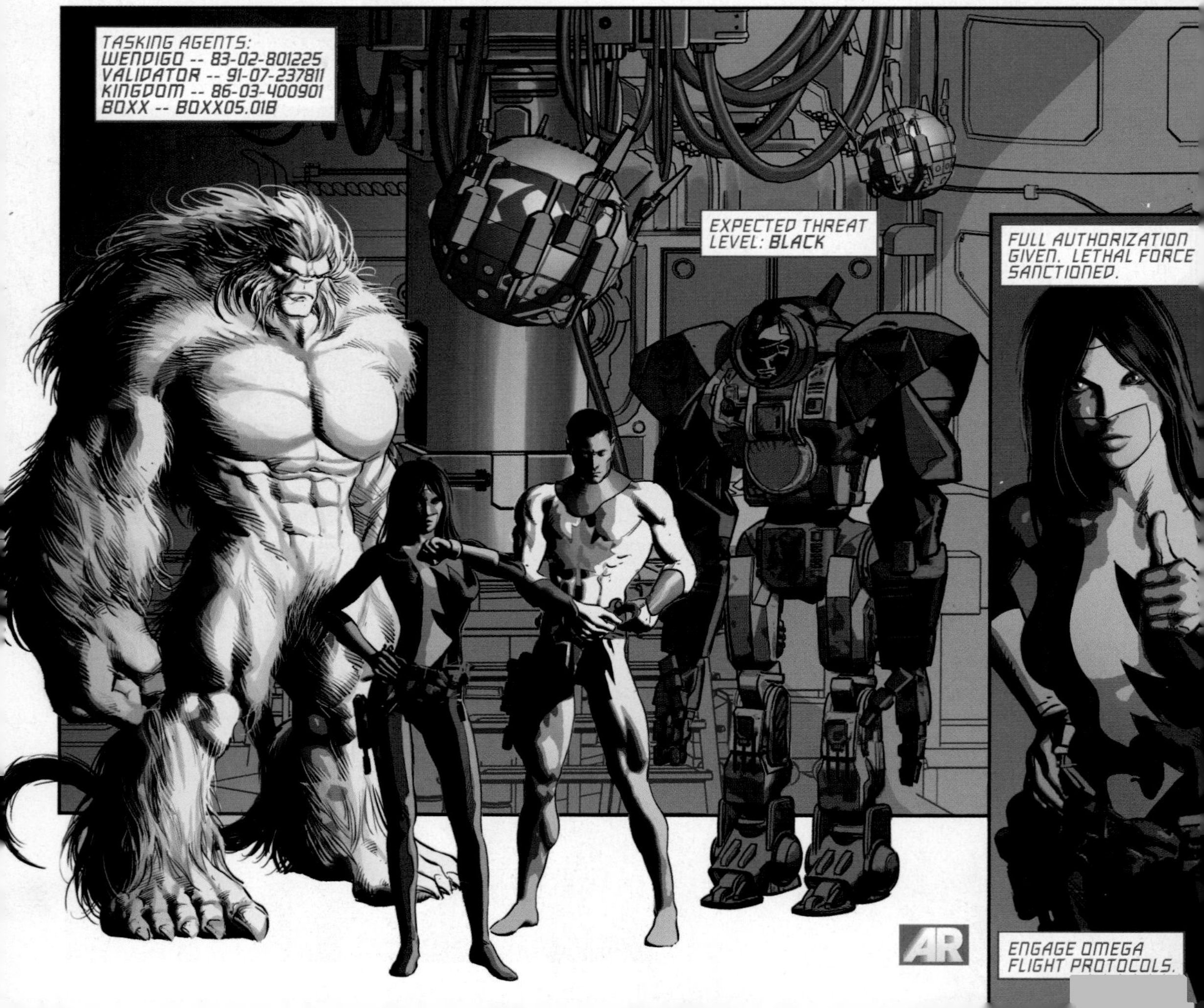
TASKING AGENTS:
WENDIGO -- 83-02-801225
VALIDATOR -- 91-07-237811
KINGDOM -- 86-03-400901
BOXX -- BOXX05.01B
EXPECTED THREAT LEVEL: BLACK
FULL AUTHORIZATION GIVEN. LETHAL FORCE SANCTIONED.
ENGAGE OMEGA FLIGHT PROTOCOLS.
AR

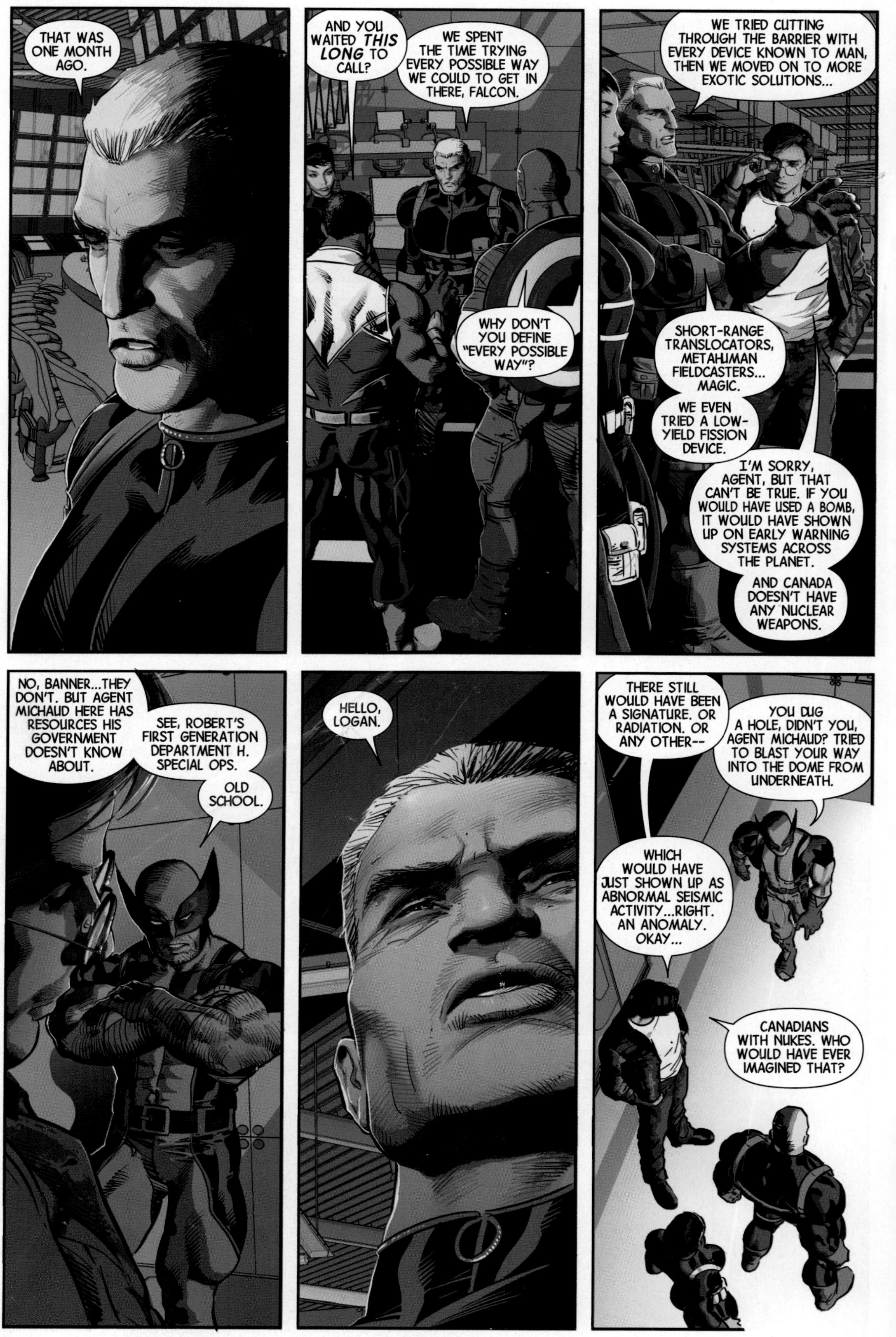
THAT WAS ONE MONTH AGO.
AND YOU WAITED THIS LONG TO CALL?
WE SPENT THE TIME TRYING EVERY POSSIBLE WAY WE COULD TO GET IN THERE, FALCON.
WHY DON'T YOU DEFINE "EVERY POSSIBLE WAY"?
WE TRIED CUTTING THROUGH THE BARRIER WITH EVERY DEVICE KNOWN TO MAN, THEN WE MOVED ON TO MORE EXOTIC SOLUTIONS...
SHORT-RANGE TRANSLOCATORS, METAHUMAN FIELDCASTERS... MAGIC.
WE EVEN TRIED A LOW-YIELD FISSION DEVICE.
I'M SORRY, AGENT, BUT THAT CAN'T BE TRUE. IF YOU WOULD HAVE USED A BOMB, IT WOULD HAVE SHOWN UP ON EARLY WARNING SYSTEMS ACROSS THE PLANET.
AND CANADA DOESN'T HAVE ANY NUCLEAR WEAPONS.
NO, BANNER...THEY DON'T. BUT AGENT MICHAUD HERE HAS RESOURCES HIS GOVERNMENT DOESN'T KNOW ABOUT.
SEE, ROBERT'S FIRST GENERATION DEPARTMENT H. SPECIAL OPS.
OLD SCHOOL.
HELLO, LOGAN.
THERE STILL WOULD HAVE BEEN A SIGNATURE. OR RADIATION. OR ANY OTHER--
YOU DUG A HOLE, DIDN'T YOU, AGENT MICHAUD? TRIED TO BLAST YOUR WAY INTO THE DOME FROM UNDERNEATH.
WHICH WOULD HAVE JUST SHOWN UP AS ABNORMAL SEISMIC ACTIVITY...RIGHT. AN ANOMALY. OKAY...
CANADIANS WITH NUKES. WHO WOULD HAVE EVER IMAGINED THAT?

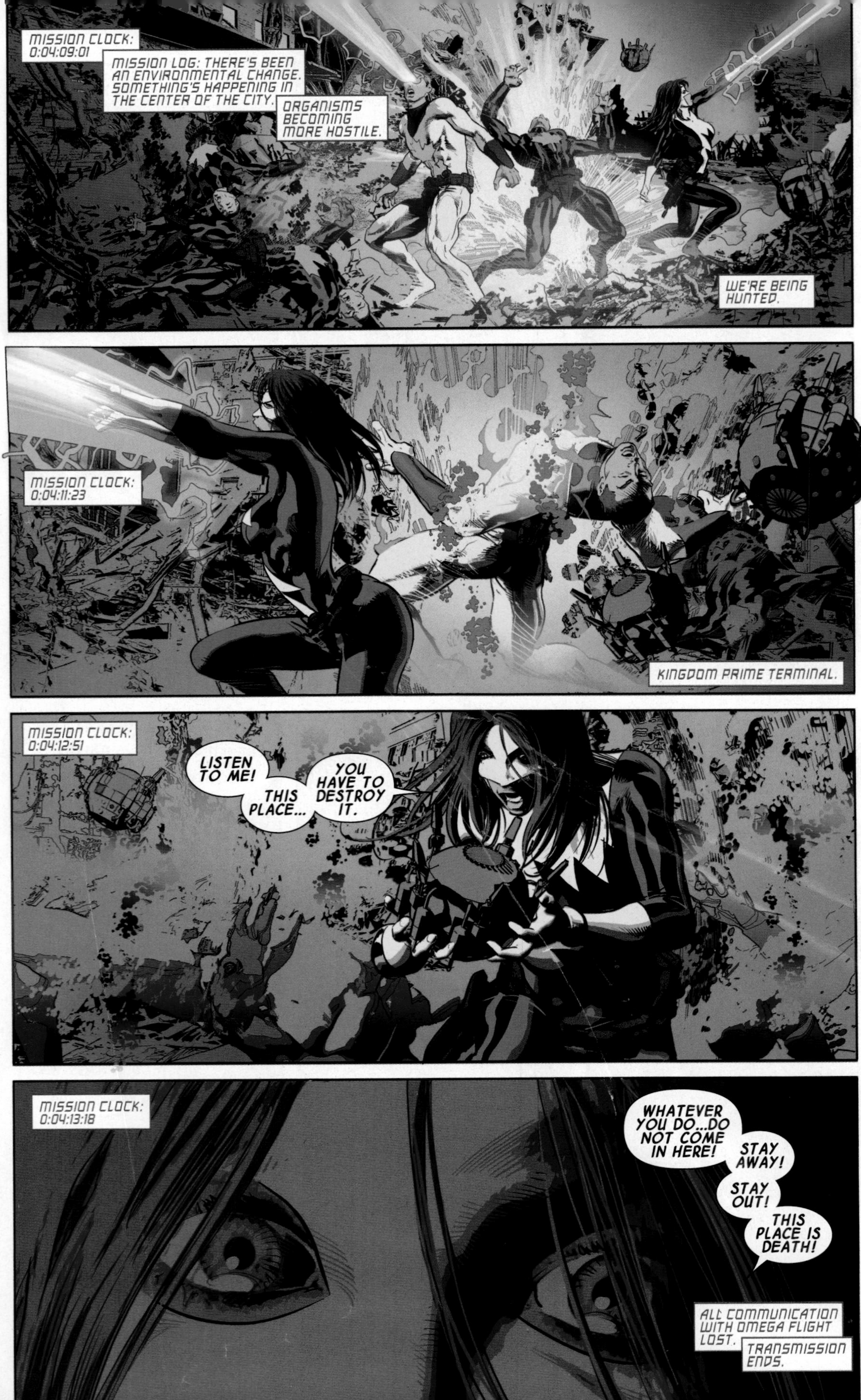
MISSION CLOCK: 0:04:09:01
MISSION LOG: THERE'S BEEN AN ENVIRONMENTAL CHANGE. SOMETHING'S HAPPENING IN THE CENTER OF THE CITY.
ORGANISMS BECOMING MORE HOSTILE.
WE'RE BEING HUNTED.
MISSION CLOCK: 0:04:11:23
KINGDOM PRIME TERMINAL.
MISSION CLOCK: 0:04:12:51
LISTEN TO ME!
THIS PLACE...
YOU HAVE TO DESTROY IT.
MISSION CLOCK: 0:04:13:18
WHATEVER YOU DO...DO NOT COME IN HERE!
STAY AWAY!
STAY OUT!
THIS PLACE IS DEATH!
ALL COMMUNICATION WITH OMEGA FLIGHT LOST.
TRANSMISSION ENDS.

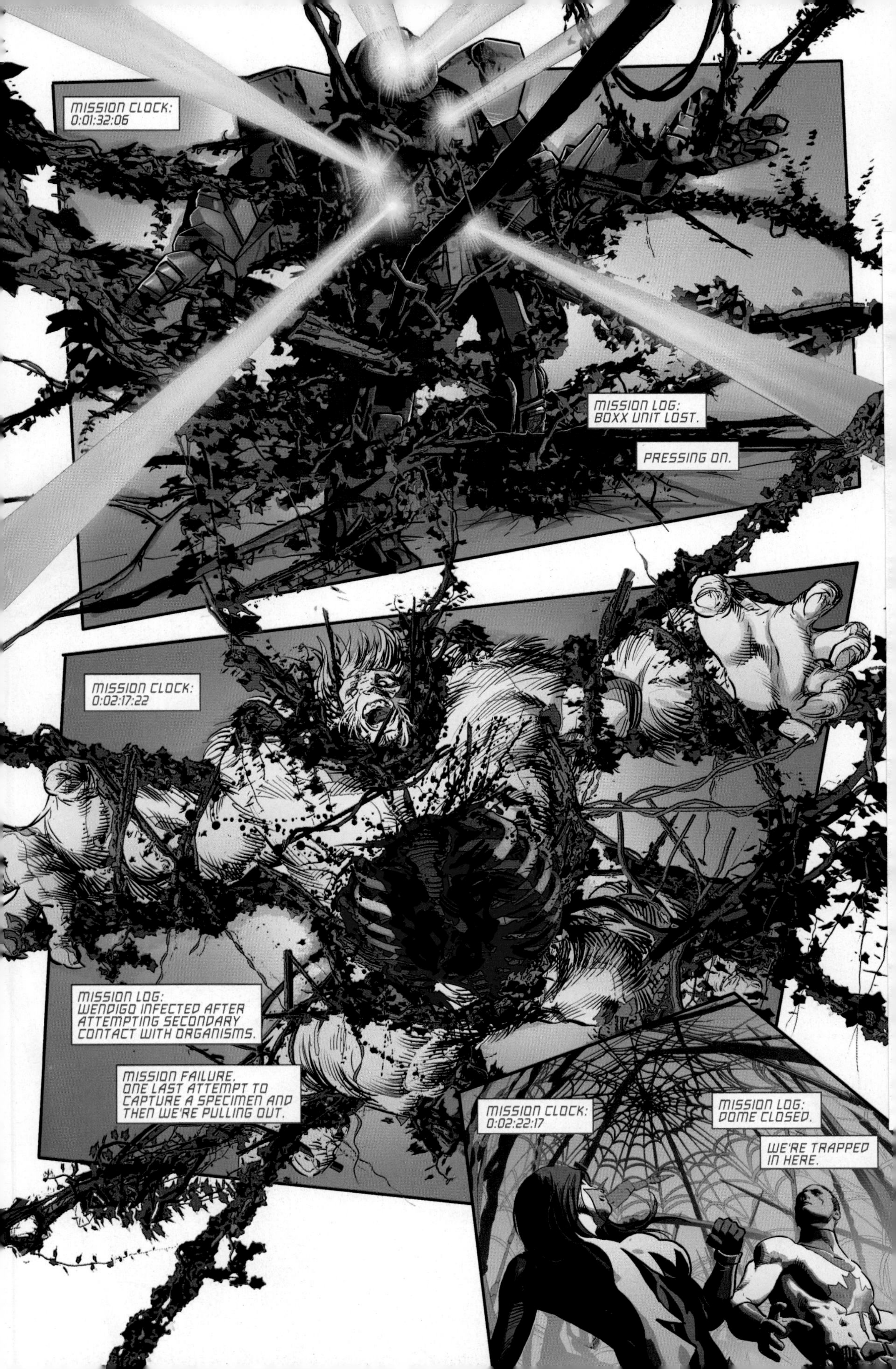
MISSION CLOCK:
0:01:32:06
MISSION LOG:
BOXX UNIT LOST.
PRESSING ON.
MISSION CLOCK:
0:02:17:22
MISSION LOG:
WENDIGO INFECTED AFTER
ATTEMPTING SECONDARY
CONTACT WITH ORGANISMS.
MISSION FAILURE.
ONE LAST ATTEMPT TO
CAPTURE A SPECIMEN AND
THEN WE'RE PULLING OUT.
MISSION CLOCK:
0:02:22:17
MISSION LOG:
DOME CLOSED.
WE'RE TRAPPED
IN HERE.

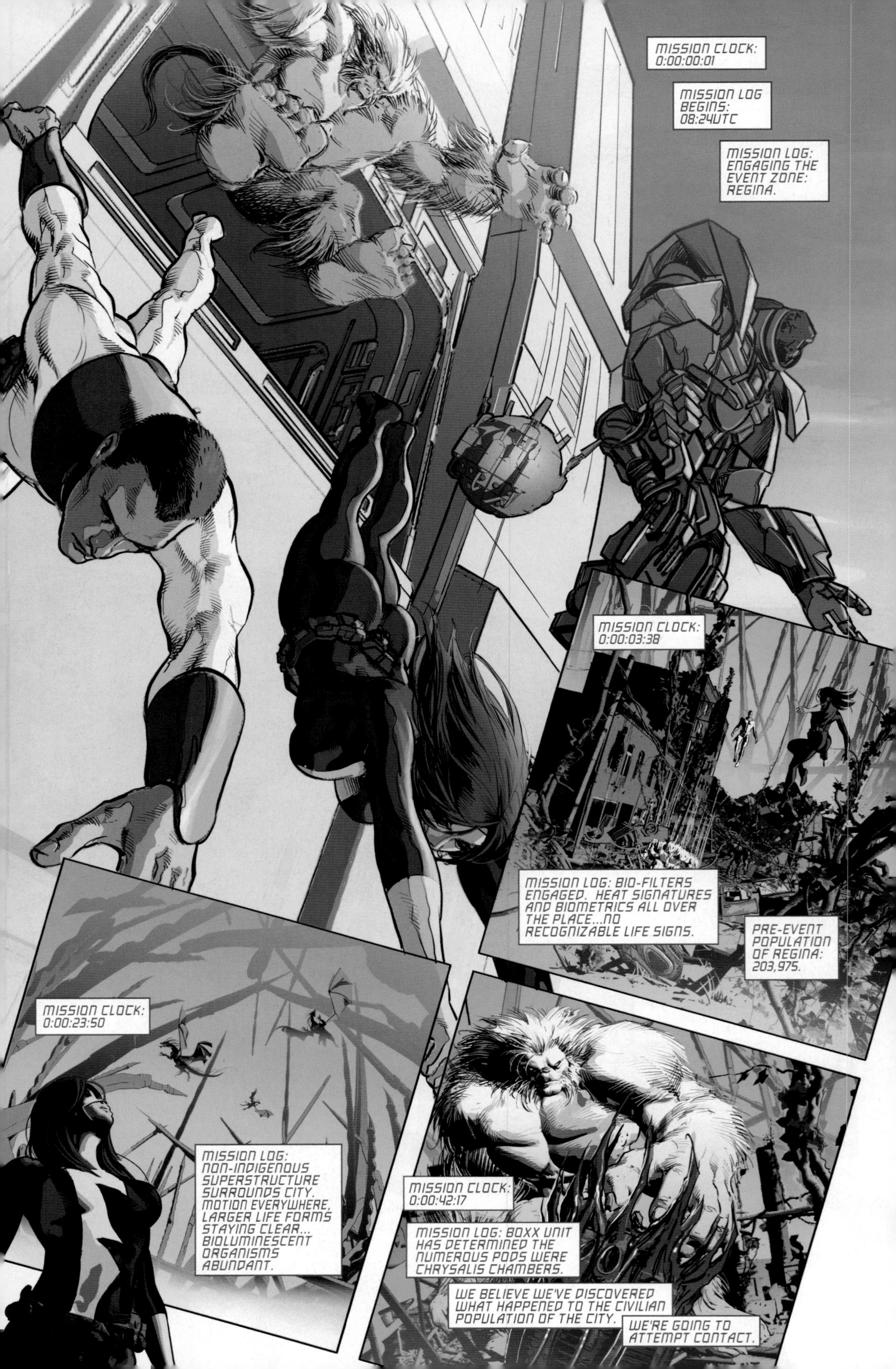
MISSION CLOCK: 0:00:00:01
MISSION LOG BEGINS: 08:24UTC
MISSION LOG: ENGAGING THE EVENT ZONE: REGINA.
MISSION CLOCK: 0:00:03:38
MISSION LOG: BIO-FILTERS ENGAGED. HEAT SIGNATURES AND BIOMETRICS ALL OVER THE PLACE...NO RECOGNIZABLE LIFE SIGNS.
PRE-EVENT POPULATION OF REGINA: 203,975.
MISSION CLOCK: 0:00:23:50
MISSION LOG: NON-INDIGENOUS SUPERSTRUCTURE SURROUNDS CITY. MOTION EVERYWHERE, LARGER LIFE FORMS STAYING CLEAR... BIOLUMINESCENT ORGANISMS ABUNDANT.
MISSION CLOCK: 0:00:42:17
MISSION LOG: BOXX UNIT HAS DETERMINED THE NUMEROUS PODS WERE CHRYSALIS CHAMBERS.
WE BELIEVE WE'VE DISCOVERED WHAT HAPPENED TO THE CIVILIAN POPULATION OF THE CITY.
WE'RE GOING TO ATTEMPT CONTACT.

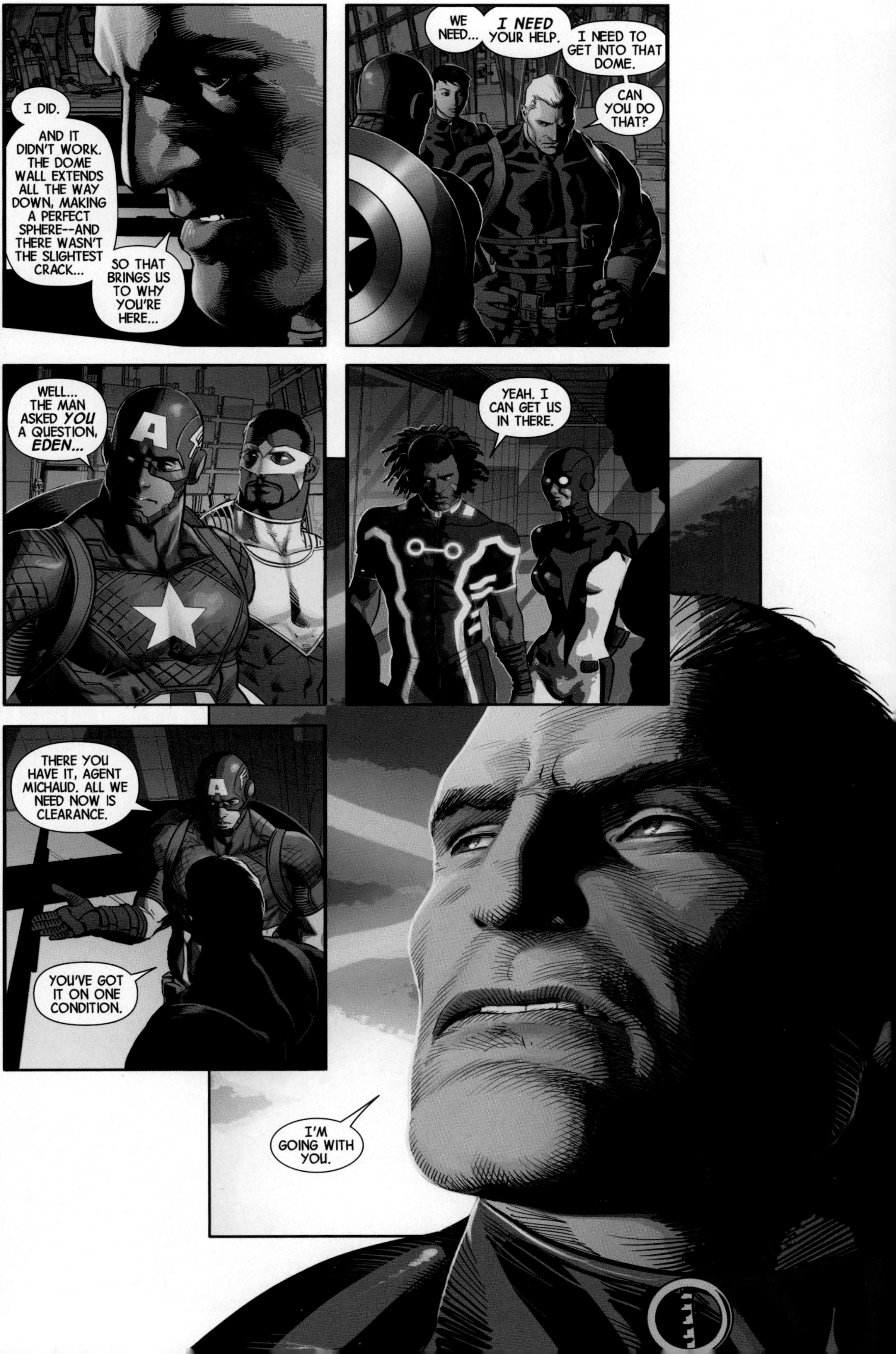
I DID.
AND IT DIDN'T WORK. THE DOME WALL EXTENDS ALL THE WAY DOWN, MAKING A PERFECT SPHERE--AND THERE WASN'T THE SLIGHTEST CRACK...
SO THAT BRINGS US TO WHY YOU'RE HERE...
WE NEED...
I NEED YOUR HELP.
I NEED TO GET INTO THAT DOME.
CAN YOU DO THAT?
WELL... THE MAN ASKED YOU A QUESTION, EDEN...
YEAH. I CAN GET US IN THERE.
THERE YOU HAVE IT, AGENT MICHAUD. ALL WE NEED NOW IS CLEARANCE.
YOU'VE GOT IT ON ONE CONDITION.
I'M GOING WITH YOU.

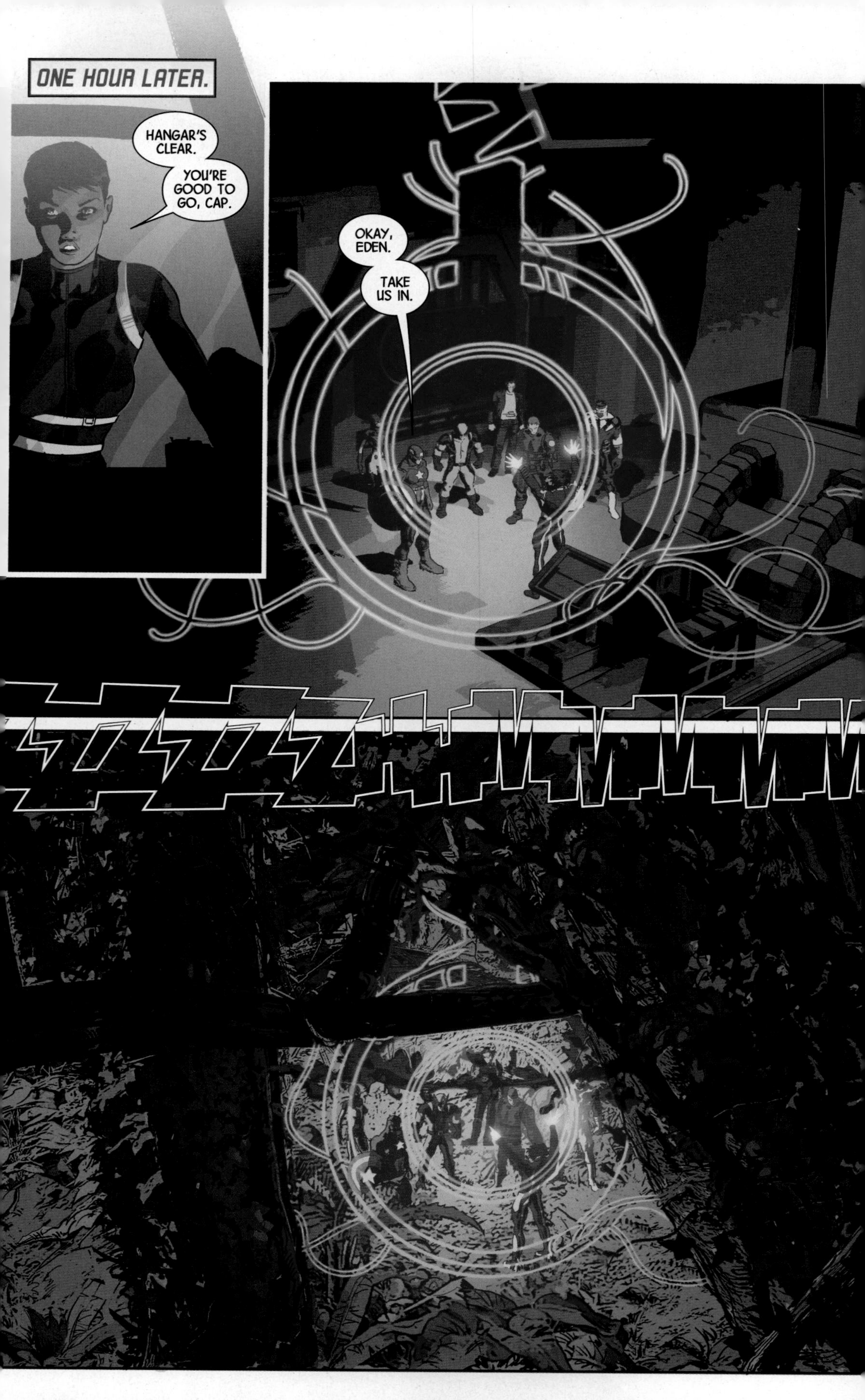
ONE HOUR LATER.
HANGAR'S CLEAR.
YOU'RE GOOD TO GO, CAP.
OKAY, EDEN.
TAKE US IN.

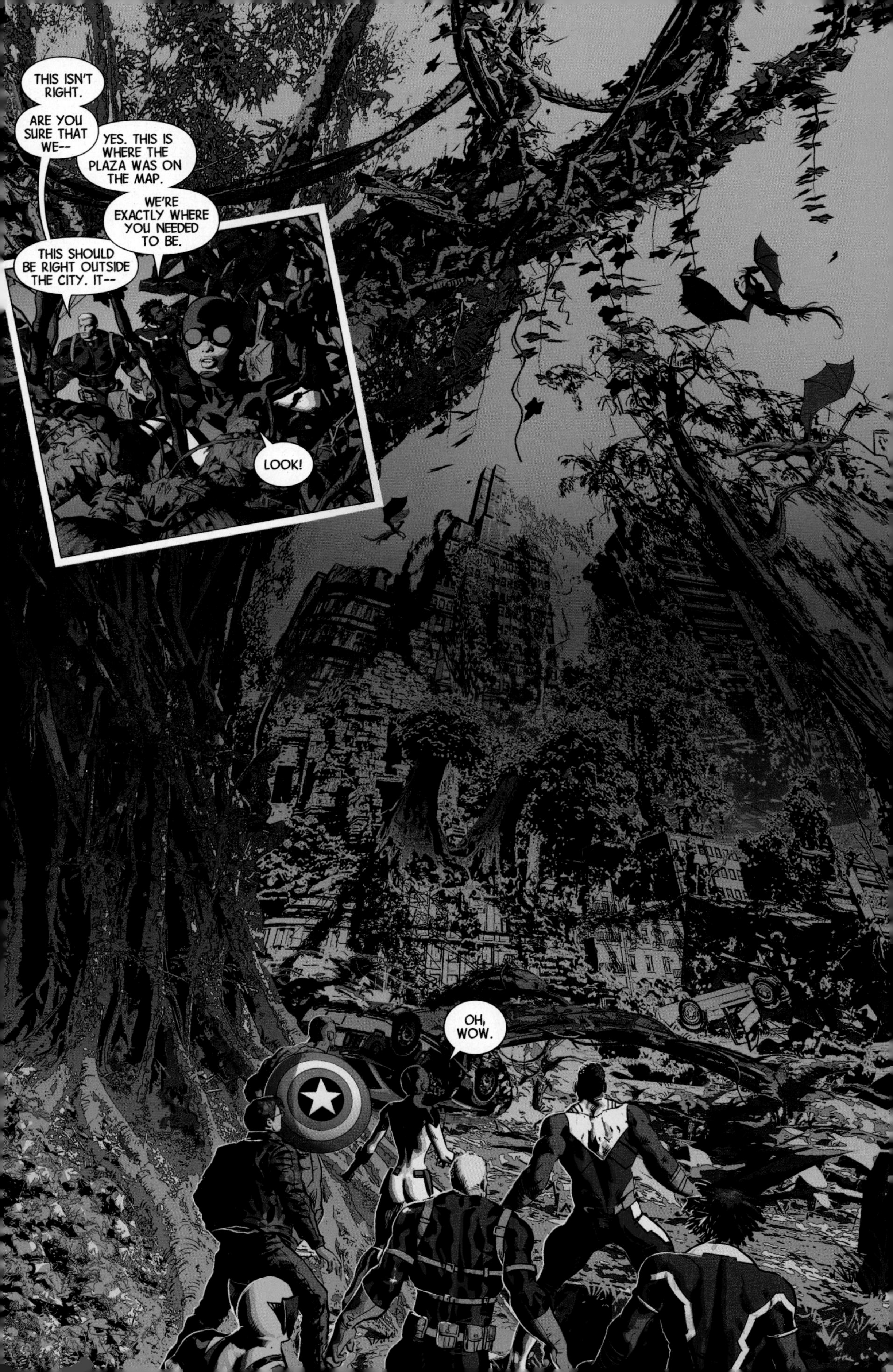
THIS ISN'T RIGHT.
ARE YOU SURE THAT WE--
YES. THIS IS WHERE THE PLAZA WAS ON THE MAP.
WE'RE EXACTLY WHERE YOU NEEDED TO BE.
THIS SHOULD BE RIGHT OUTSIDE THE CITY. IT--
LOOK!
OH, WOW.

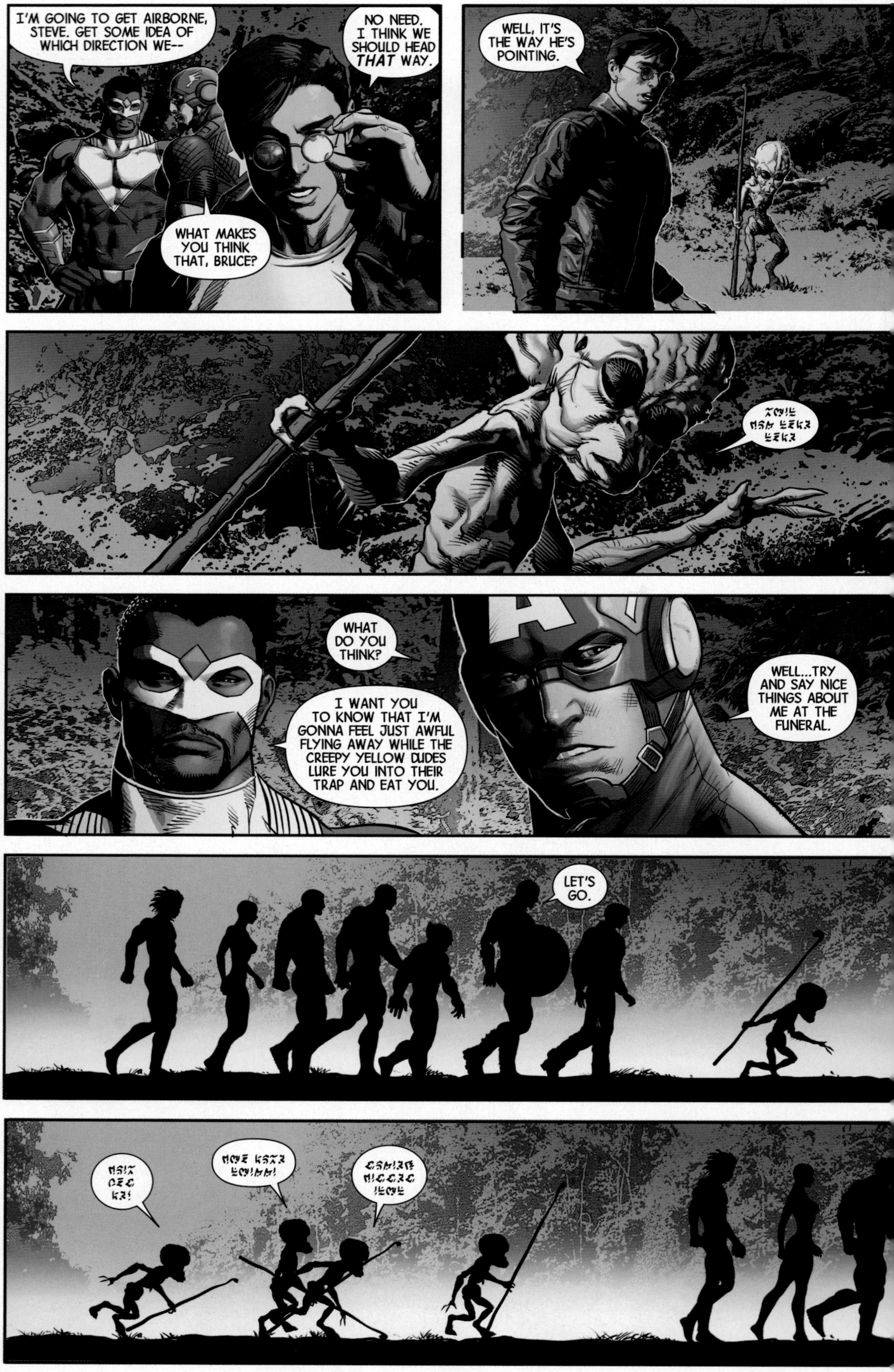
I'M GOING TO GET AIRBORNE, STEVE. GET SOME IDEA OF WHICH DIRECTION WE--
NO NEED. I THINK WE SHOULD HEAD *THAT* WAY.
WHAT MAKES YOU THINK THAT, BRUCE?
WELL, IT'S THE WAY HE'S POINTING.
WHAT DO YOU THINK?
I WANT YOU TO KNOW THAT I'M GONNA FEEL JUST AWFUL FLYING AWAY WHILE THE CREEPY YELLOW DUDES LURE YOU INTO THEIR TRAP AND EAT YOU.
WELL...TRY AND SAY NICE THINGS ABOUT ME AT THE FUNERAL.
LET'S GO.

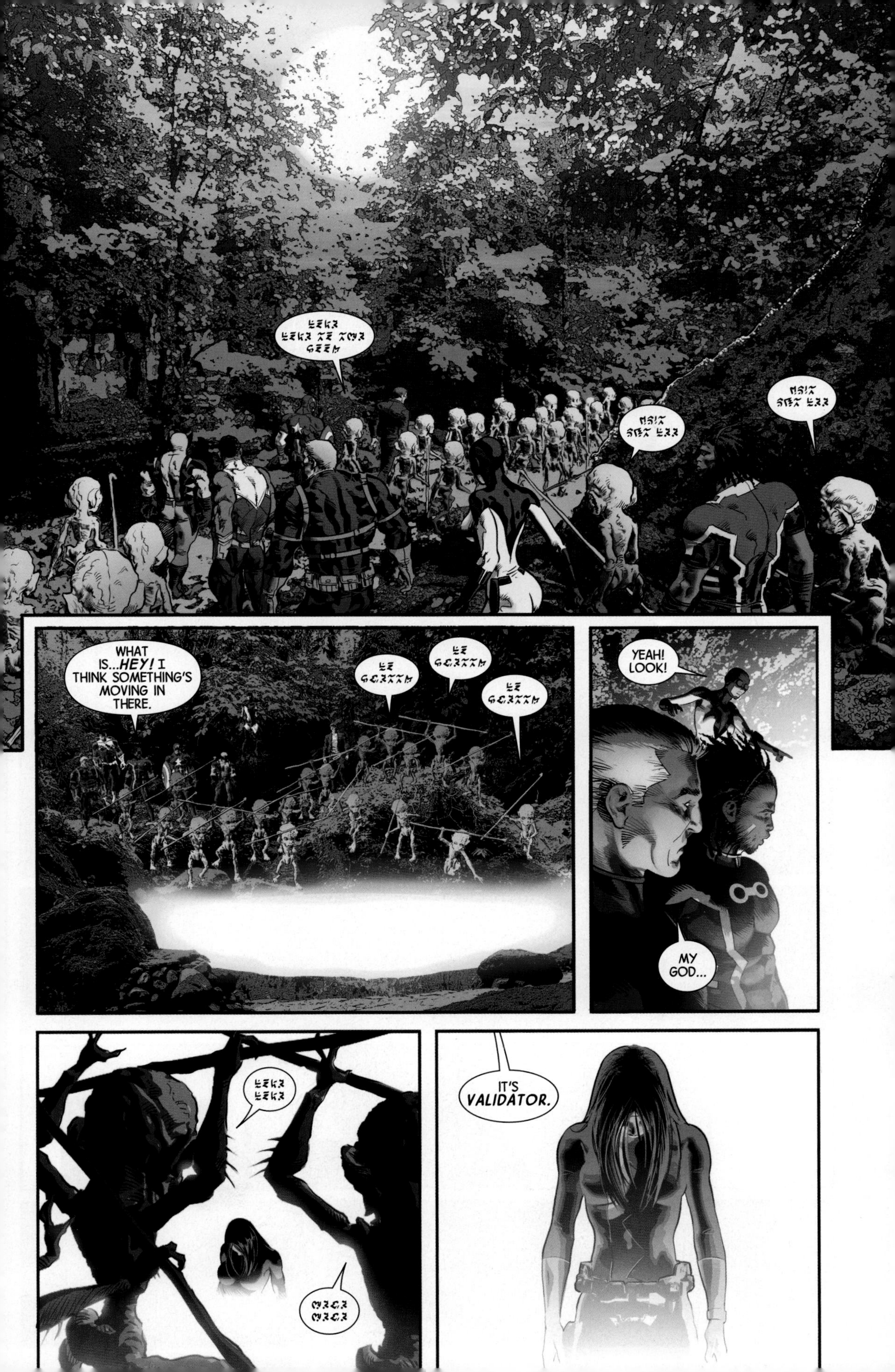
WHAT IS...HEY! I THINK SOMETHING'S MOVING IN THERE.
YEAH! LOOK!
MY GOD...
IT'S VALIDATOR.

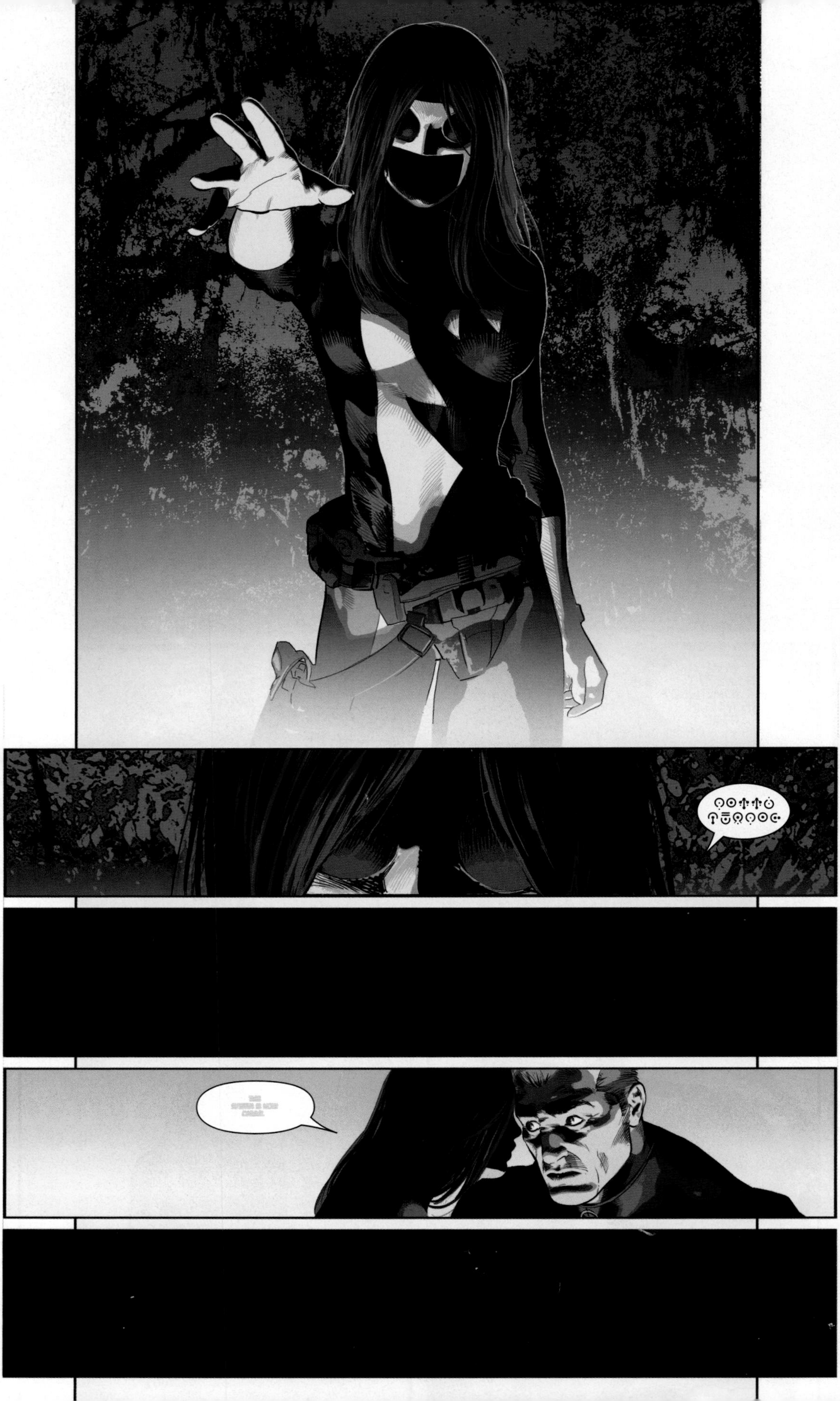

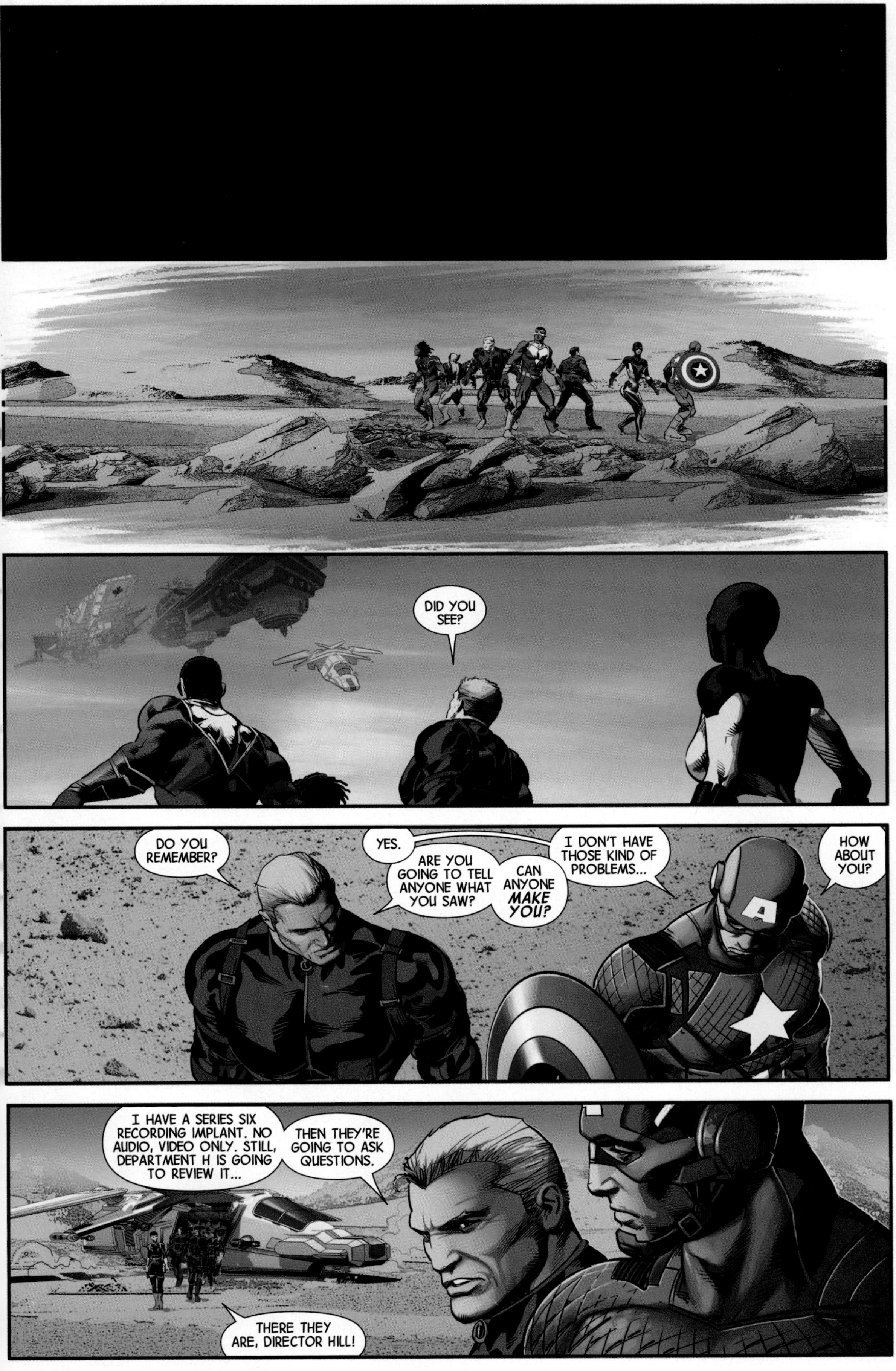
DID YOU SEE?
DO YOU REMEMBER?
YES.
ARE YOU GOING TO TELL ANYONE WHAT YOU SAW?
CAN ANYONE *MAKE YOU*?
I DON'T HAVE THOSE KIND OF PROBLEMS...
HOW ABOUT YOU?
I HAVE A SERIES SIX RECORDING IMPLANT. NO AUDIO, VIDEO ONLY. STILL, DEPARTMENT H IS GOING TO REVIEW IT...
THEN THEY'RE GOING TO ASK QUESTIONS.
THERE THEY ARE, DIRECTOR HILL!

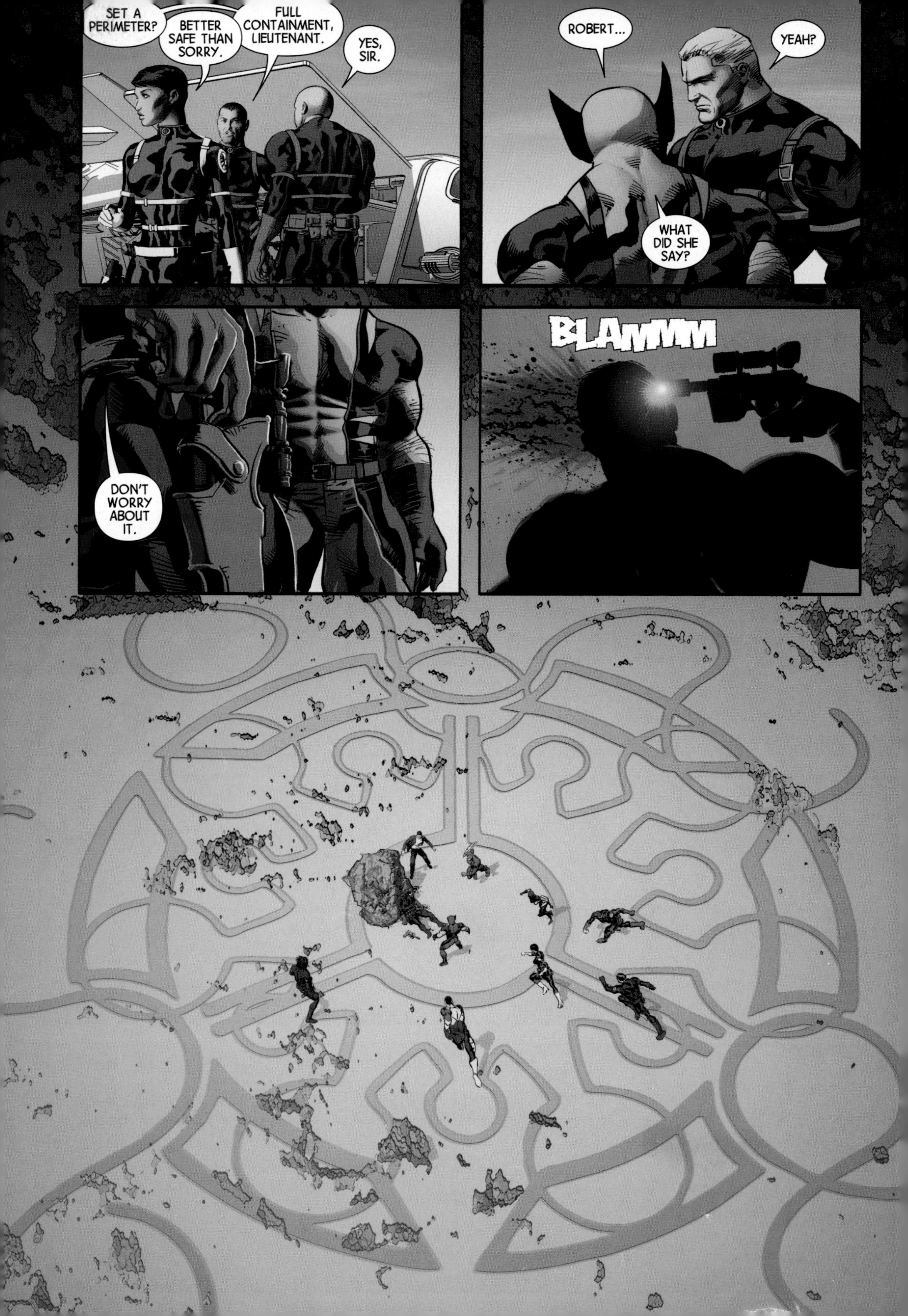
SET A PERIMETER?
BETTER SAFE THAN SORRY.
FULL CONTAINMENT, LIEUTENANT.
YES, SIR.
ROBERT...
YEAH?
WHAT DID SHE SAY?
DON'T WORRY ABOUT IT.
BLAMMM

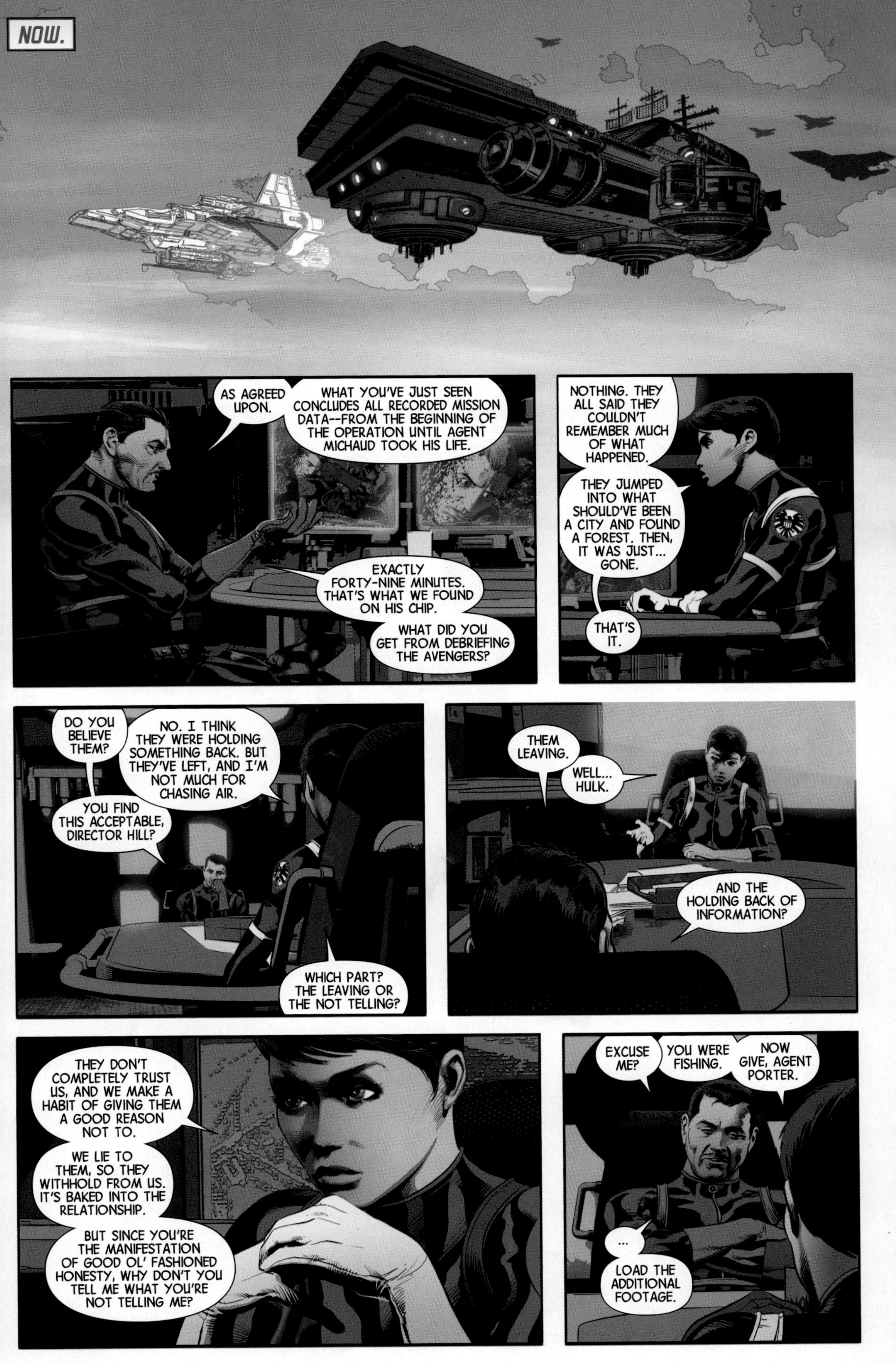
NOW.
AS AGREED UPON.
WHAT YOU'VE JUST SEEN CONCLUDES ALL RECORDED MISSION DATA--FROM THE BEGINNING OF THE OPERATION UNTIL AGENT MICHAUD TOOK HIS LIFE.
EXACTLY FORTY-NINE MINUTES. THAT'S WHAT WE FOUND ON HIS CHIP.
WHAT DID YOU GET FROM DEBRIEFING THE AVENGERS?
NOTHING. THEY ALL SAID THEY COULDN'T REMEMBER MUCH OF WHAT HAPPENED.
THEY JUMPED INTO WHAT SHOULD'VE BEEN A CITY AND FOUND A FOREST. THEN, IT WAS JUST... GONE.
THAT'S IT.
DO YOU BELIEVE THEM?
NO. I THINK THEY WERE HOLDING SOMETHING BACK. BUT THEY'VE LEFT, AND I'M NOT MUCH FOR CHASING AIR.
YOU FIND THIS ACCEPTABLE, DIRECTOR HILL?
WHICH PART? THE LEAVING OR THE NOT TELLING?
THEM LEAVING.
WELL... HULK.
AND THE HOLDING BACK OF INFORMATION?
THEY DON'T COMPLETELY TRUST US, AND WE MAKE A HABIT OF GIVING THEM A GOOD REASON NOT TO.
WE LIE TO THEM, SO THEY WITHHOLD FROM US. IT'S BAKED INTO THE RELATIONSHIP.
BUT SINCE YOU'RE THE MANIFESTATION OF GOOD OL' FASHIONED HONESTY, WHY DON'T YOU TELL ME WHAT YOU'RE NOT TELLING ME?
EXCUSE ME?
YOU WERE FISHING.
NOW GIVE, AGENT PORTER.
...
LOAD THE ADDITIONAL FOOTAGE.

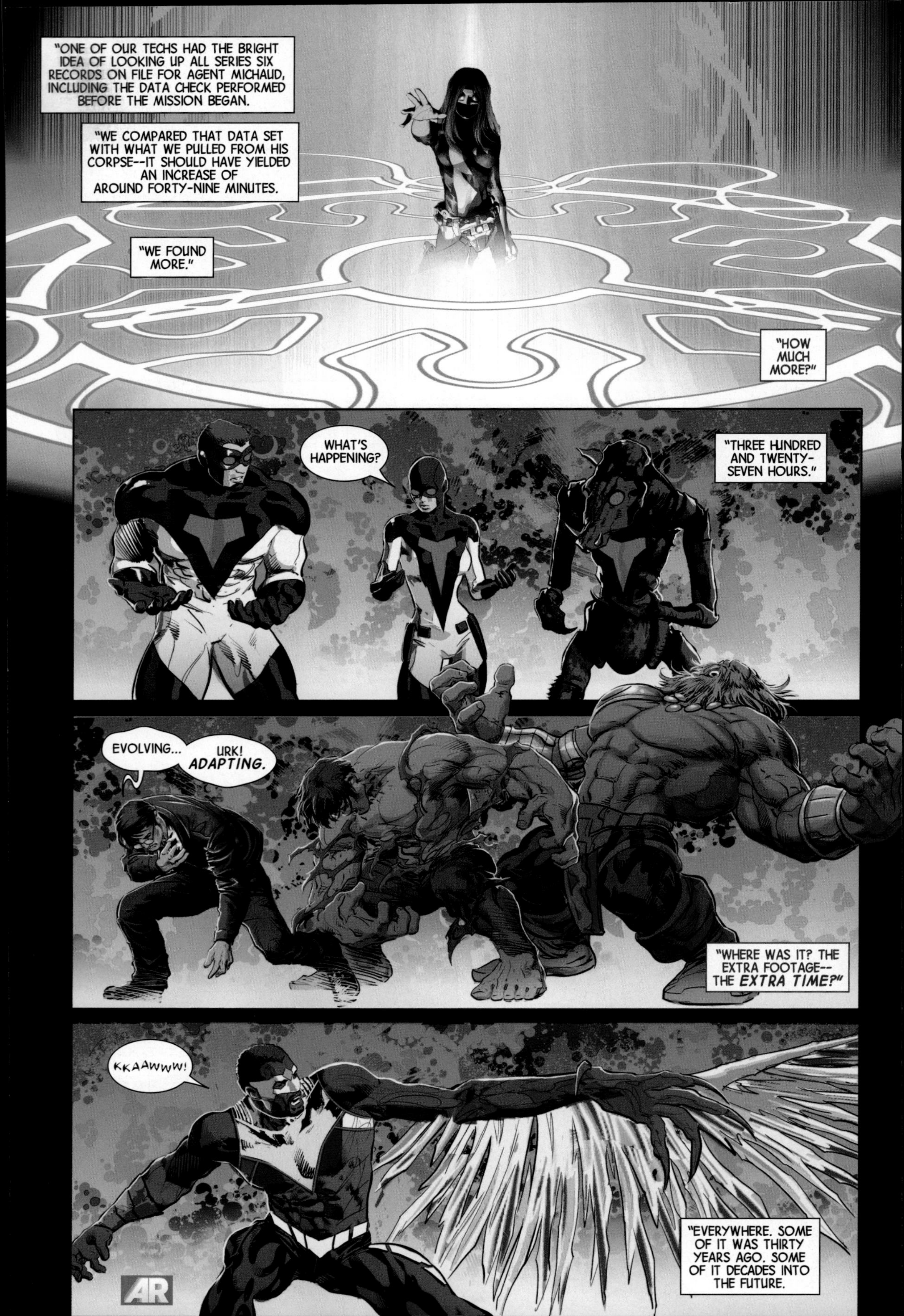
"ONE OF OUR TECHS HAD THE BRIGHT IDEA OF LOOKING UP ALL SERIES SIX RECORDS ON FILE FOR AGENT MICHAUD, INCLUDING THE DATA CHECK PERFORMED BEFORE THE MISSION BEGAN.
"WE COMPARED THAT DATA SET WITH WHAT WE PULLED FROM HIS CORPSE--IT SHOULD HAVE YIELDED AN INCREASE OF AROUND FORTY-NINE MINUTES.
"WE FOUND MORE."
"HOW MUCH MORE?"
WHAT'S HAPPENING?
"THREE HUNDRED AND TWENTY-SEVEN HOURS."
EVOLVING...
URK! ADAPTING.
"WHERE WAS IT? THE EXTRA FOOTAGE-- THE EXTRA TIME?"
KKAAWWW!
"EVERYWHERE. SOME OF IT WAS THIRTY YEARS AGO. SOME OF IT DECADES INTO THE FUTURE.

"THE EFFECTS APPEAR TO BE VARIABLE.

"SPECIFIC TO EACH OF THEM.

"WHAT WE'RE INTERESTED IN IS COMING UP NOW.

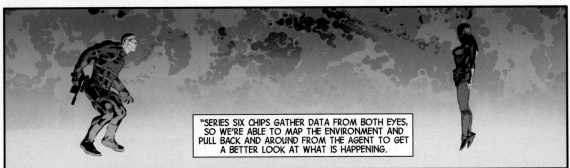

PLEASE!

STOP!

"SERIES SIX CHIPS GATHER DATA FROM BOTH EYES, SO WE'RE ABLE TO MAP THE ENVIRONMENT AND PULL BACK AND AROUND FROM THE AGENT TO GET A BETTER LOOK AT WHAT IS HAPPENING.

"THERE! SEE?

"SHE PULLS HIM CLOSE, DRAWING HIM IN...AND THEN...NOTHING.

"NOTHING HAPPENED."

DON'T BE RIDICULOUS, AGENT. ISN'T IT OBVIOUS...?

SHE WAS TELLING HIM SOMETHING.

"I THINK WE SHOULD TALK ABOUT IT. IS THAT OKAY?"

NO. NOT REALLY.

SERIOUSLY, I HAVE QUESTIONS. A TON OF THEM.

LIKE, *WHAT JUST HAPPENED?*

RIGHT. AND WHY DID WE LIE TO THE S.H.I.E.L.D. GUYS? ARE WE NOT ON THE SAME TEAM ANYMORE?

AND, THE BIG ONE: WHY DID THAT AGENT SHOOT HIMSELF?

YEAH. *THAT.*

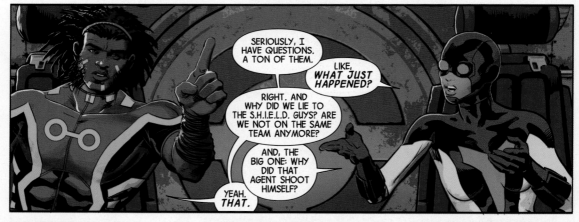

HE DID WHAT HE THOUGHT HE HAD TO DO.

HE DID WHAT SOMEONE DOES WHEN KEEPING A SECRET IS WORTH MORE THAN THEIR LIFE.

I DON'T UNDERSTAND...

WHY WOULD HE DO THAT?

BECAUSE, WHATEVER *VALIDATOR* BECAME...

IT USED TO BE HIS DAUGHTER.

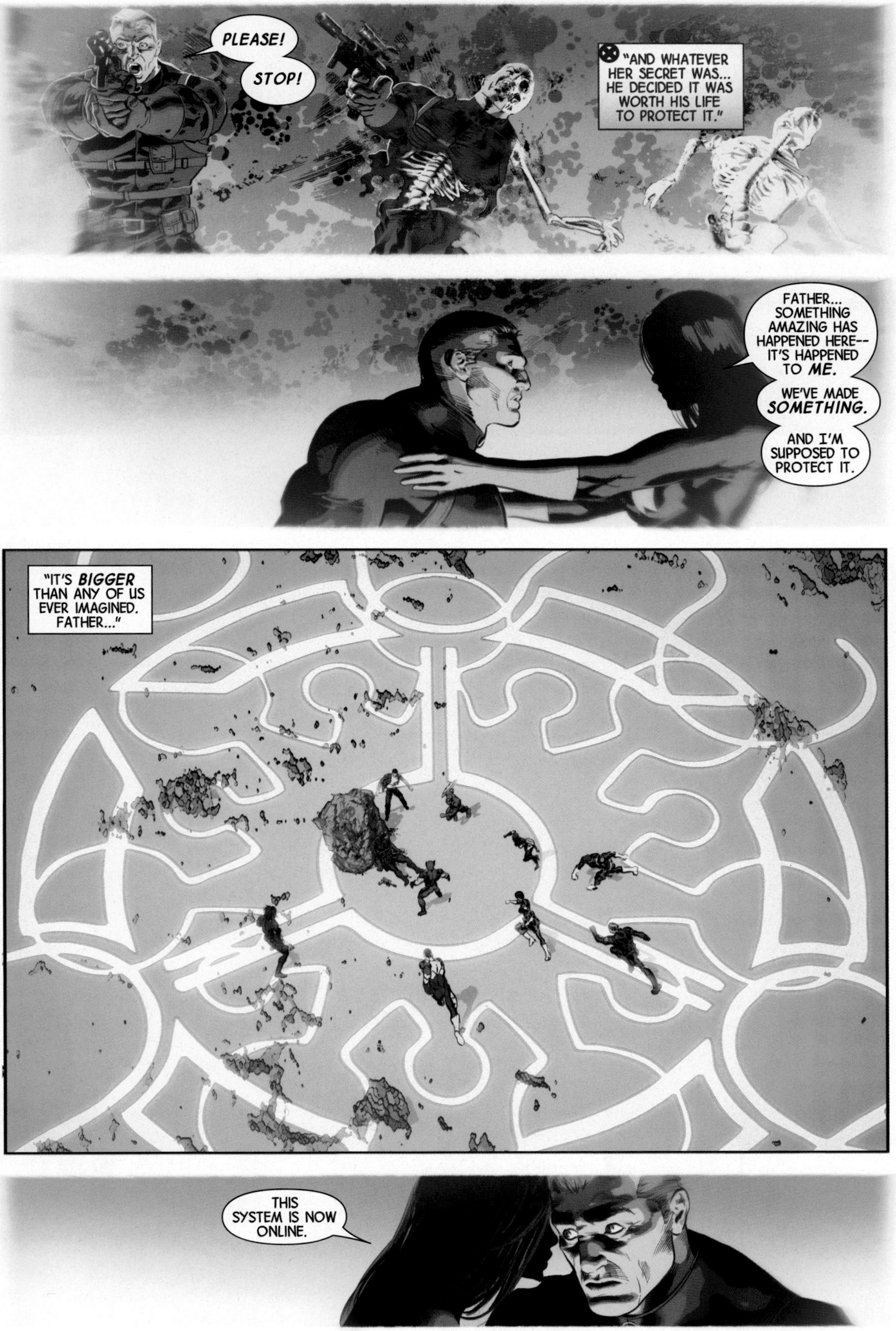
PLEASE!
STOP!
"AND WHATEVER HER SECRET WAS... HE DECIDED IT WAS WORTH HIS LIFE TO PROTECT IT."
FATHER... SOMETHING AMAZING HAS HAPPENED HERE-- IT'S HAPPENED TO ME.
WE'VE MADE SOMETHING.
AND I'M SUPPOSED TO PROTECT IT.
"IT'S BIGGER THAN ANY OF US EVER IMAGINED. FATHER..."
THIS SYSTEM IS NOW ONLINE.

"WAKE THE DRAGON"

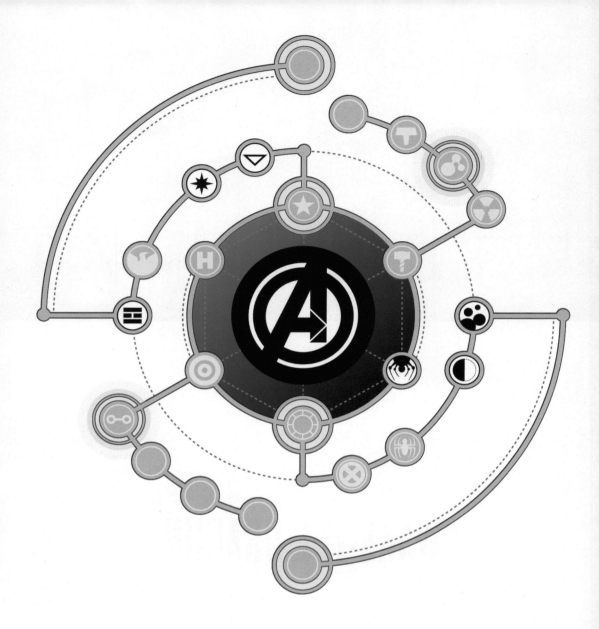

EARTH'S MIGHTIEST HEROES

CAPTAIN AMERICA · IRON MAN · THOR · HAWKEYE · BLACK WIDOW · HULK
WOLVERINE · SPIDER-MAN · CAPTAIN MARVEL · SPIDER-WOMAN
FALCON · SHANG-CHI · SUNSPOT · CANNONBALL · MANIFOLD
SMASHER · CAPTAIN UNIVERSE · HYPERION

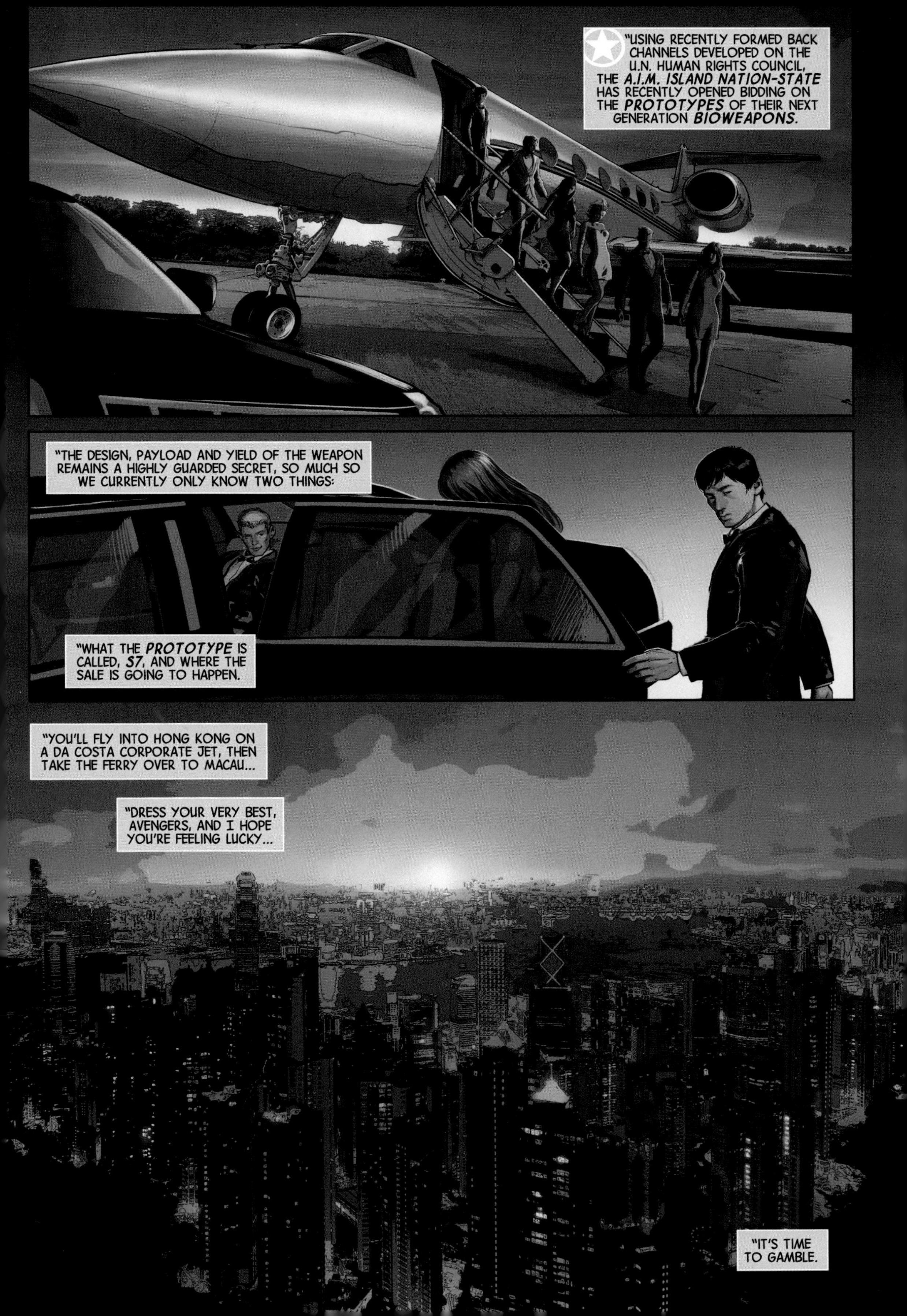
"USING RECENTLY FORMED BACK CHANNELS DEVELOPED ON THE U.N. HUMAN RIGHTS COUNCIL, THE A.I.M. ISLAND NATION-STATE HAS RECENTLY OPENED BIDDING ON THE PROTOTYPES OF THEIR NEXT GENERATION BIOWEAPONS.
"THE DESIGN, PAYLOAD AND YIELD OF THE WEAPON REMAINS A HIGHLY GUARDED SECRET, SO MUCH SO WE CURRENTLY ONLY KNOW TWO THINGS:
"WHAT THE PROTOTYPE IS CALLED, S7, AND WHERE THE SALE IS GOING TO HAPPEN.
"YOU'LL FLY INTO HONG KONG ON A DA COSTA CORPORATE JET, THEN TAKE THE FERRY OVER TO MACAU...
"DRESS YOUR VERY BEST, AVENGERS, AND I HOPE YOU'RE FEELING LUCKY...
"IT'S TIME TO GAMBLE.

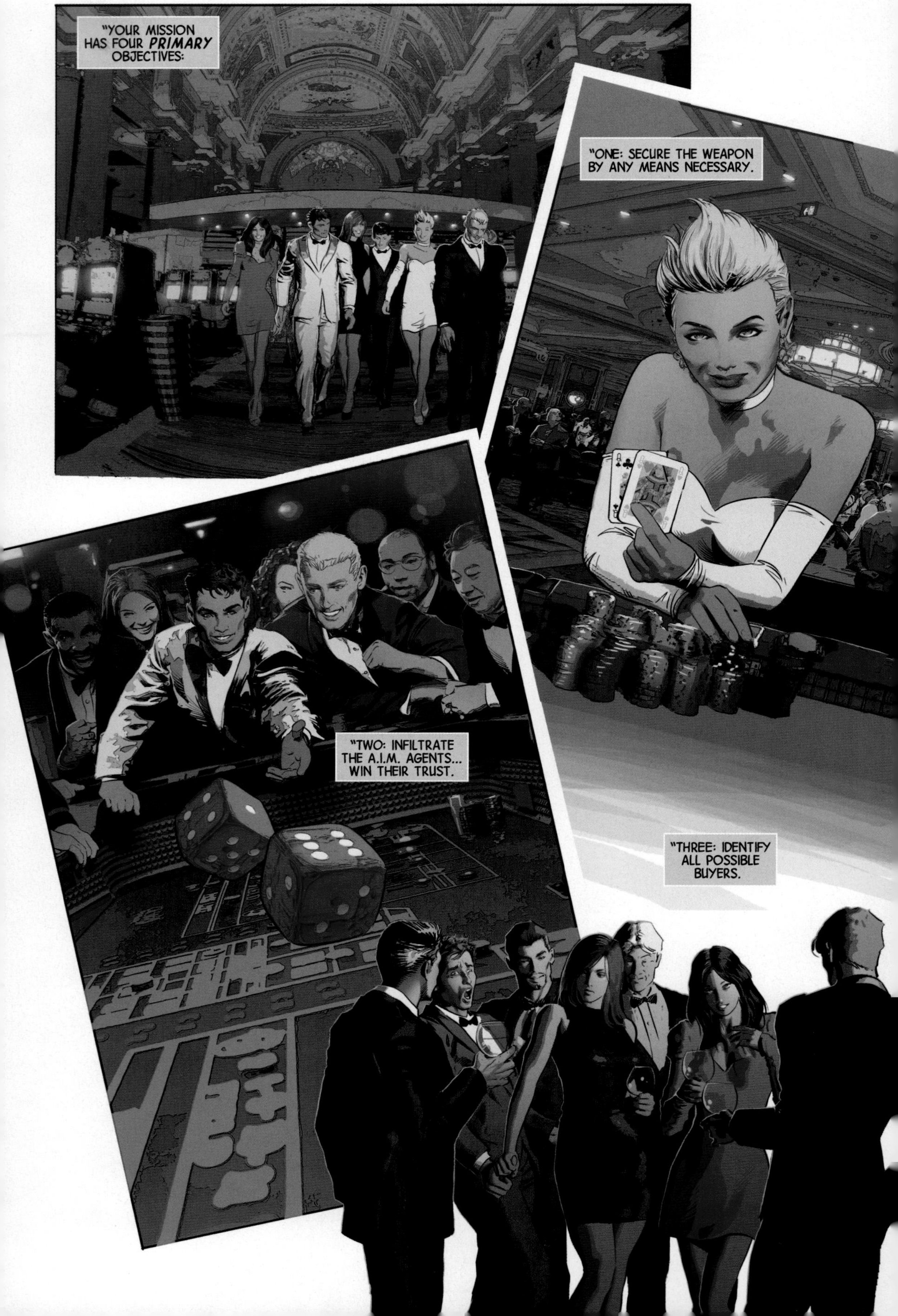
"YOUR MISSION HAS FOUR *PRIMARY* OBJECTIVES:
"ONE: SECURE THE WEAPON BY ANY MEANS NECESSARY.
"TWO: INFILTRATE THE A.I.M. AGENTS... WIN THEIR TRUST.
"THREE: IDENTIFY ALL POSSIBLE BUYERS.

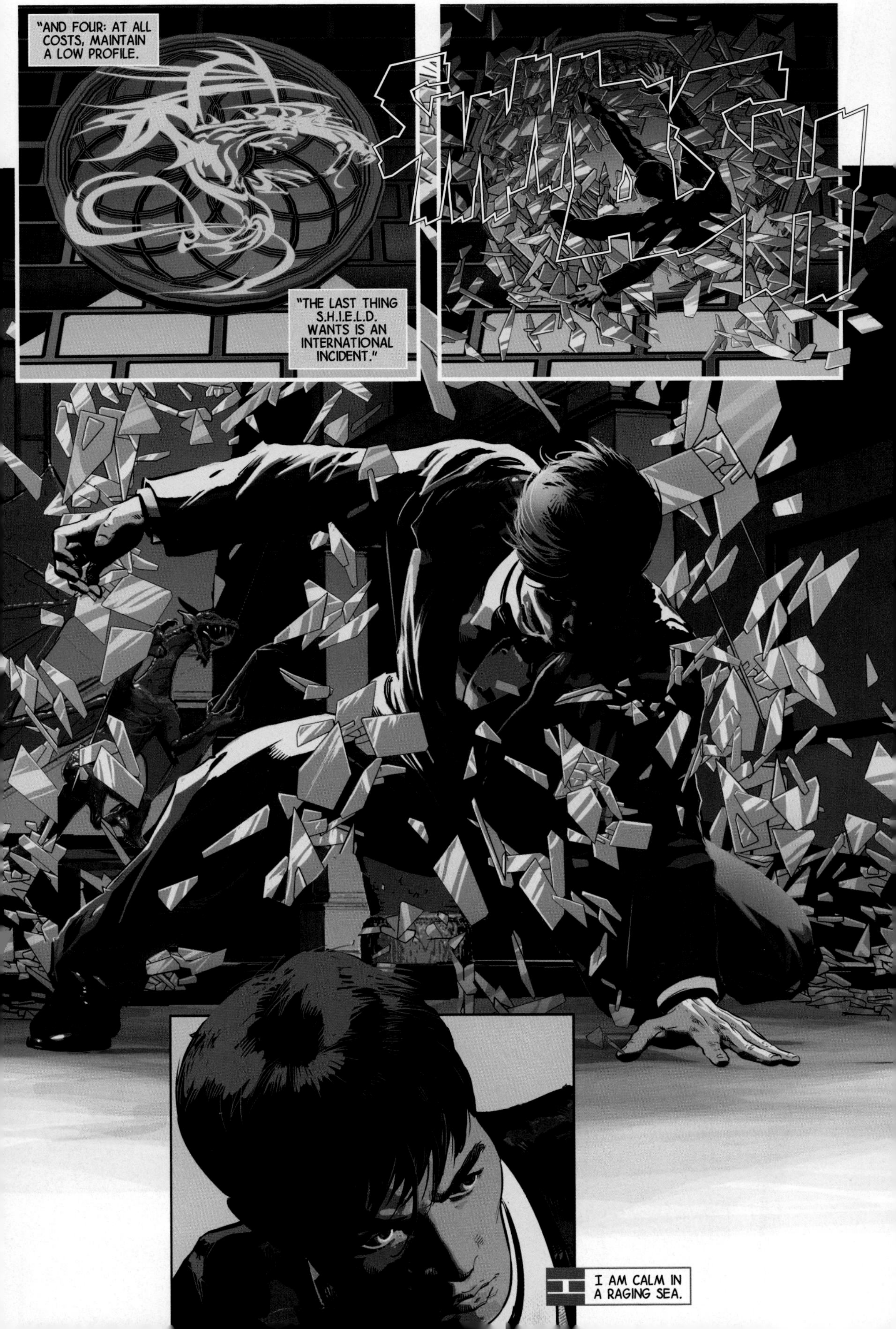
"AND FOUR: AT ALL COSTS, MAINTAIN A LOW PROFILE.
"THE LAST THING S.H.I.E.L.D. WANTS IS AN INTERNATIONAL INCIDENT."
I AM CALM IN A RAGING SEA.

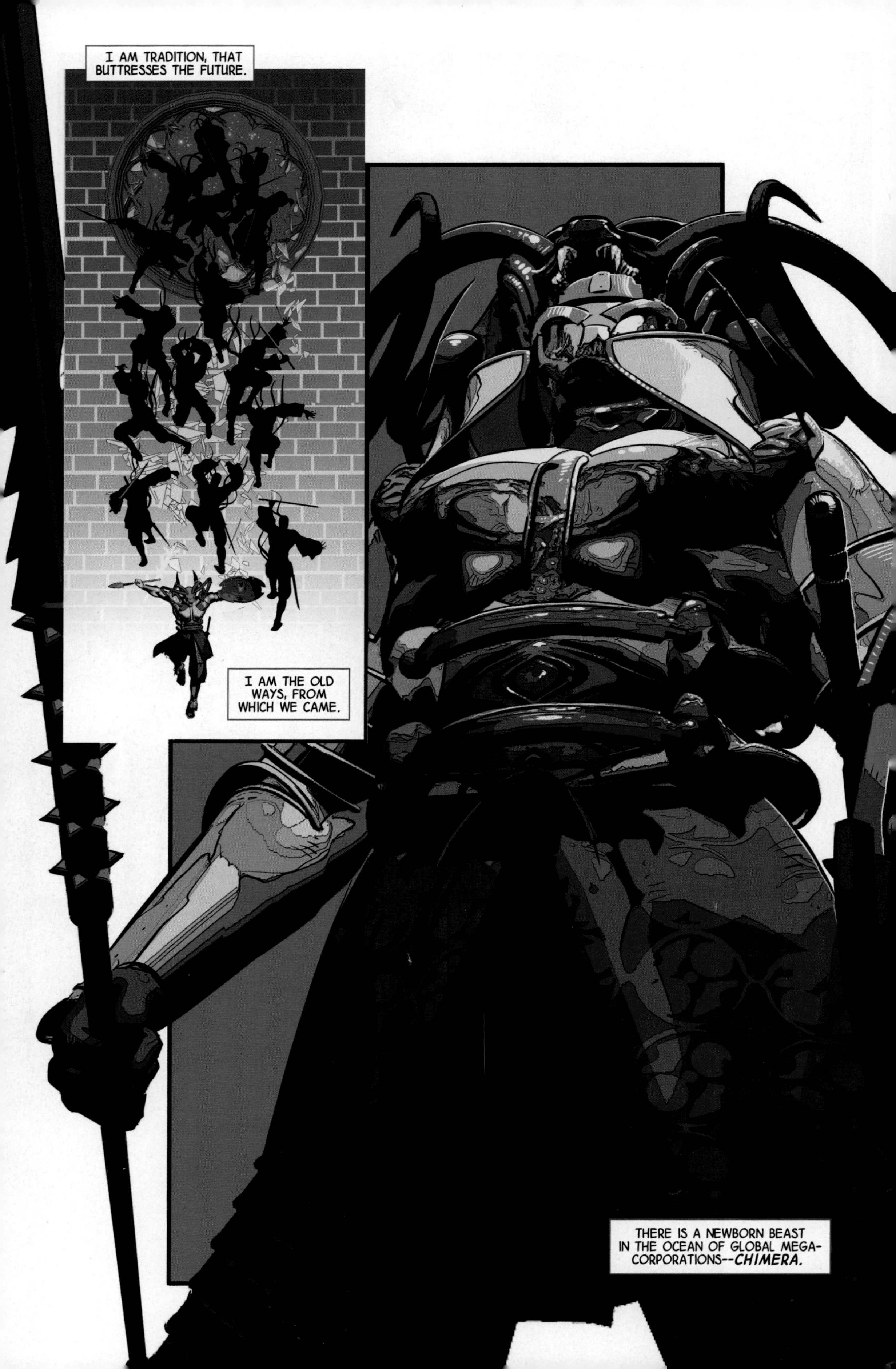
I AM TRADITION, THAT BUTTRESSES THE FUTURE.
I AM THE OLD WAYS, FROM WHICH WE CAME.
THERE IS A NEWBORN BEAST IN THE OCEAN OF GLOBAL MEGA-CORPORATIONS--*CHIMERA.*

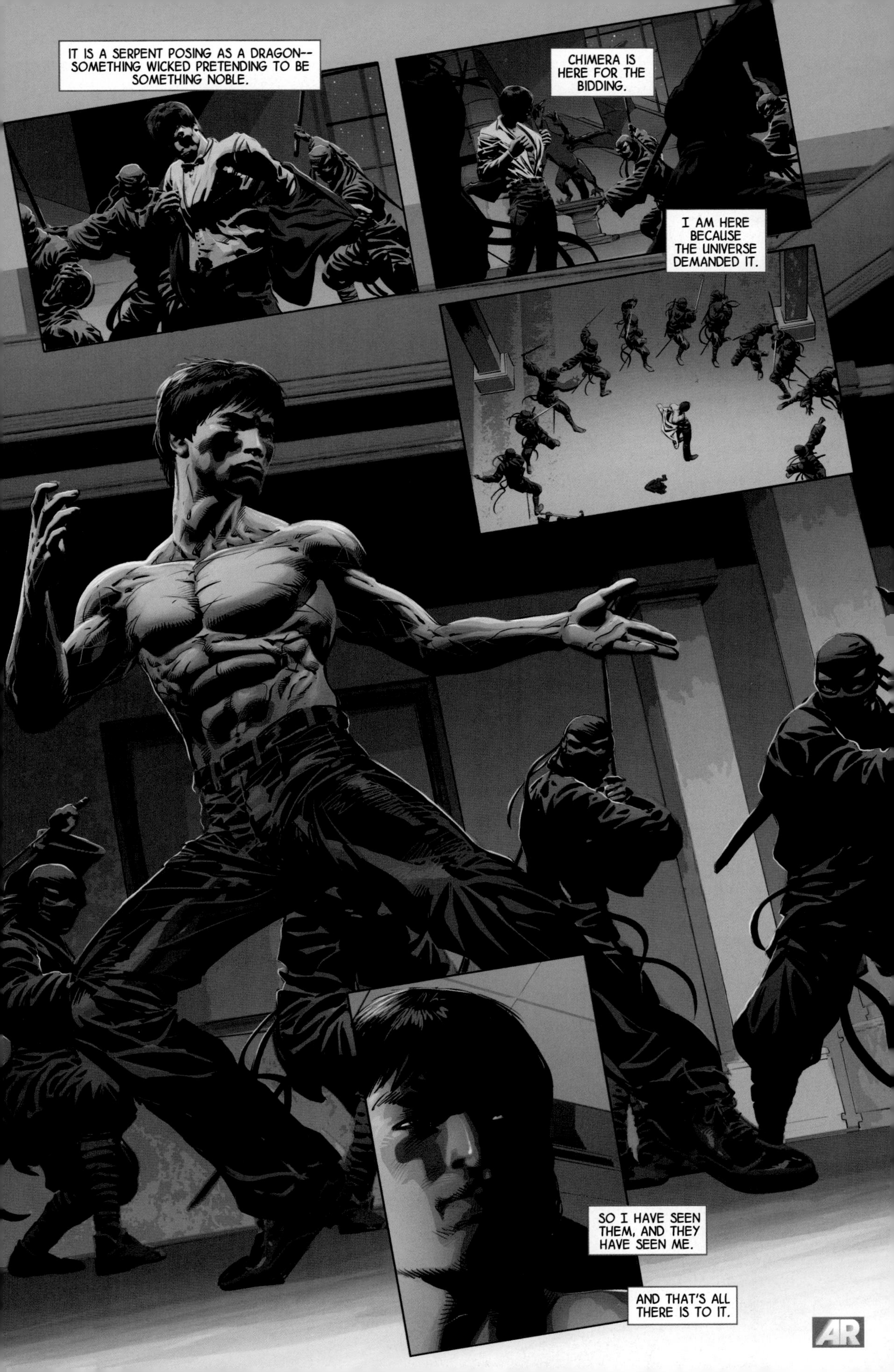
IT IS A SERPENT POSING AS A DRAGON-- SOMETHING WICKED PRETENDING TO BE SOMETHING NOBLE.
CHIMERA IS HERE FOR THE BIDDING.
I AM HERE BECAUSE THE UNIVERSE DEMANDED IT.
SO I HAVE SEEN THEM, AND THEY HAVE SEEN ME.
AND THAT'S ALL THERE IS TO IT.

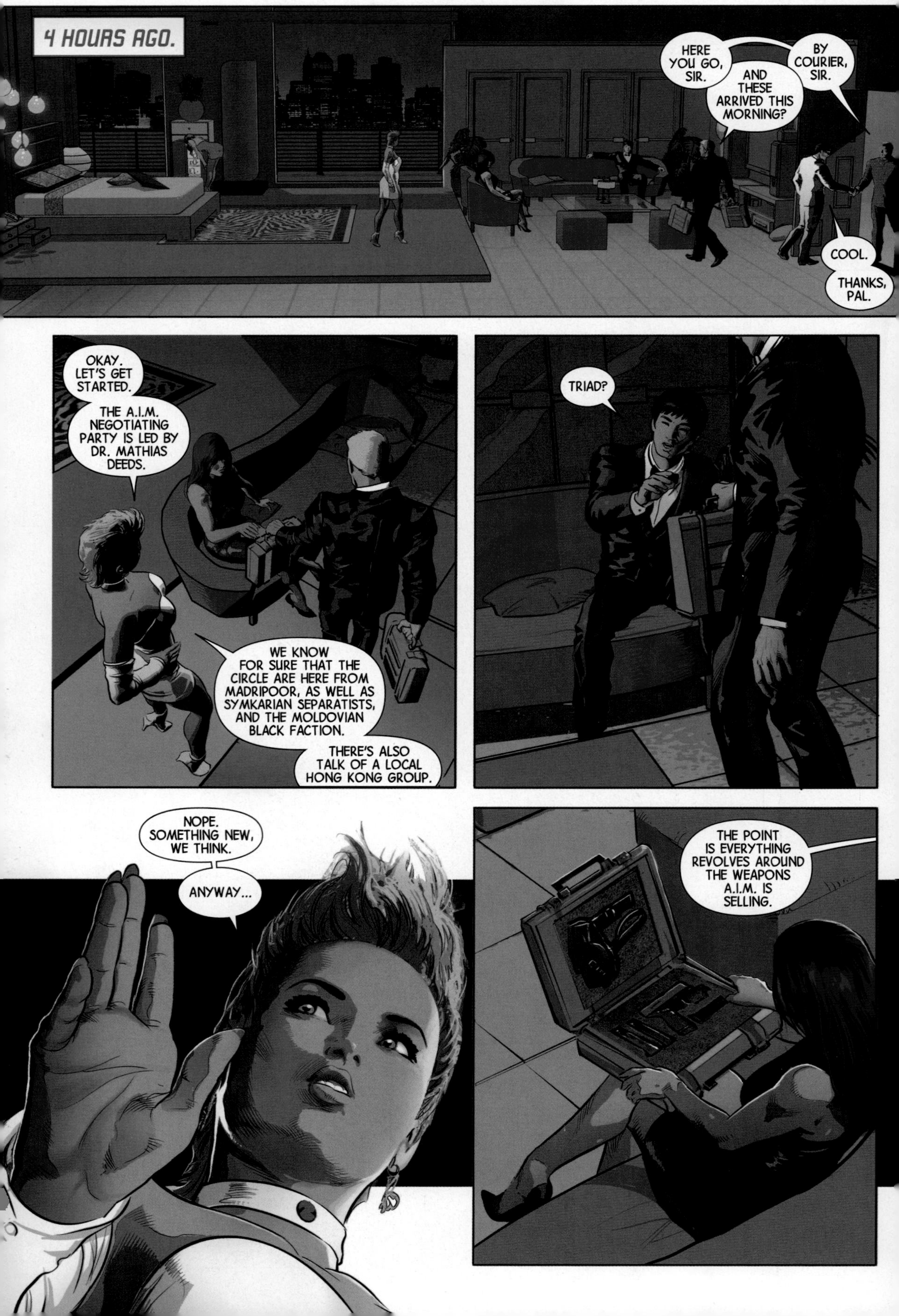

4 HOURS AGO.
HERE YOU GO, SIR.
AND THESE ARRIVED THIS MORNING?
BY COURIER, SIR.
COOL.
THANKS, PAL.
OKAY. LET'S GET STARTED.
THE A.I.M. NEGOTIATING PARTY IS LED BY DR. MATHIAS DEEDS.
WE KNOW FOR SURE THAT THE CIRCLE ARE HERE FROM MADRIPOOR, AS WELL AS SYMKARIAN SEPARATISTS, AND THE MOLDOVIAN BLACK FACTION.
THERE'S ALSO TALK OF A LOCAL HONG KONG GROUP.
TRIAD?
NOPE. SOMETHING NEW, WE THINK.
ANYWAY...
THE POINT IS EVERYTHING REVOLVES AROUND THE WEAPONS A.I.M. IS SELLING.

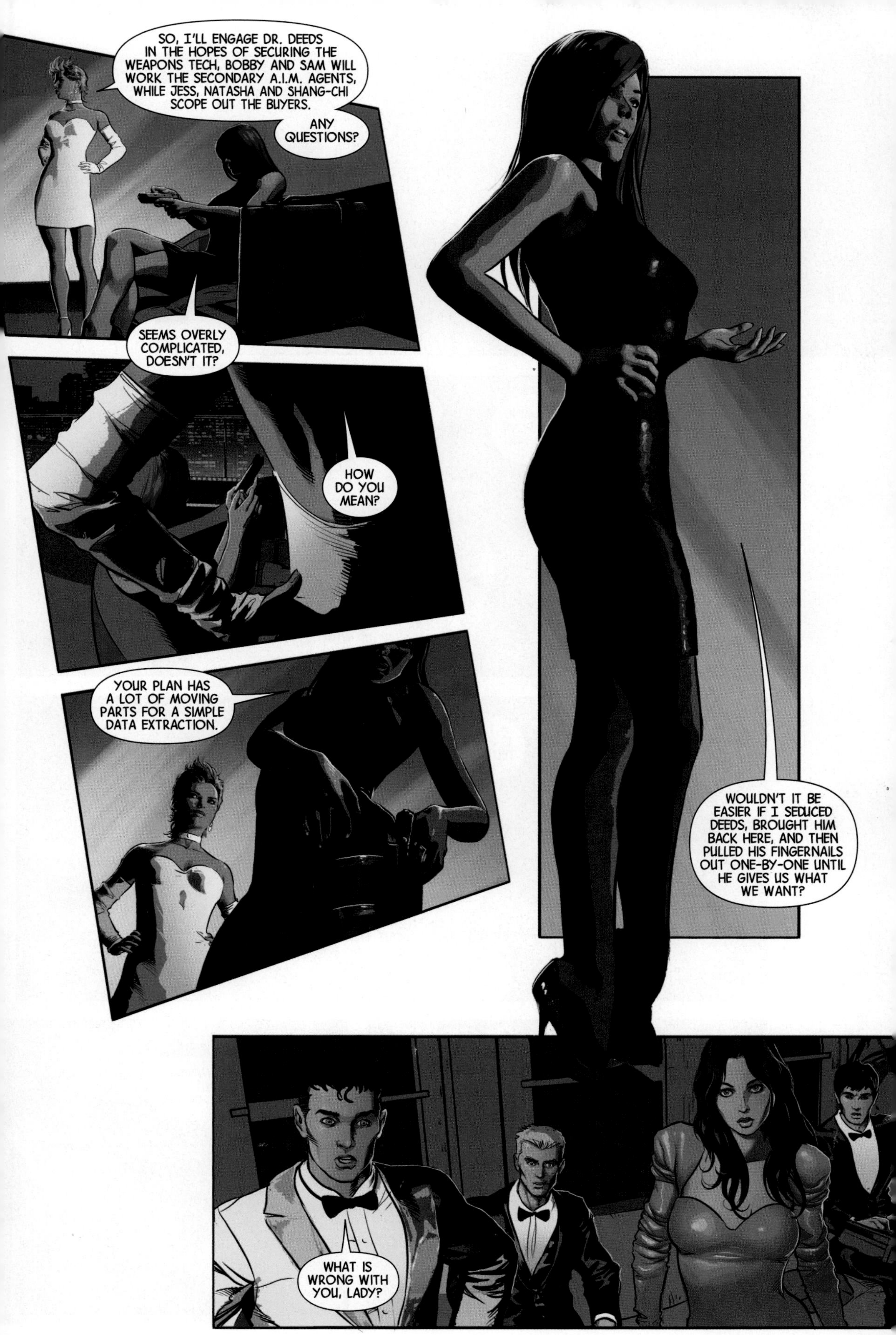
SO, I'LL ENGAGE DR. DEEDS IN THE HOPES OF SECURING THE WEAPONS TECH, BOBBY AND SAM WILL WORK THE SECONDARY A.I.M. AGENTS, WHILE JESS, NATASHA AND SHANG-CHI SCOPE OUT THE BUYERS.
ANY QUESTIONS?
SEEMS OVERLY COMPLICATED, DOESN'T IT?
HOW DO YOU MEAN?
YOUR PLAN HAS A LOT OF MOVING PARTS FOR A SIMPLE DATA EXTRACTION.
WOULDN'T IT BE EASIER IF I SEDUCED DEEDS, BROUGHT HIM BACK HERE, AND THEN PULLED HIS FINGERNAILS OUT ONE-BY-ONE UNTIL HE GIVES US WHAT WE WANT?
WHAT IS WRONG WITH YOU, LADY?

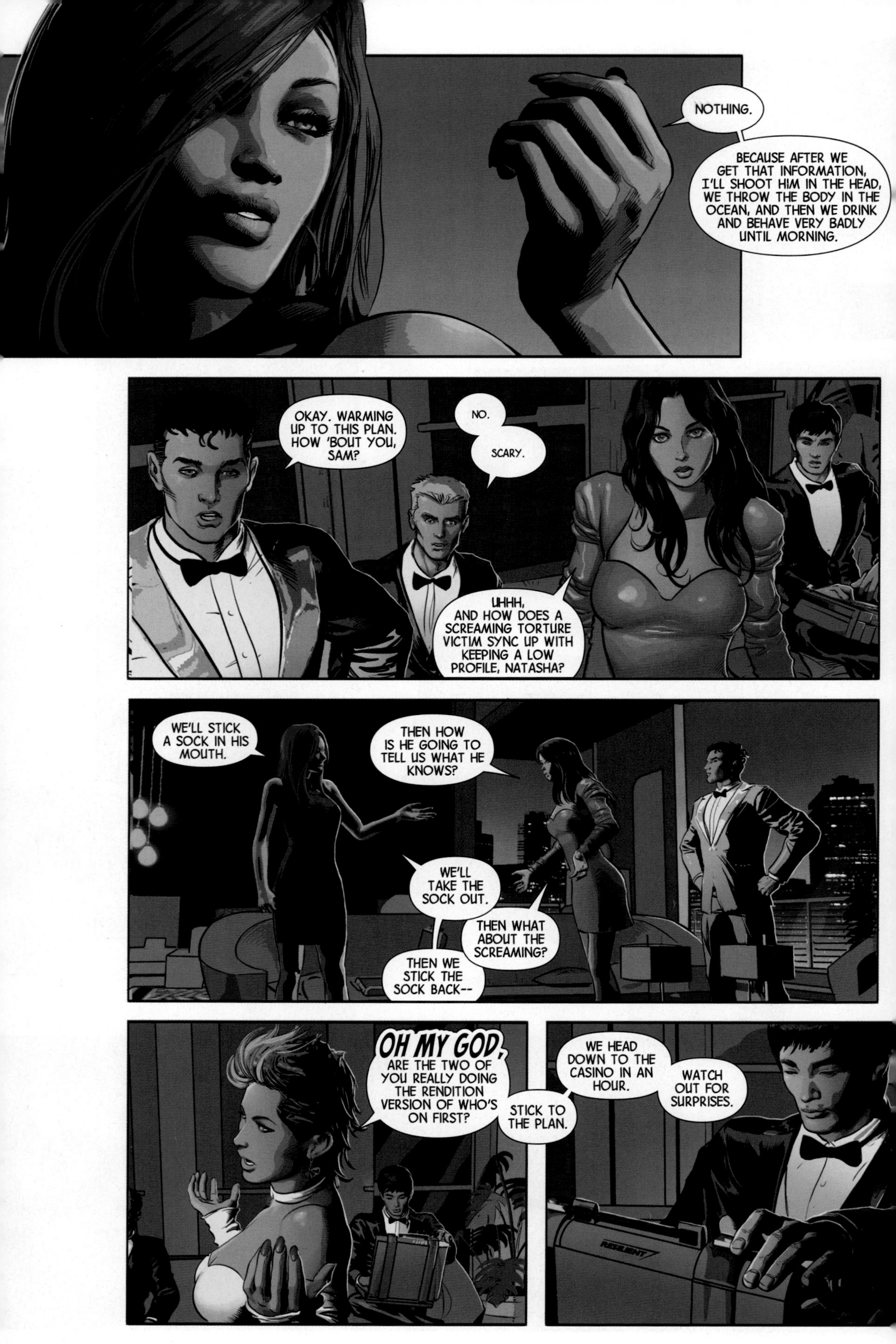
NOTHING.
BECAUSE AFTER WE GET THAT INFORMATION, I'LL SHOOT HIM IN THE HEAD, WE THROW THE BODY IN THE OCEAN, AND THEN WE DRINK AND BEHAVE VERY BADLY UNTIL MORNING.
OKAY. WARMING UP TO THIS PLAN. HOW 'BOUT YOU, SAM?
NO.
SCARY.
UHHH, AND HOW DOES A SCREAMING TORTURE VICTIM SYNC UP WITH KEEPING A LOW PROFILE, NATASHA?
WE'LL STICK A SOCK IN HIS MOUTH.
THEN HOW IS HE GOING TO TELL US WHAT HE KNOWS?
WE'LL TAKE THE SOCK OUT.
THEN WHAT ABOUT THE SCREAMING?
THEN WE STICK THE SOCK BACK--
OH MY GOD, ARE THE TWO OF YOU REALLY DOING THE RENDITION VERSION OF WHO'S ON FIRST?
STICK TO THE PLAN.
WE HEAD DOWN TO THE CASINO IN AN HOUR.
WATCH OUT FOR SURPRISES.
RESILIENT

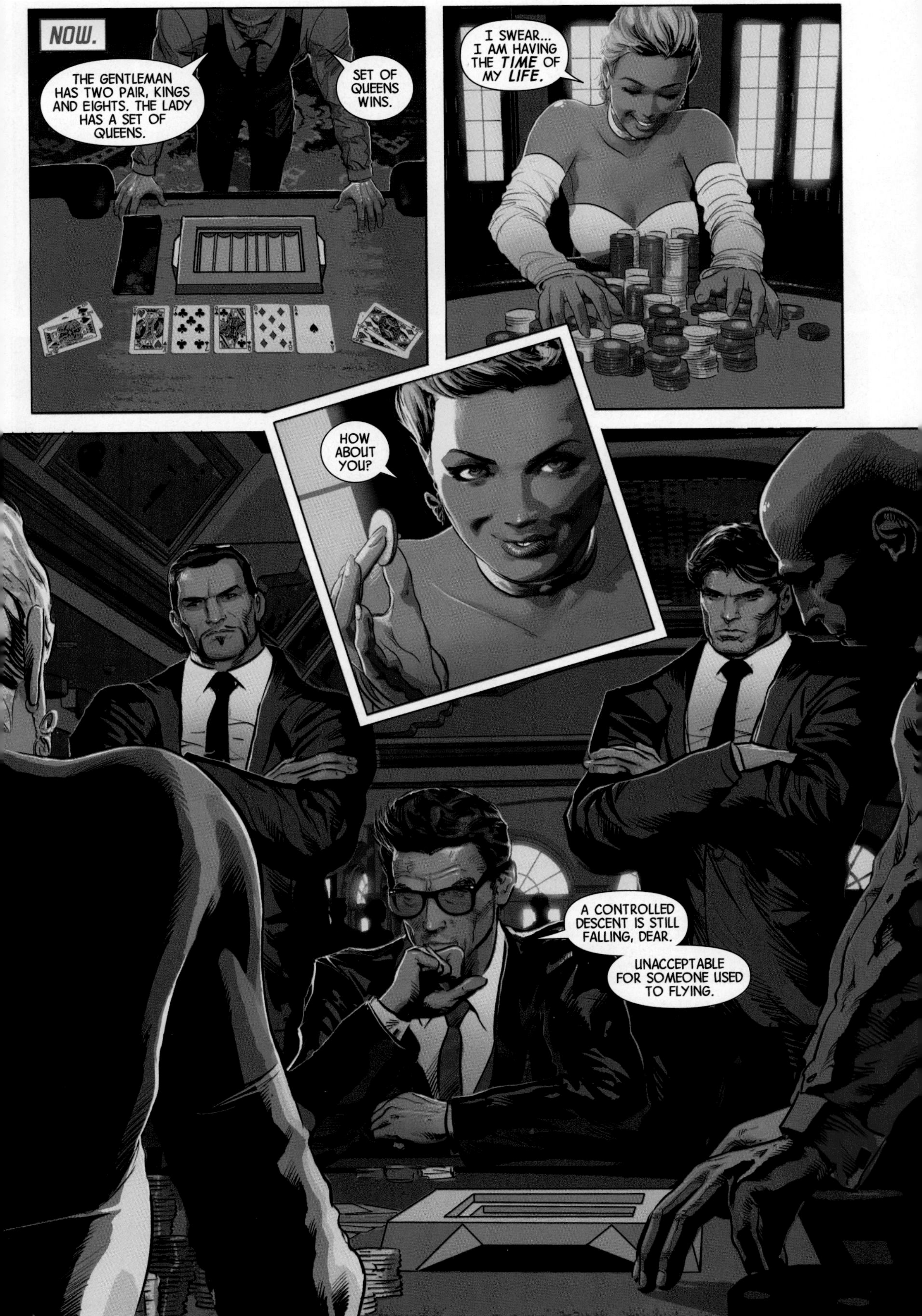
NOW.
THE GENTLEMAN HAS TWO PAIR, KINGS AND EIGHTS. THE LADY HAS A SET OF QUEENS.
SET OF QUEENS WINS.
I SWEAR... I AM HAVING THE *TIME* OF MY *LIFE*.
HOW ABOUT YOU?
A CONTROLLED DESCENT IS STILL FALLING, DEAR.
UNACCEPTABLE FOR SOMEONE USED TO FLYING.

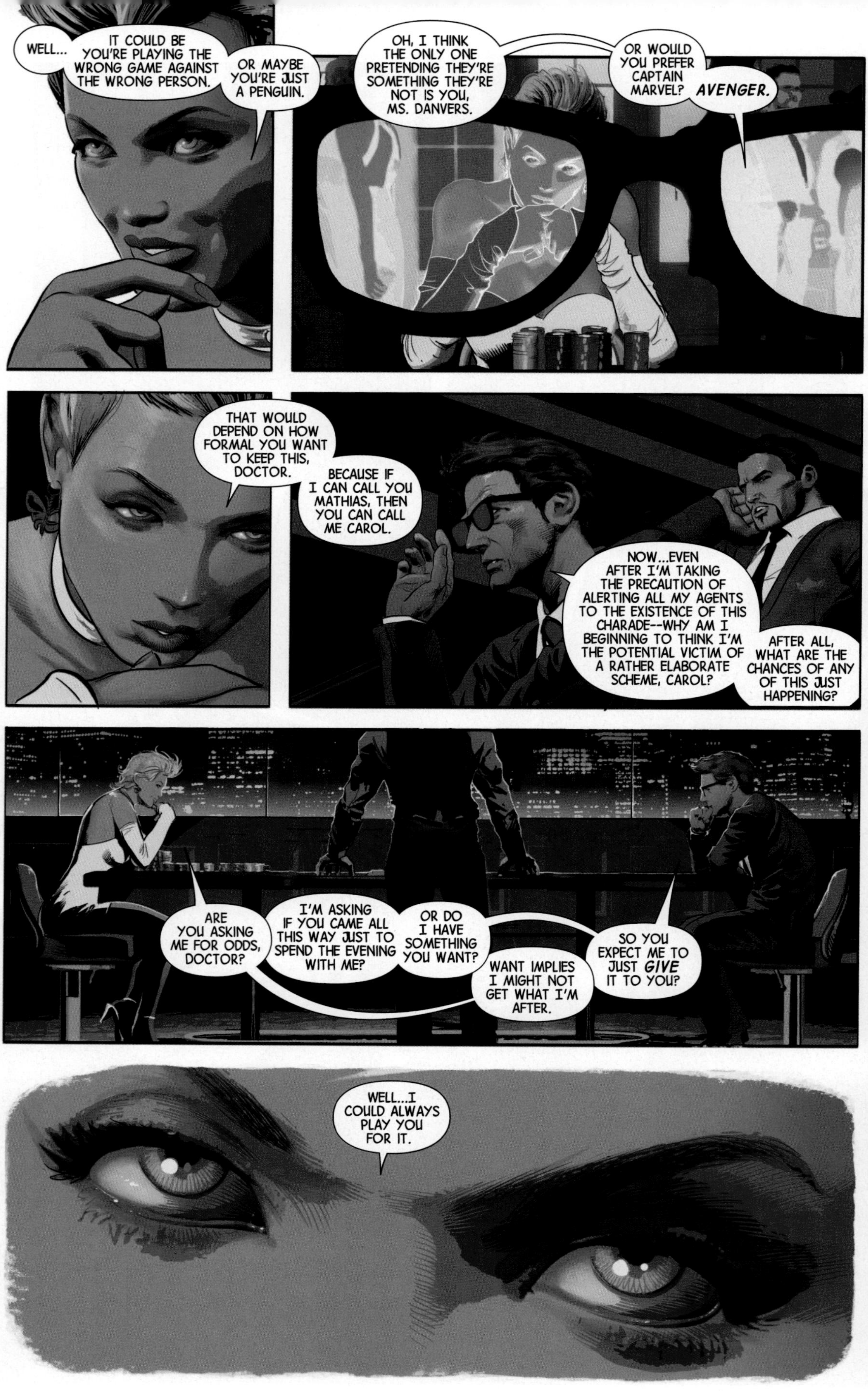
WELL...
IT COULD BE YOU'RE PLAYING THE WRONG GAME AGAINST THE WRONG PERSON.
OR MAYBE YOU'RE JUST A PENGUIN.
OH, I THINK THE ONLY ONE PRETENDING THEY'RE SOMETHING THEY'RE NOT IS YOU, MS. DANVERS.
OR WOULD YOU PREFER CAPTAIN MARVEL?
AVENGER.
THAT WOULD DEPEND ON HOW FORMAL YOU WANT TO KEEP THIS, DOCTOR.
BECAUSE IF I CAN CALL YOU MATHIAS, THEN YOU CAN CALL ME CAROL.
NOW...EVEN AFTER I'M TAKING THE PRECAUTION OF ALERTING ALL MY AGENTS TO THE EXISTENCE OF THIS CHARADE--WHY AM I BEGINNING TO THINK I'M THE POTENTIAL VICTIM OF A RATHER ELABORATE SCHEME, CAROL?
AFTER ALL, WHAT ARE THE CHANCES OF ANY OF THIS JUST HAPPENING?
ARE YOU ASKING ME FOR ODDS, DOCTOR?
I'M ASKING IF YOU CAME ALL THIS WAY JUST TO SPEND THE EVENING WITH ME?
OR DO I HAVE SOMETHING YOU WANT?
WANT IMPLIES I MIGHT NOT GET WHAT I'M AFTER.
SO YOU EXPECT ME TO JUST GIVE IT TO YOU?
WELL...I COULD ALWAYS PLAY YOU FOR IT.

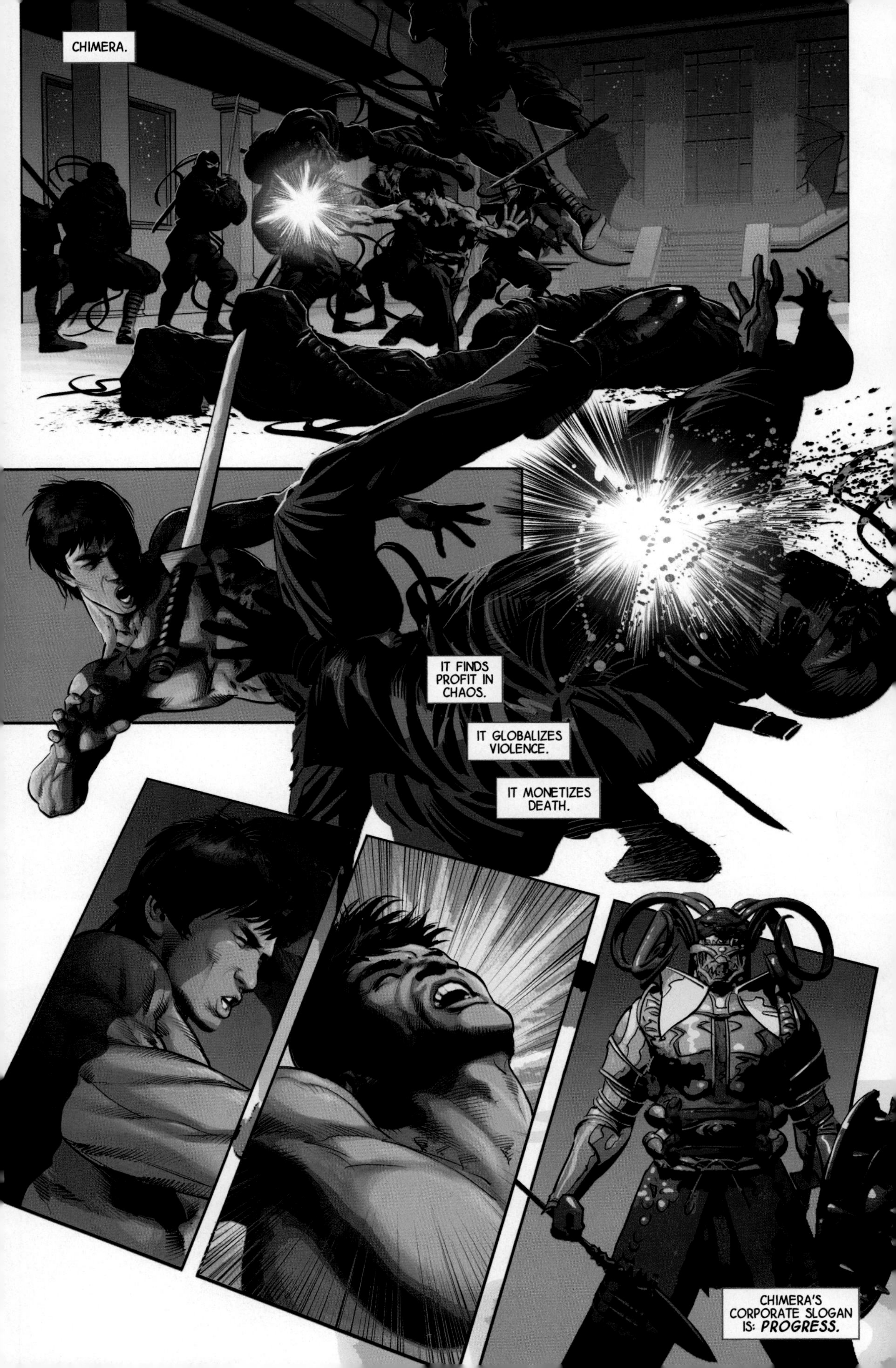
CHIMERA.
IT FINDS PROFIT IN CHAOS.
IT GLOBALIZES VIOLENCE.
IT MONETIZES DEATH.
CHIMERA'S CORPORATE SLOGAN IS: *PROGRESS.*

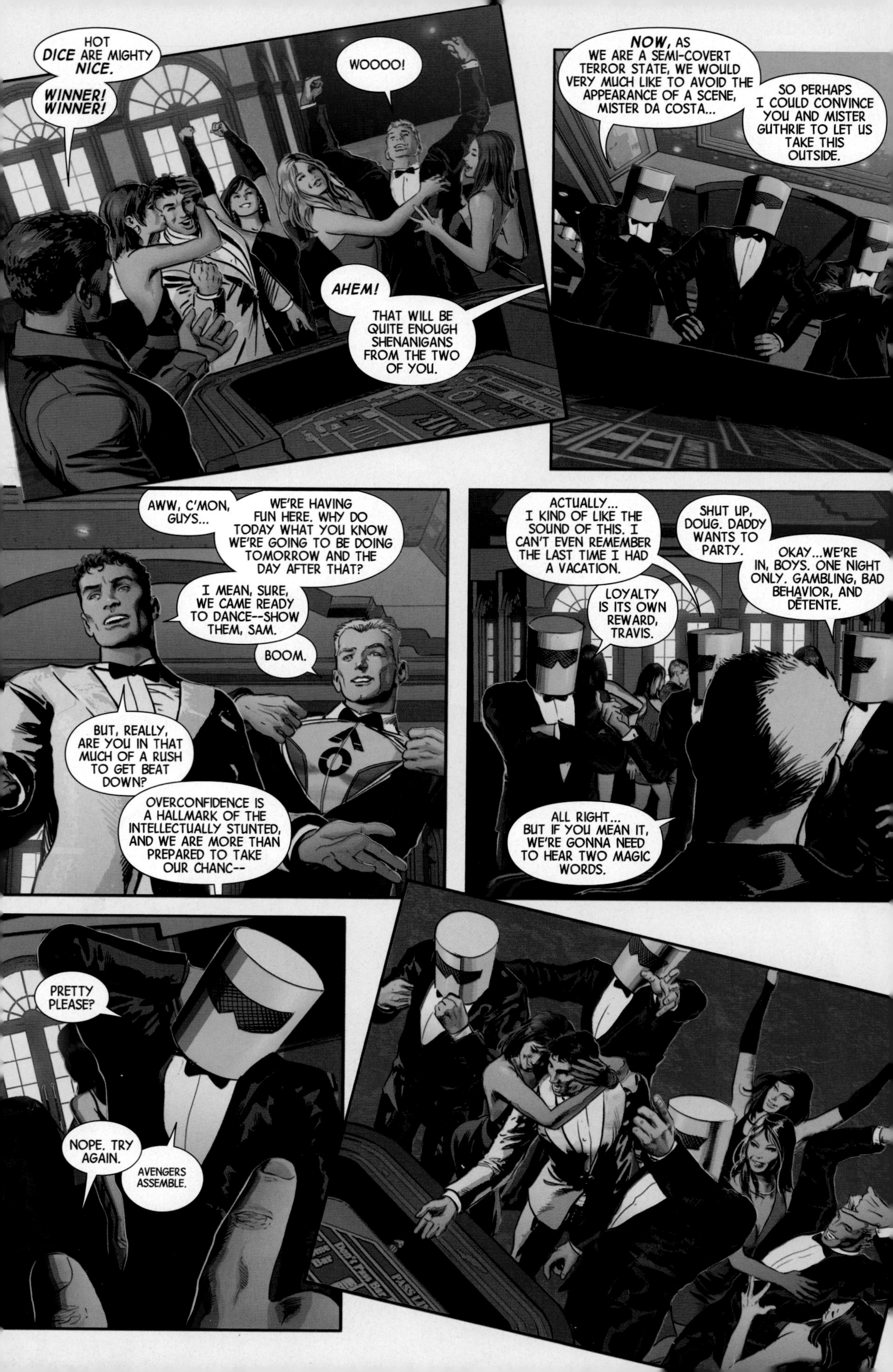
HOT DICE ARE MIGHTY NICE.
WINNER! WINNER!
WOOOO!
AHEM!
THAT WILL BE QUITE ENOUGH SHENANIGANS FROM THE TWO OF YOU.
NOW, AS WE ARE A SEMI-COVERT TERROR STATE, WE WOULD VERY MUCH LIKE TO AVOID THE APPEARANCE OF A SCENE, MISTER DA COSTA...
SO PERHAPS I COULD CONVINCE YOU AND MISTER GUTHRIE TO LET US TAKE THIS OUTSIDE.
AWW, C'MON, GUYS...
WE'RE HAVING FUN HERE. WHY DO TODAY WHAT YOU KNOW WE'RE GOING TO BE DOING TOMORROW AND THE DAY AFTER THAT?
I MEAN, SURE, WE CAME READY TO DANCE--SHOW THEM, SAM.
BOOM.
BUT, REALLY, ARE YOU IN THAT MUCH OF A RUSH TO GET BEAT DOWN?
OVERCONFIDENCE IS A HALLMARK OF THE INTELLECTUALLY STUNTED, AND WE ARE MORE THAN PREPARED TO TAKE OUR CHANC--
ACTUALLY... I KIND OF LIKE THE SOUND OF THIS. I CAN'T EVEN REMEMBER THE LAST TIME I HAD A VACATION.
LOYALTY IS ITS OWN REWARD, TRAVIS.
SHUT UP, DOUG. DADDY WANTS TO PARTY.
OKAY...WE'RE IN, BOYS. ONE NIGHT ONLY. GAMBLING, BAD BEHAVIOR, AND DÉTENTE.
ALL RIGHT... BUT IF YOU MEAN IT, WE'RE GONNA NEED TO HEAR TWO MAGIC WORDS.
PRETTY PLEASE?
NOPE. TRY AGAIN.
AVENGERS ASSEMBLE.

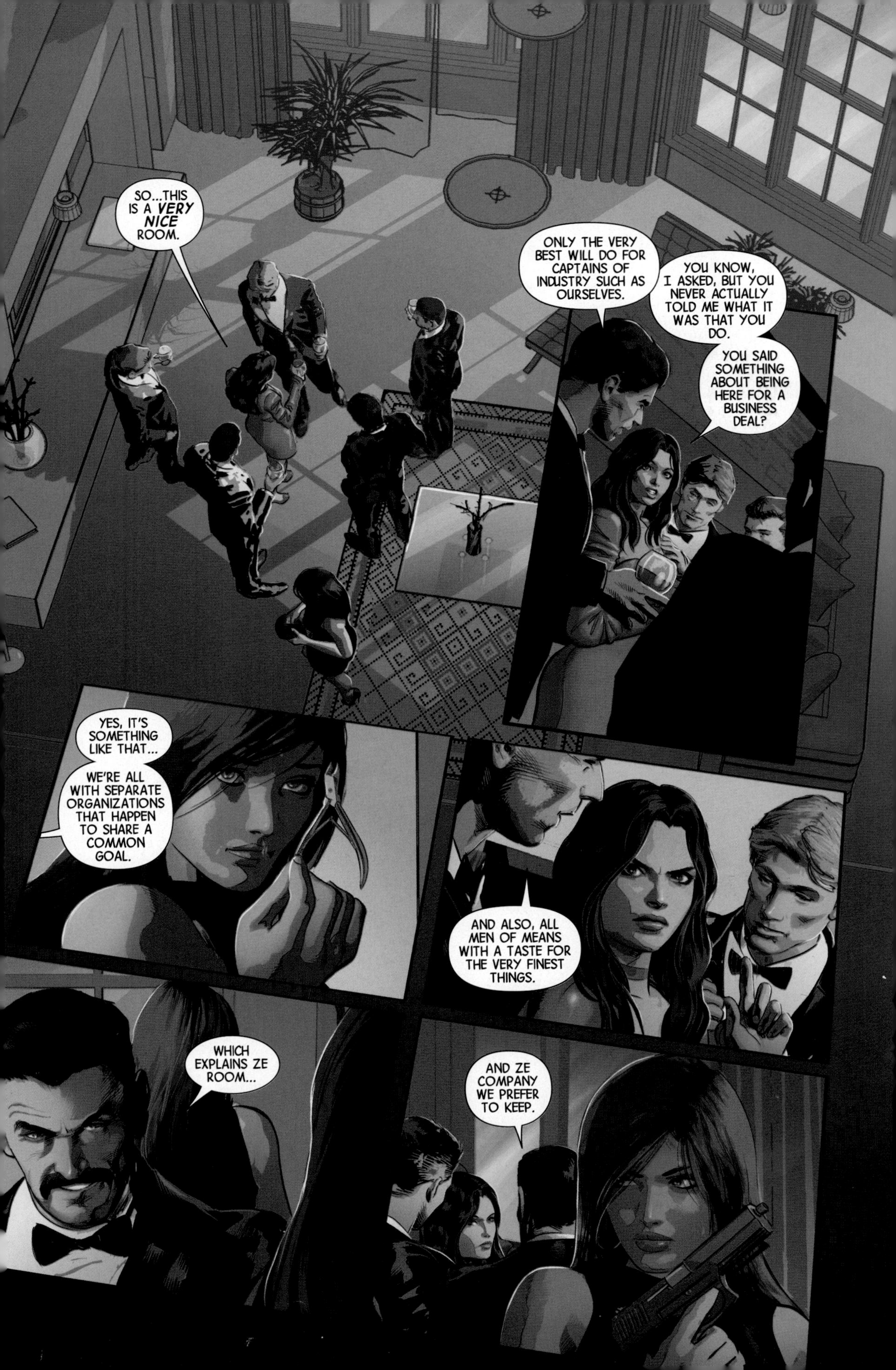
SO...THIS IS A VERY NICE ROOM.
ONLY THE VERY BEST WILL DO FOR CAPTAINS OF INDUSTRY SUCH AS OURSELVES.
YOU KNOW, I ASKED, BUT YOU NEVER ACTUALLY TOLD ME WHAT IT WAS THAT YOU DO.
YOU SAID SOMETHING ABOUT BEING HERE FOR A BUSINESS DEAL?
YES, IT'S SOMETHING LIKE THAT...
WE'RE ALL WITH SEPARATE ORGANIZATIONS THAT HAPPEN TO SHARE A COMMON GOAL.
AND ALSO, ALL MEN OF MEANS WITH A TASTE FOR THE VERY FINEST THINGS.
WHICH EXPLAINS ZE ROOM...
AND ZE COMPANY WE PREFER TO KEEP.

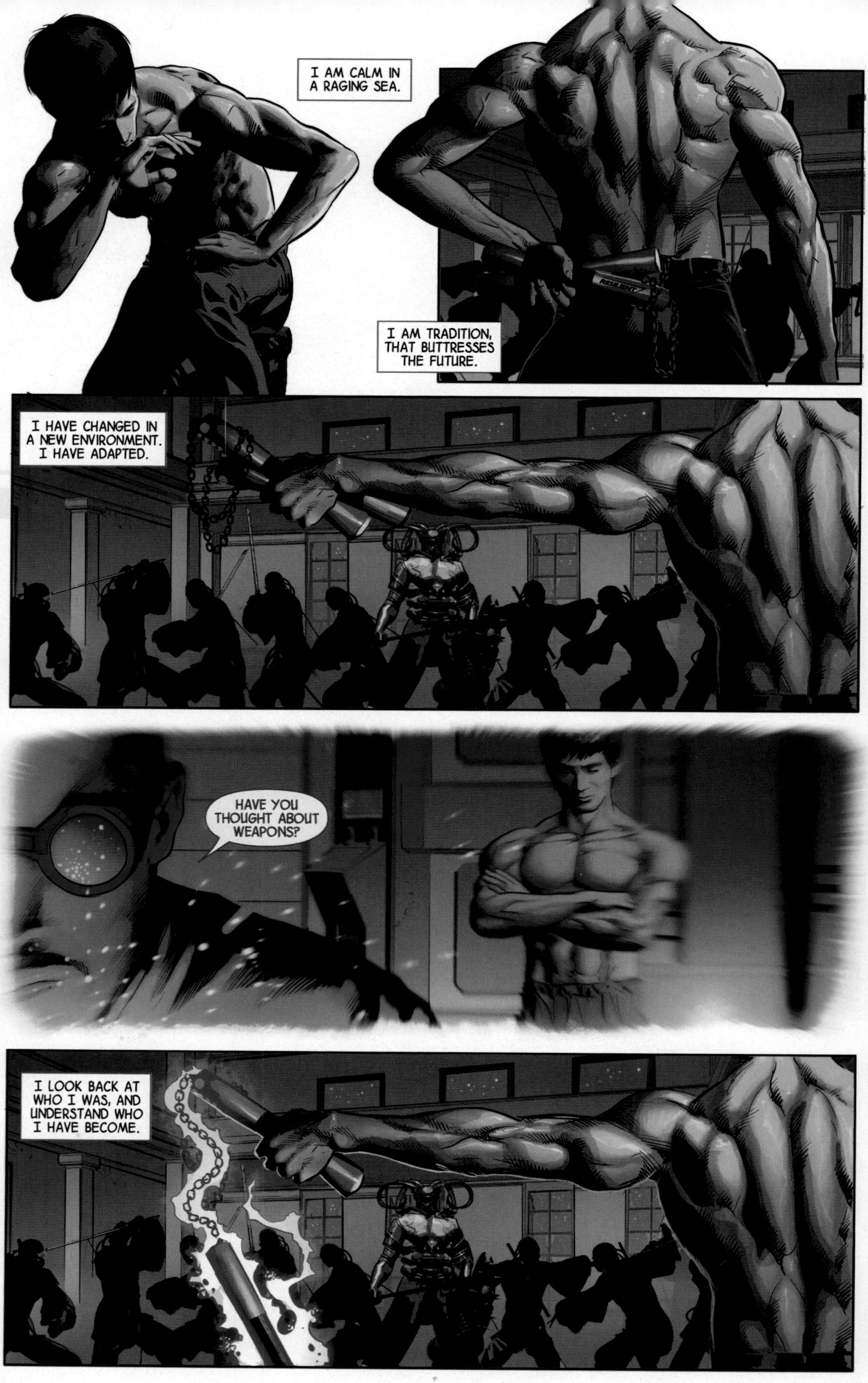
I AM CALM IN A RAGING SEA.
I AM TRADITION, THAT BUTTRESSES THE FUTURE.
I HAVE CHANGED IN A NEW ENVIRONMENT. I HAVE ADAPTED.
HAVE YOU THOUGHT ABOUT WEAPONS?
I LOOK BACK AT WHO I WAS, AND UNDERSTAND WHO I HAVE BECOME.

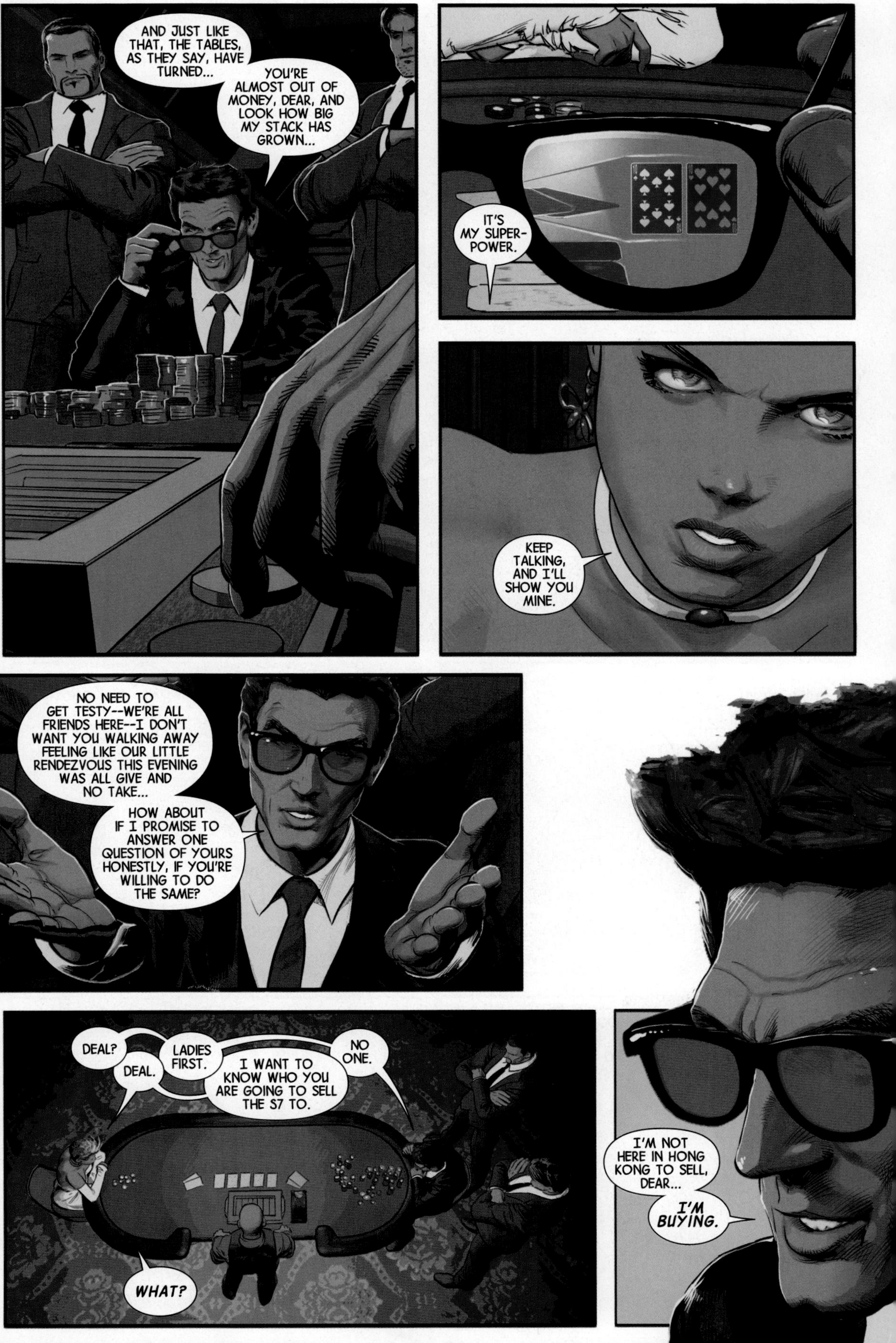
AND JUST LIKE THAT, THE TABLES, AS THEY SAY, HAVE TURNED...
YOU'RE ALMOST OUT OF MONEY, DEAR, AND LOOK HOW BIG MY STACK HAS GROWN...
IT'S MY SUPER-POWER.
KEEP TALKING, AND I'LL SHOW YOU MINE.
NO NEED TO GET TESTY--WE'RE ALL FRIENDS HERE--I DON'T WANT YOU WALKING AWAY FEELING LIKE OUR LITTLE RENDEZVOUS THIS EVENING WAS ALL GIVE AND NO TAKE...
HOW ABOUT IF I PROMISE TO ANSWER ONE QUESTION OF YOURS HONESTLY, IF YOU'RE WILLING TO DO THE SAME?
DEAL?
DEAL.
LADIES FIRST.
I WANT TO KNOW WHO YOU ARE GOING TO SELL THE S7 TO.
NO ONE.
WHAT?
I'M NOT HERE IN HONG KONG TO SELL, DEAR...
I'M BUYING.

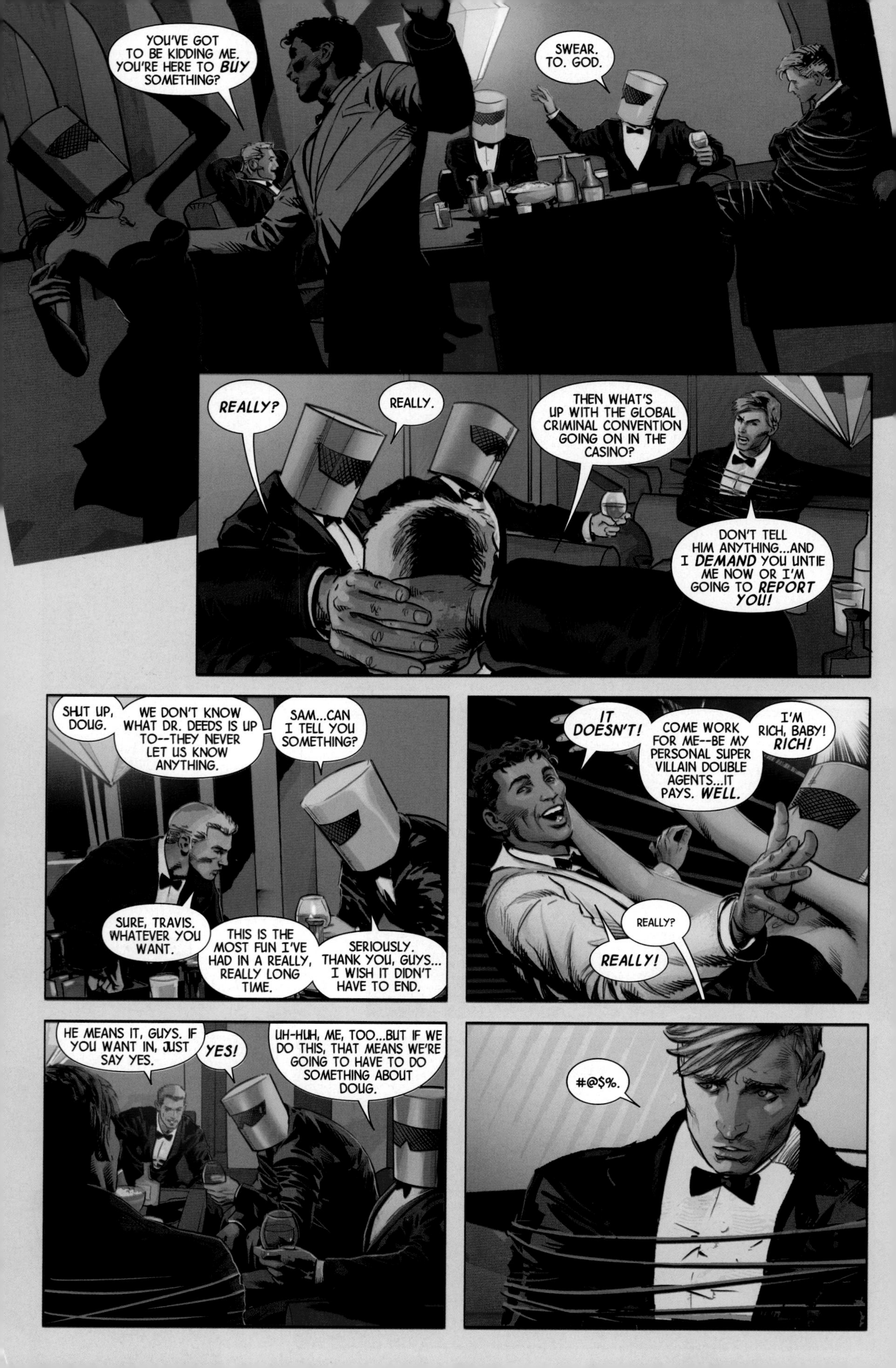

YOU'VE GOT TO BE KIDDING ME. YOU'RE HERE TO BUY SOMETHING?
SWEAR. TO. GOD.
REALLY?
REALLY.
THEN WHAT'S UP WITH THE GLOBAL CRIMINAL CONVENTION GOING ON IN THE CASINO?
DON'T TELL HIM ANYTHING...AND I DEMAND YOU UNTIE ME NOW OR I'M GOING TO REPORT YOU!
SHUT UP, DOUG.
WE DON'T KNOW WHAT DR. DEEDS IS UP TO--THEY NEVER LET US KNOW ANYTHING.
SAM...CAN I TELL YOU SOMETHING?
SURE, TRAVIS. WHATEVER YOU WANT.
THIS IS THE MOST FUN I'VE HAD IN A REALLY, REALLY LONG TIME.
SERIOUSLY. THANK YOU, GUYS... I WISH IT DIDN'T HAVE TO END.
IT DOESN'T!
COME WORK FOR ME--BE MY PERSONAL SUPER VILLAIN DOUBLE AGENTS...IT PAYS. WELL.
I'M RICH, BABY! RICH!
REALLY?
REALLY!
HE MEANS IT, GUYS. IF YOU WANT IN, JUST SAY YES.
YES!
UH-HUH, ME, TOO...BUT IF WE DO THIS, THAT MEANS WE'RE GOING TO HAVE TO DO SOMETHING ABOUT DOUG.
#@$%.

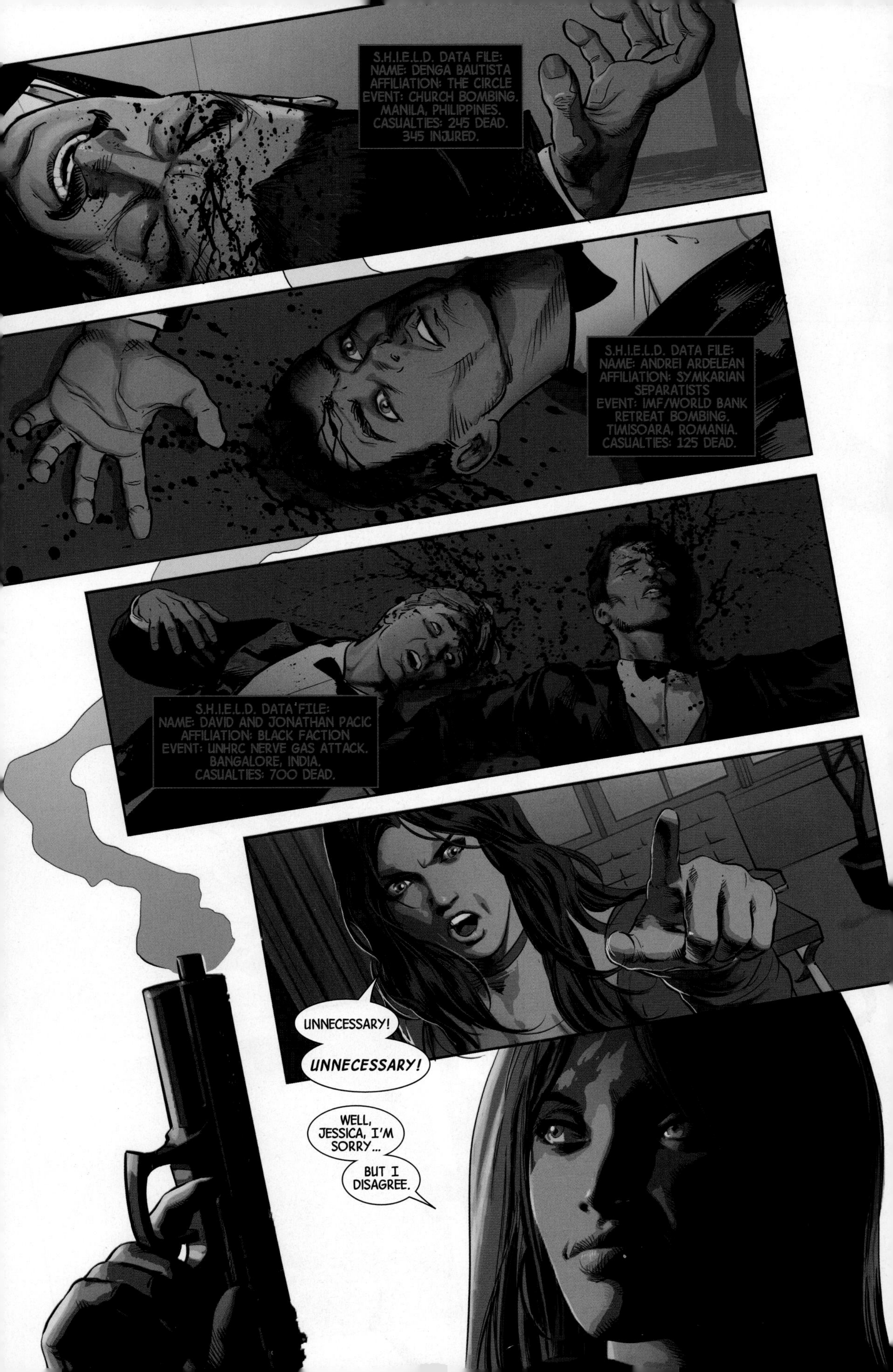

S.H.I.E.L.D. DATA FILE:
NAME: DENGA BAUTISTA
AFFILIATION: THE CIRCLE
EVENT: CHURCH BOMBING.
MANILA, PHILIPPINES.
CASUALTIES: 245 DEAD.
345 INJURED.
S.H.I.E.L.D. DATA FILE:
NAME: ANDREI ARDELEAN
AFFILIATION: SYMKARIAN SEPARATISTS
EVENT: IMF/WORLD BANK RETREAT BOMBING.
TIMISOARA, ROMANIA.
CASUALTIES: 125 DEAD.
S.H.I.E.L.D. DATA FILE:
NAME: DAVID AND JONATHAN PACIC
AFFILIATION: BLACK FACTION
EVENT: UNHRC NERVE GAS ATTACK.
BANGALORE, INDIA.
CASUALTIES: 700 DEAD.
UNNECESSARY!
UNNECESSARY!
WELL, JESSICA, I'M SORRY...
BUT I DISAGREE.

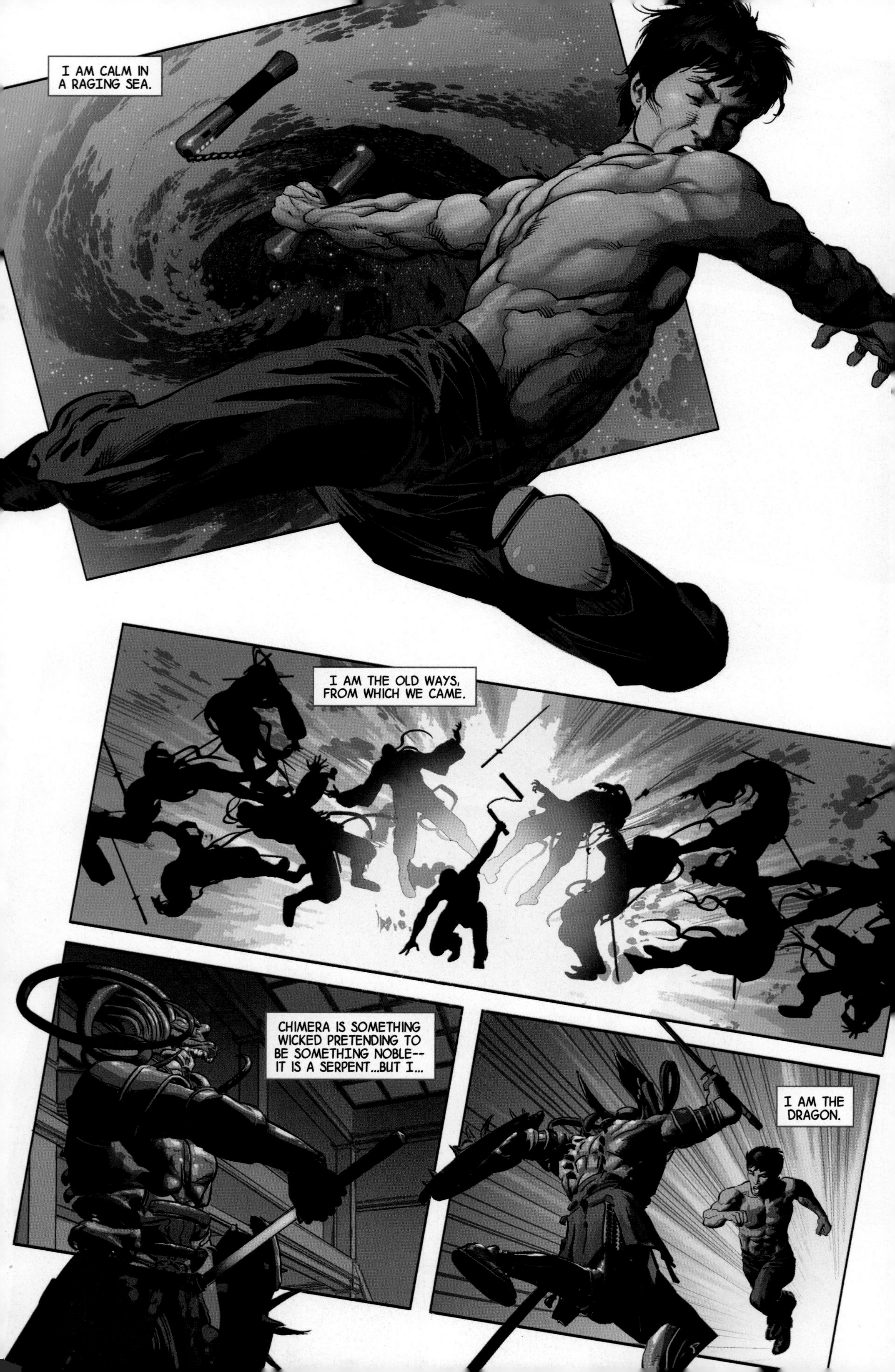
I AM CALM IN
A RAGING SEA.
I AM THE OLD WAYS,
FROM WHICH WE CAME.
CHIMERA IS SOMETHING
WICKED PRETENDING TO
BE SOMETHING NOBLE--
IT IS A SERPENT...BUT I...
I AM THE
DRAGON.

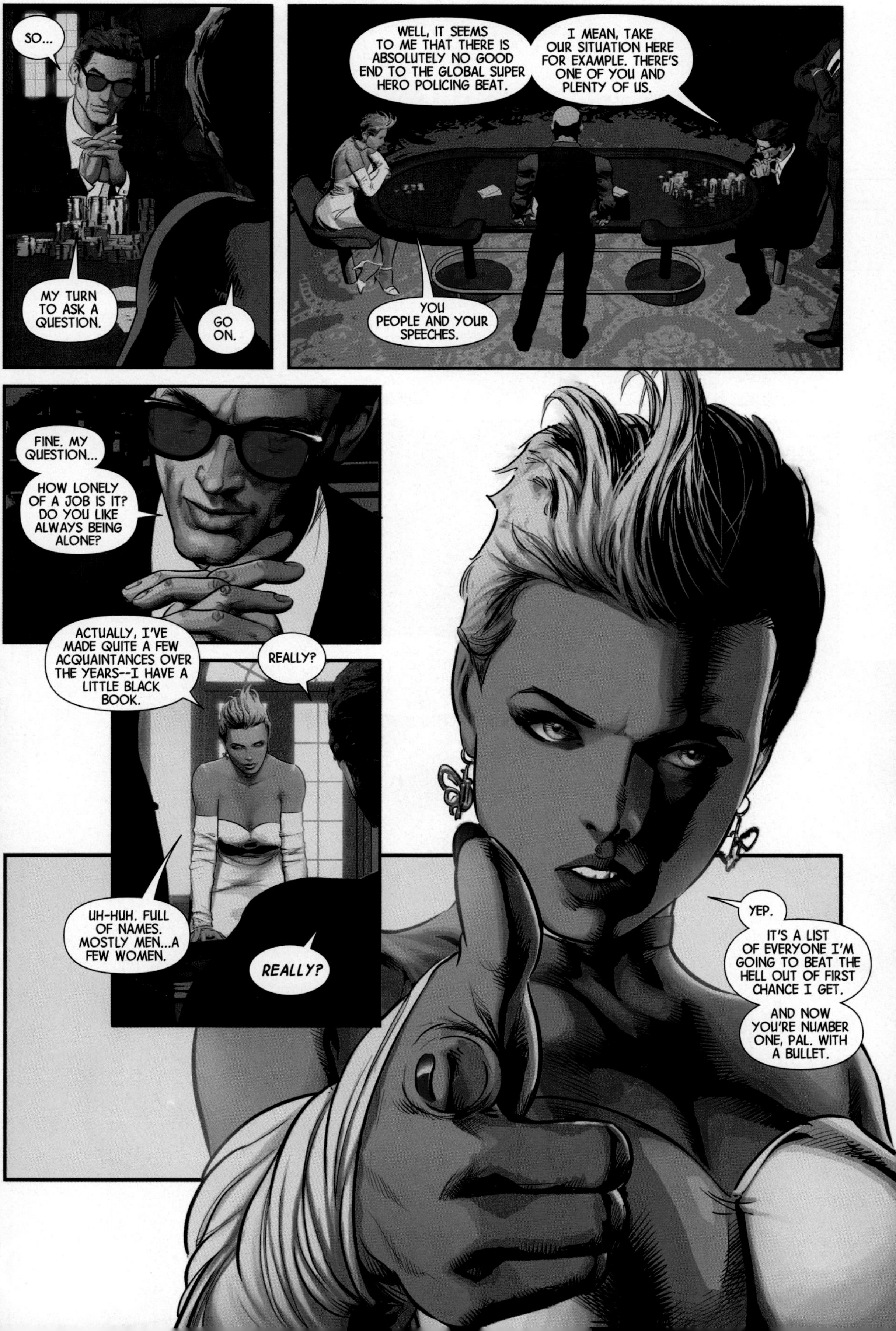
SO...
MY TURN TO ASK A QUESTION.
GO ON.
WELL, IT SEEMS TO ME THAT THERE IS ABSOLUTELY NO GOOD END TO THE GLOBAL SUPER HERO POLICING BEAT.
I MEAN, TAKE OUR SITUATION HERE FOR EXAMPLE. THERE'S ONE OF YOU AND PLENTY OF US.
YOU PEOPLE AND YOUR SPEECHES.
FINE. MY QUESTION...
HOW LONELY OF A JOB IS IT? DO YOU LIKE ALWAYS BEING ALONE?
ACTUALLY, I'VE MADE QUITE A FEW ACQUAINTANCES OVER THE YEARS--I HAVE A LITTLE BLACK BOOK.
REALLY?
UH-HUH. FULL OF NAMES. MOSTLY MEN...A FEW WOMEN.
REALLY?
YEP.
IT'S A LIST OF EVERYONE I'M GOING TO BEAT THE HELL OUT OF FIRST CHANCE I GET.
AND NOW YOU'RE NUMBER ONE, PAL. WITH A BULLET.

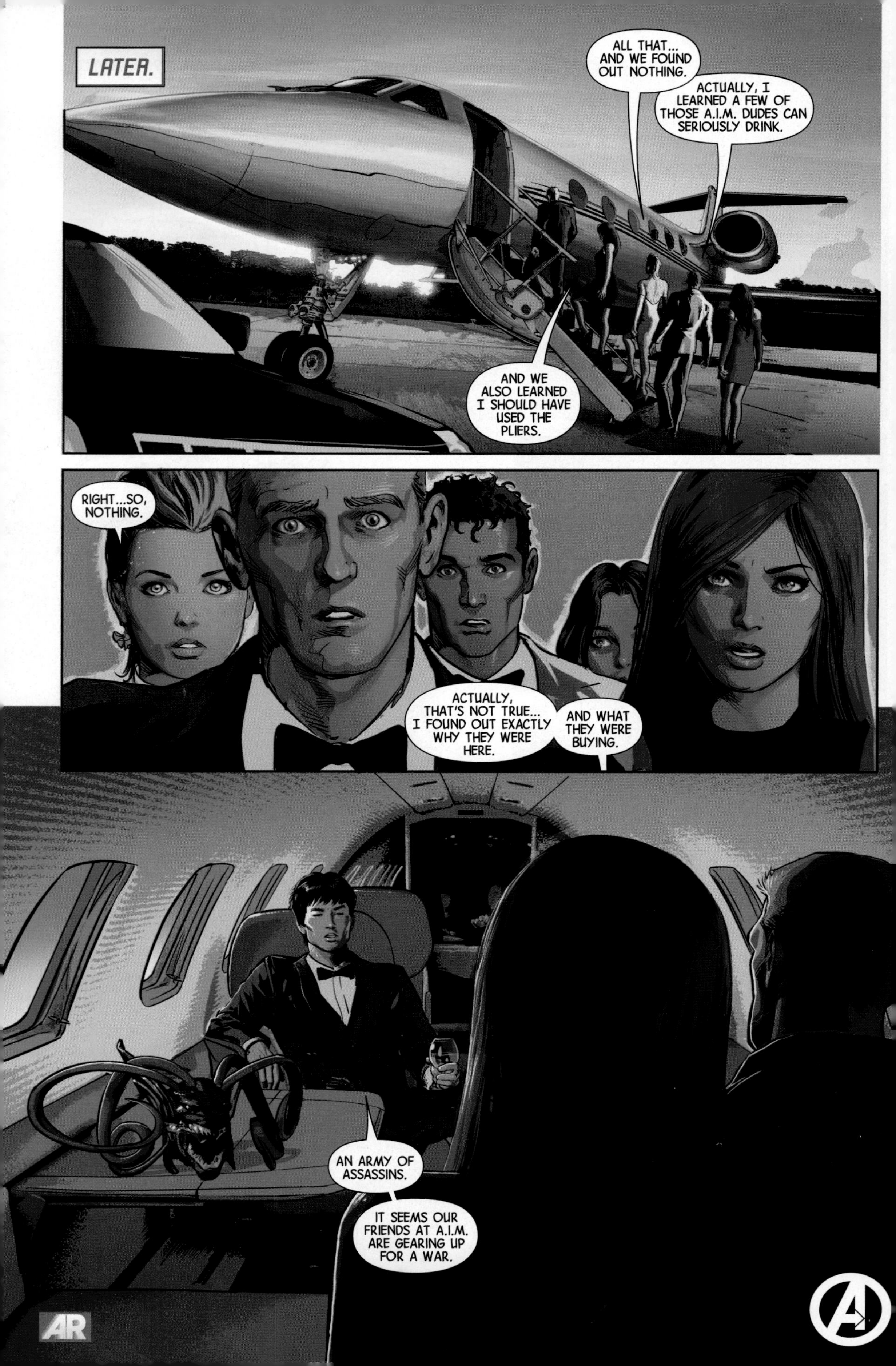
LATER.
ALL THAT... AND WE FOUND OUT NOTHING.
ACTUALLY, I LEARNED A FEW OF THOSE A.I.M. DUDES CAN SERIOUSLY DRINK.
AND WE ALSO LEARNED I SHOULD HAVE USED THE PLIERS.
RIGHT...SO, NOTHING.
ACTUALLY, THAT'S NOT TRUE... I FOUND OUT EXACTLY WHY THEY WERE HERE.
AND WHAT THEY WERE BUYING.
AN ARMY OF ASSASSINS.
IT SEEMS OUR FRIENDS AT A.I.M. ARE GEARING UP FOR A WAR.

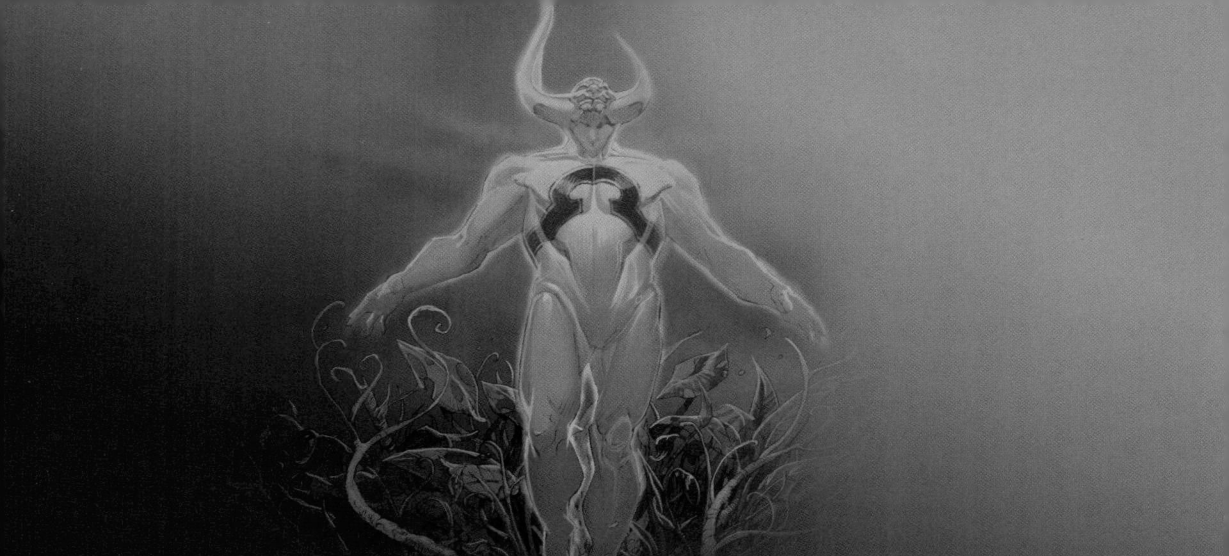

BUILDER MACHINE CODE

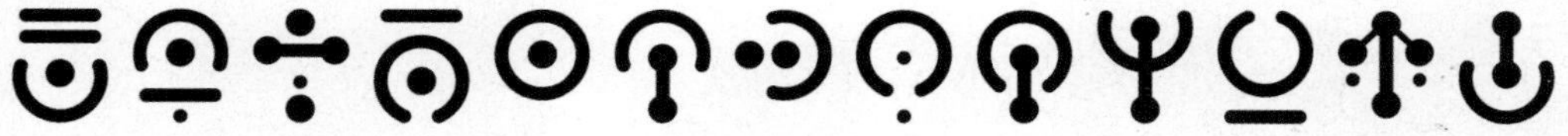

A B C D E F G H I J K L M

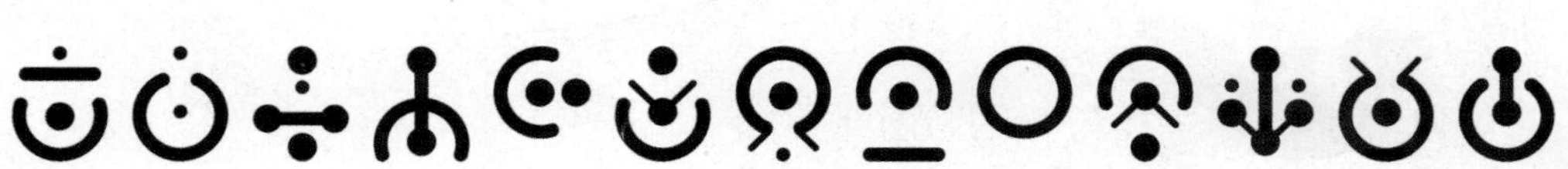

N O P Q R S T U V W X Y Z

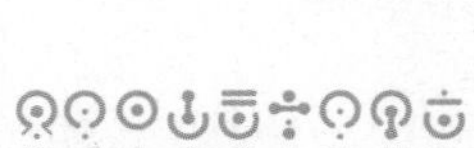

#7

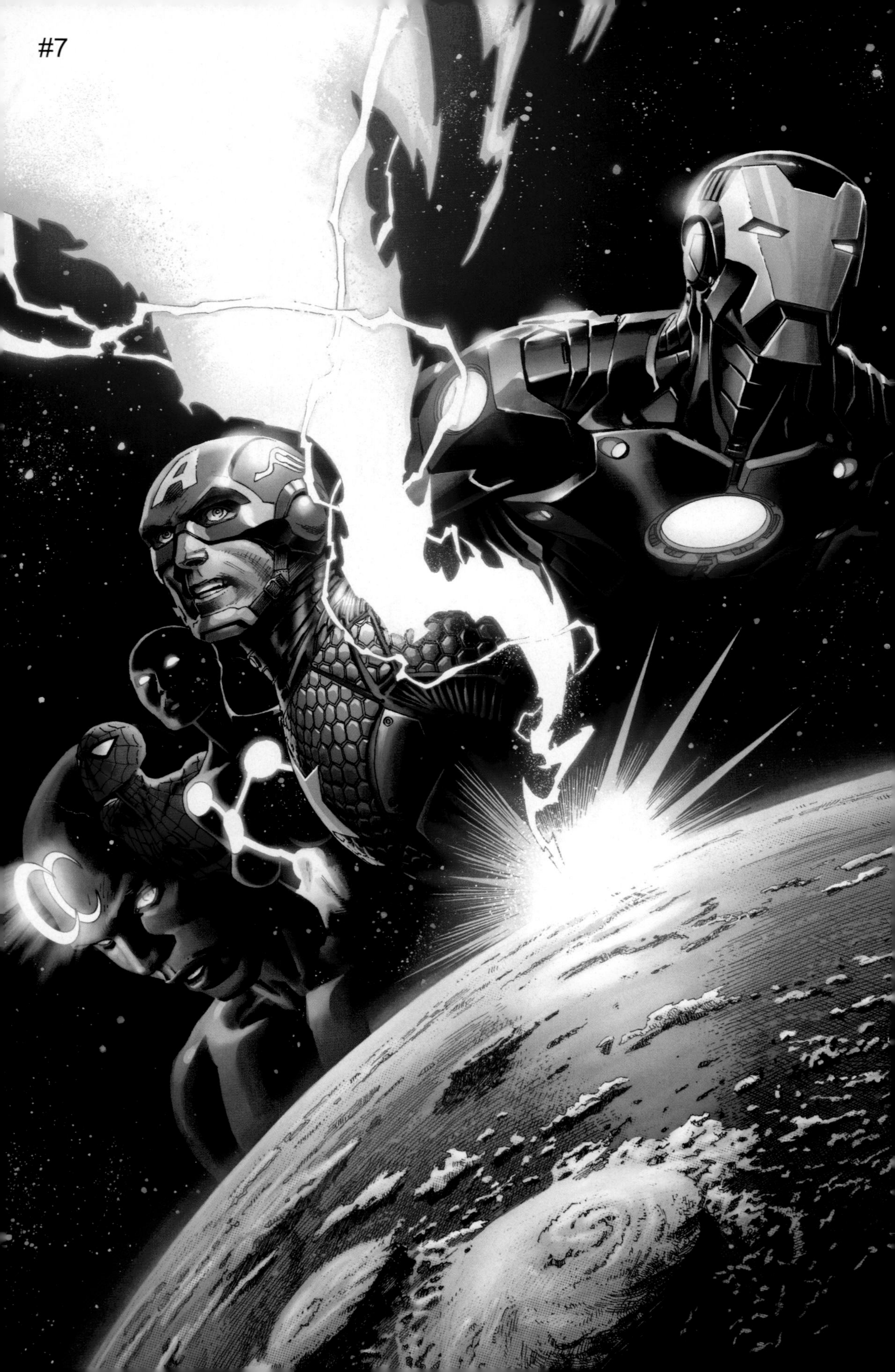

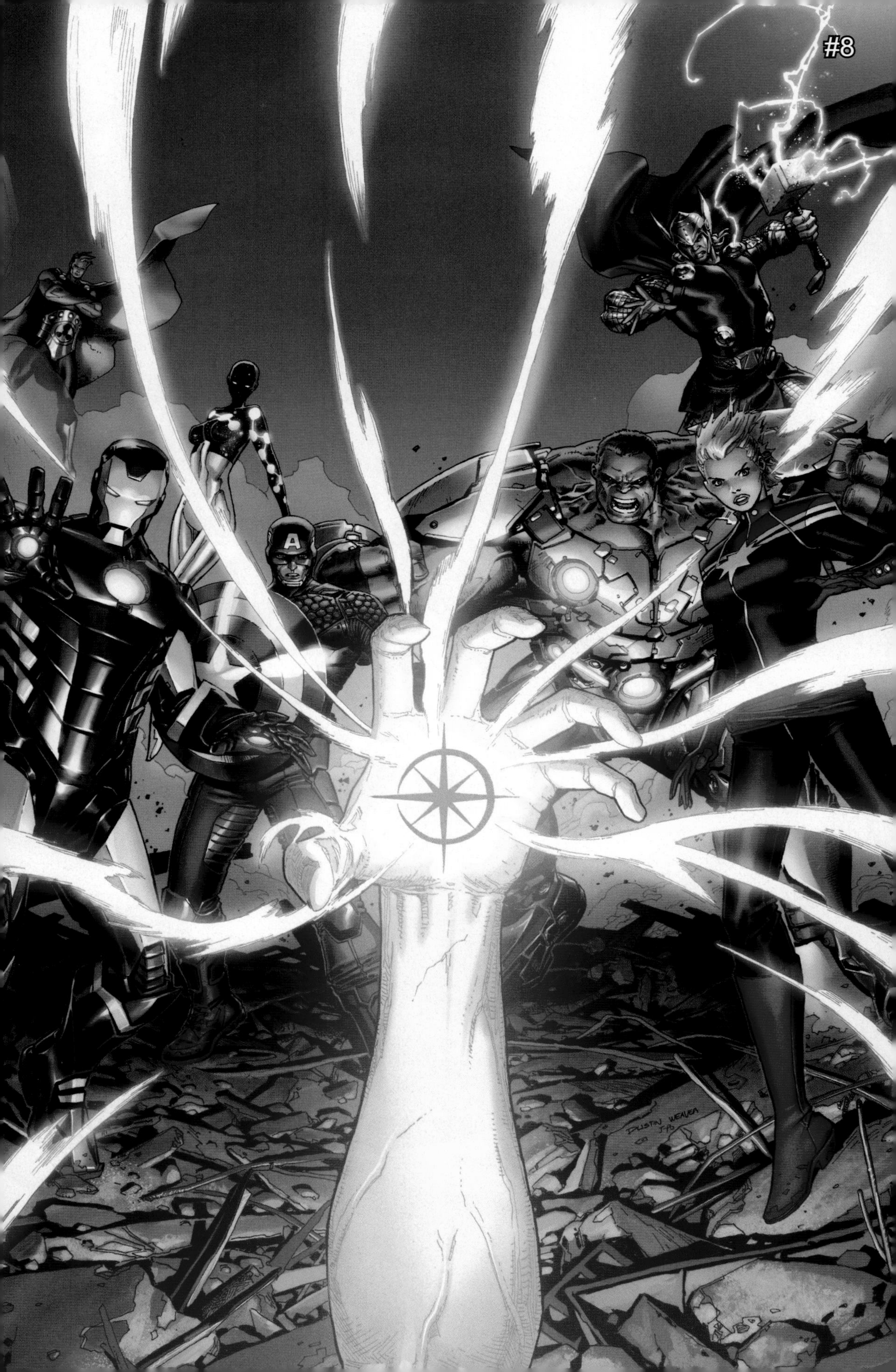
#8

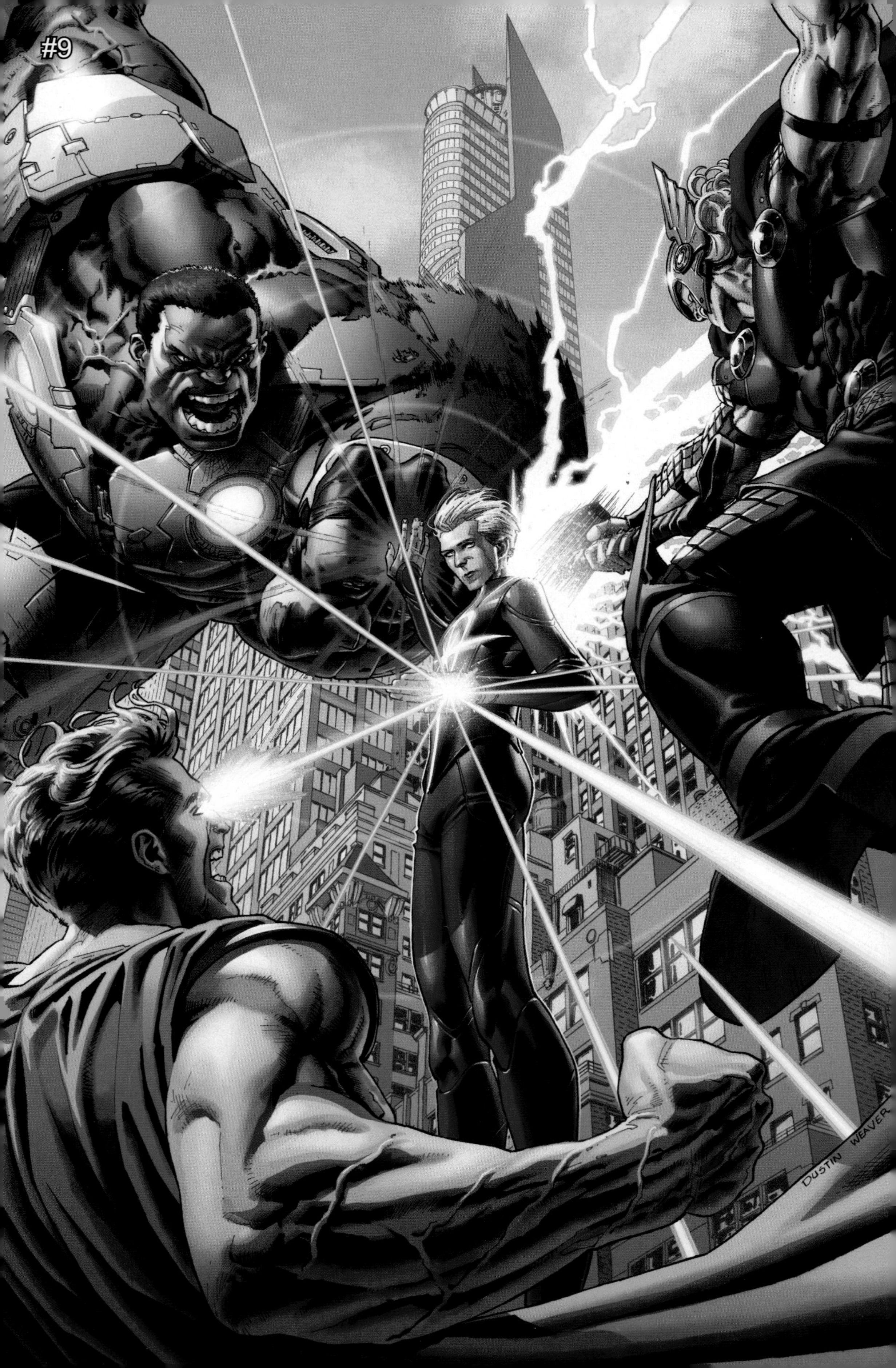
#9
DUSTIN WEAVER

#10

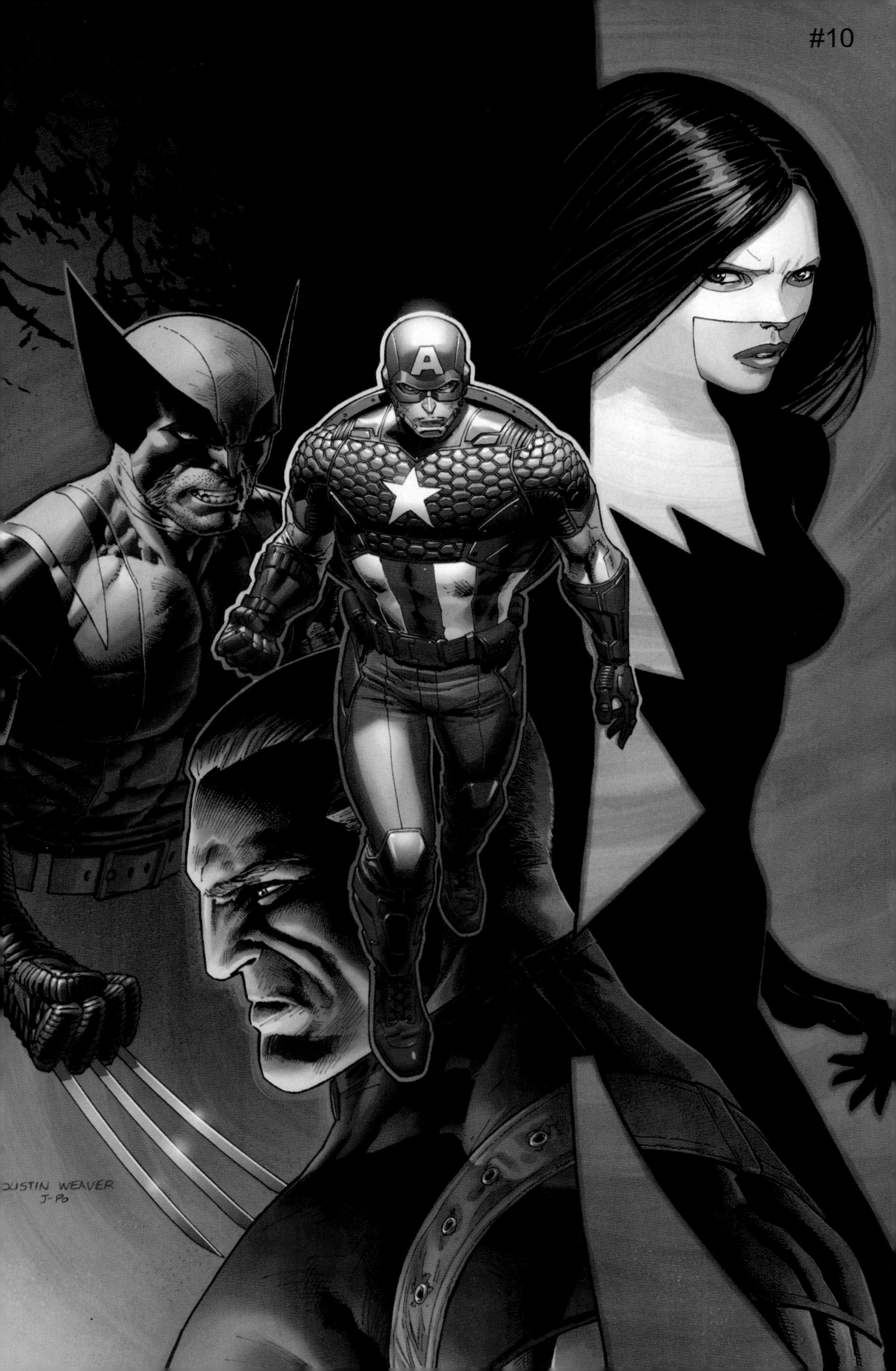
DUSTIN WEAVER
J-Po

#11

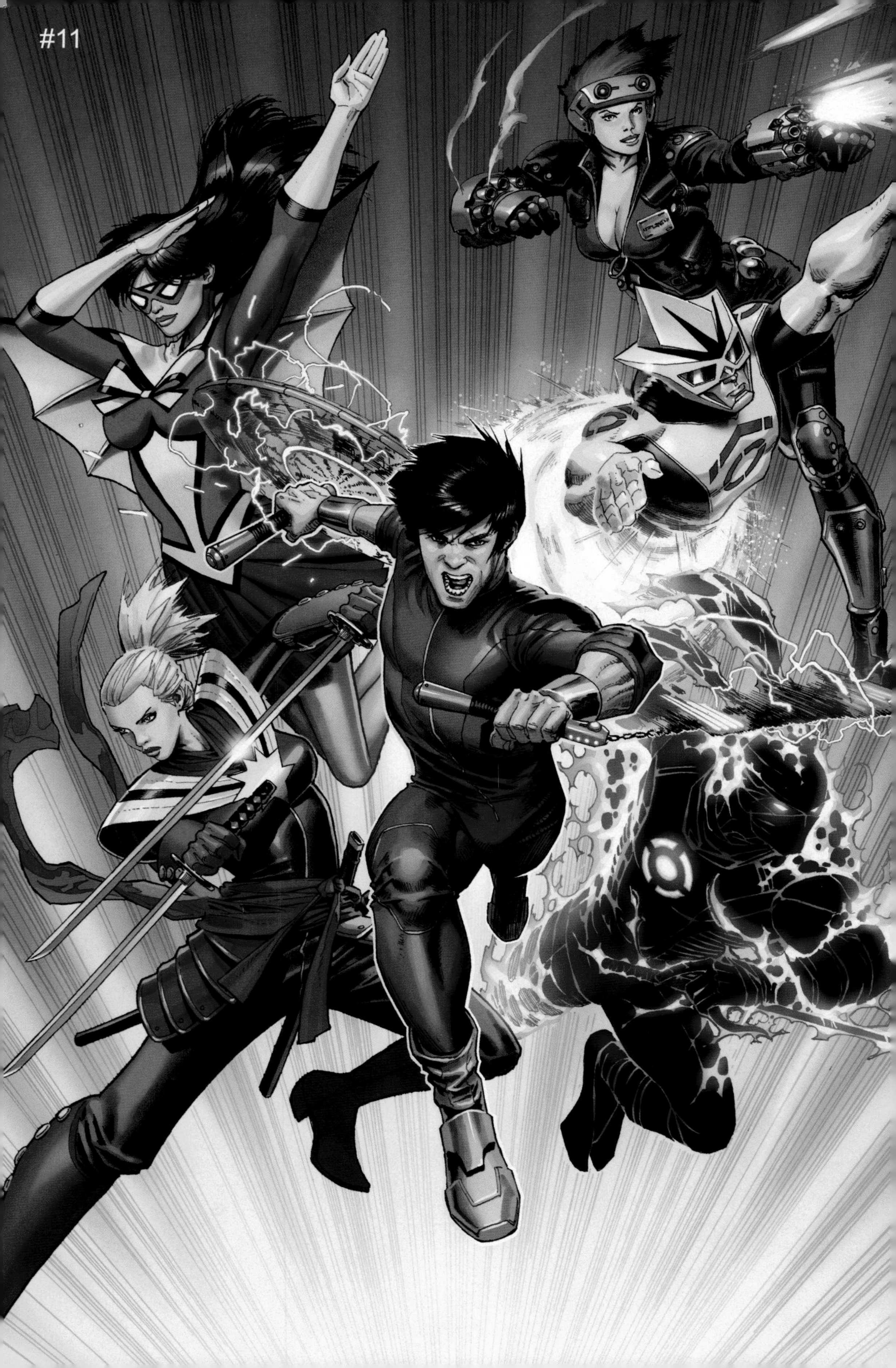

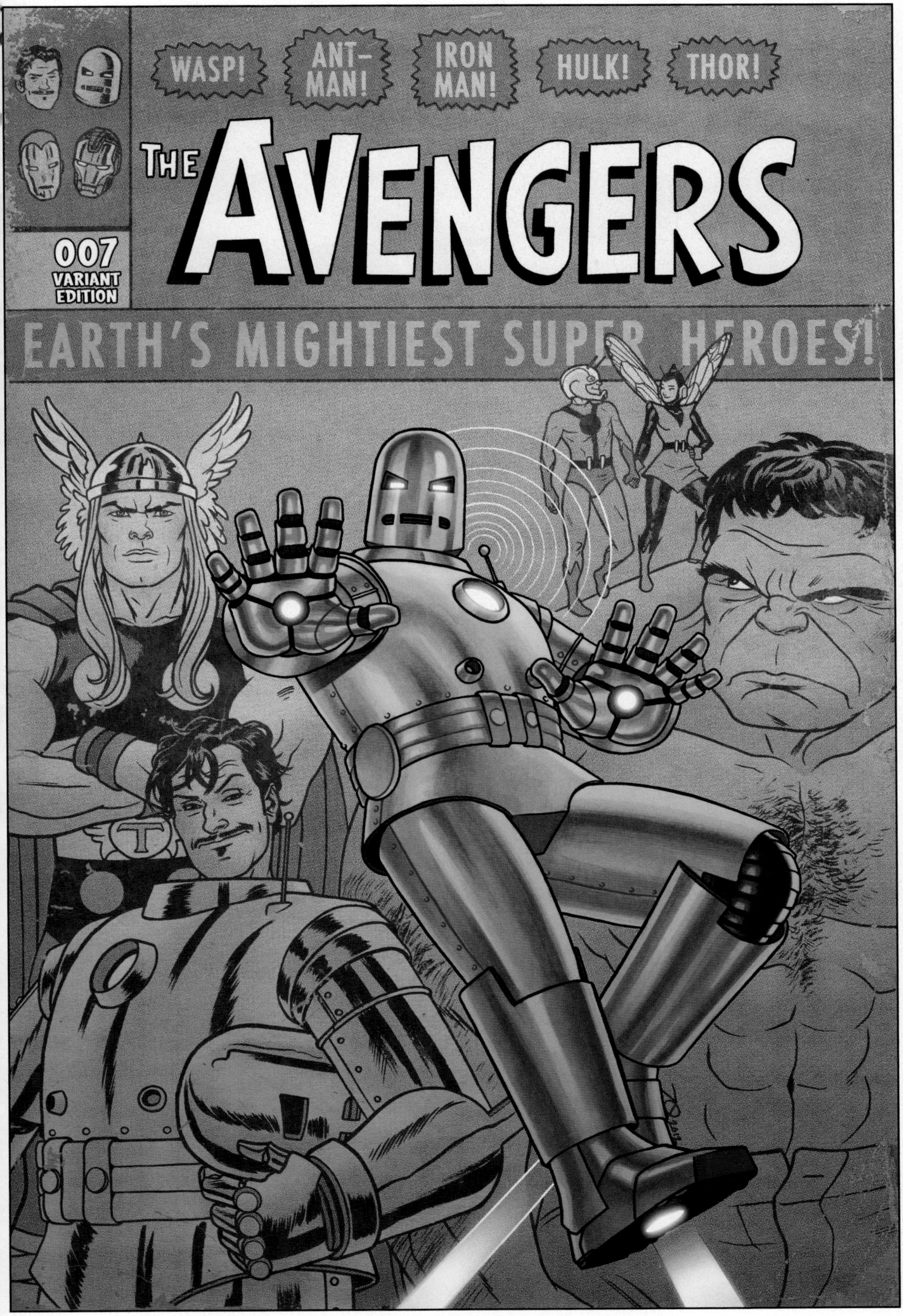
WASP!
ANT-MAN!
IRON MAN!
HULK!
THOR!
THE AVENGERS
007
VARIANT EDITION
EARTH'S MIGHTIEST SUPER HEROES!

#9 MANY ARMORS OF IRON MAN VARIANT:
DANIEL ACUÑA

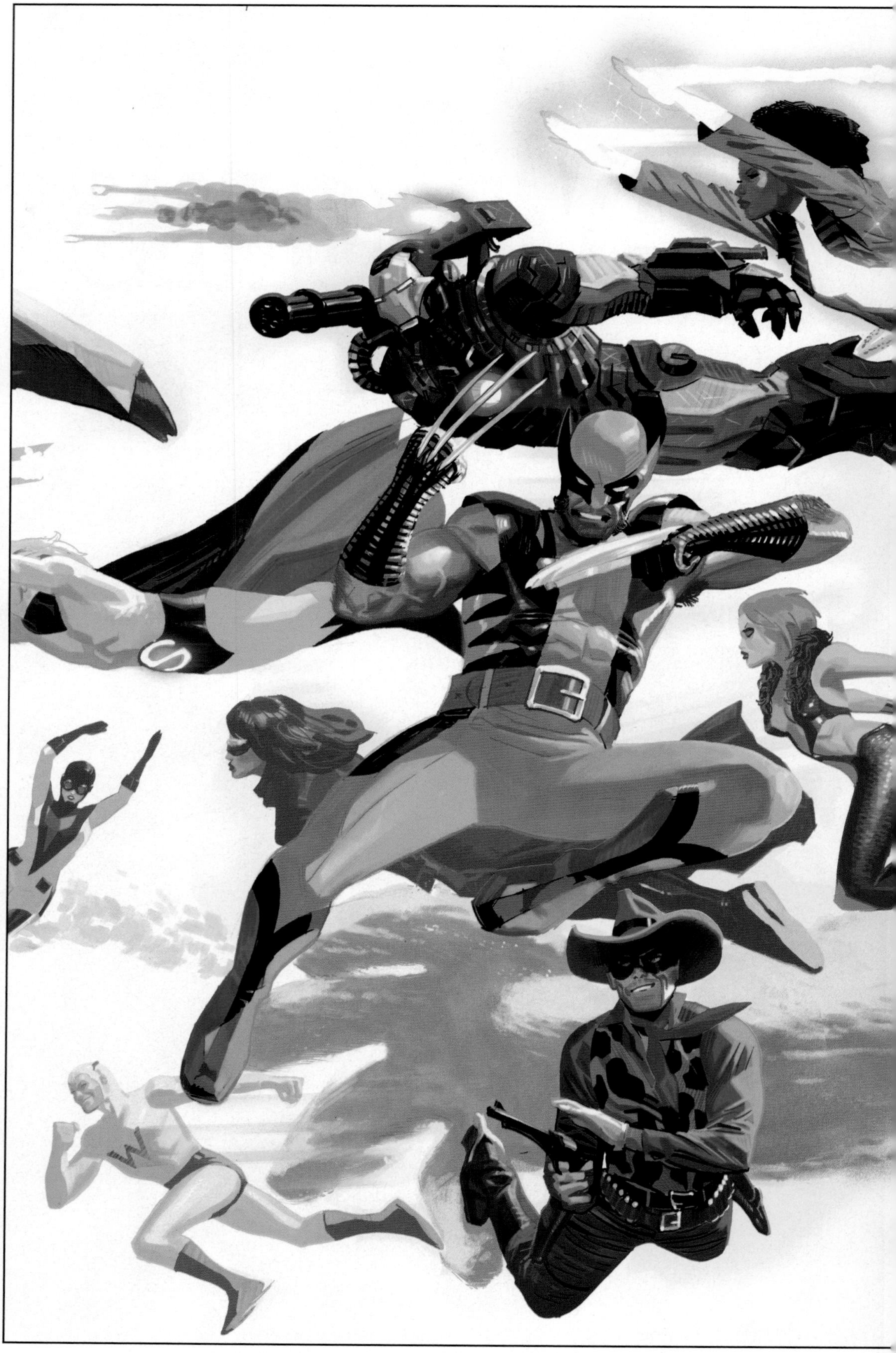

#8 & #10 AVENGERS 50TH ANNIVERSARY VARIANTS:
DANIEL ACUÑA

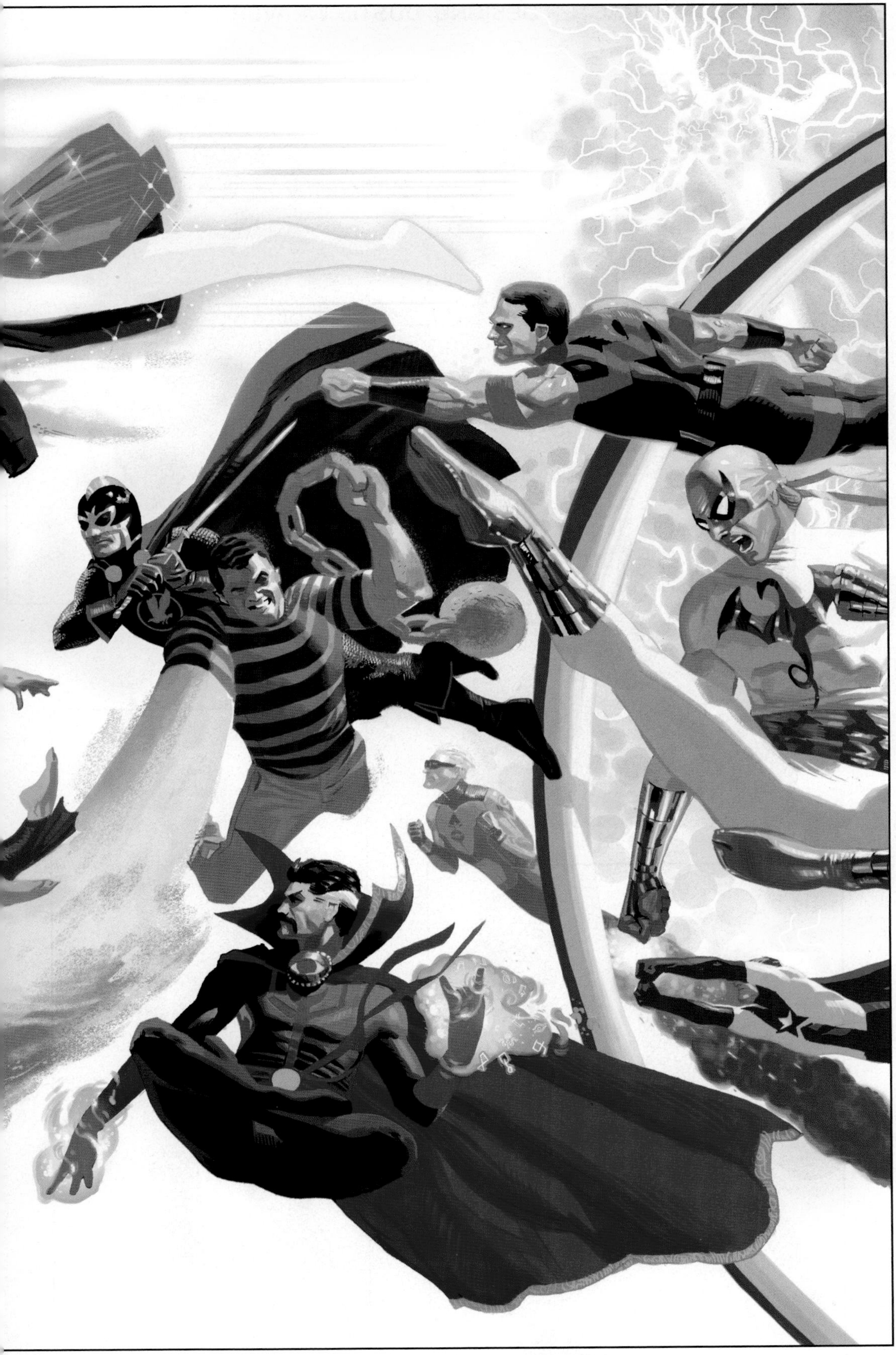

CHARACTER DESIGNS: **DUSTIN WEAVER**

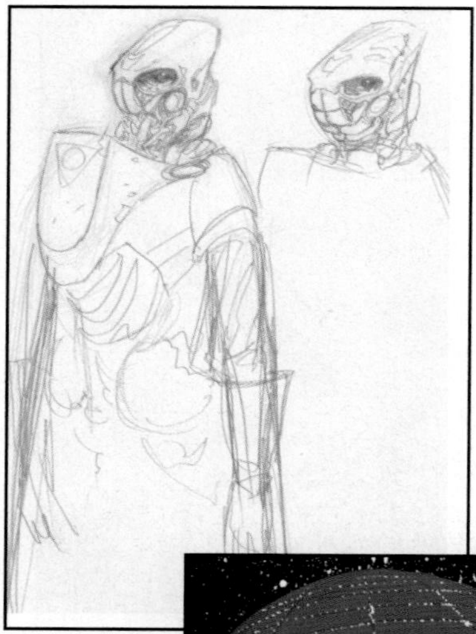

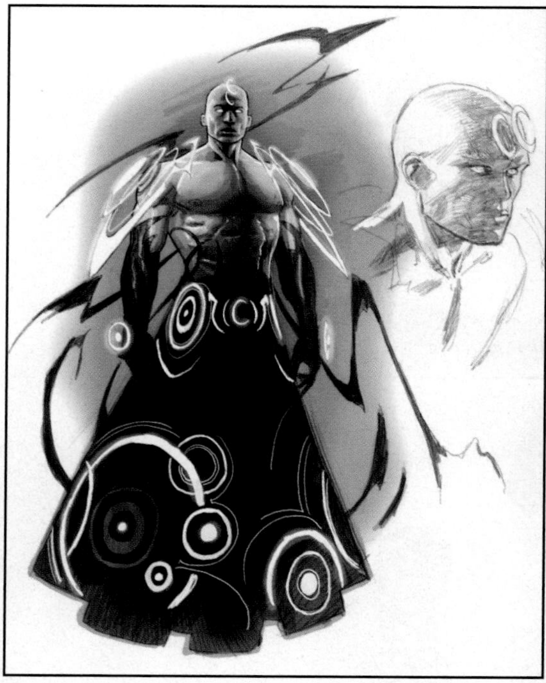

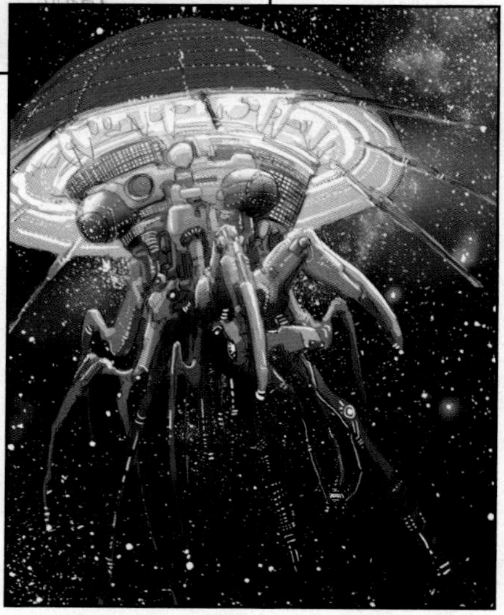

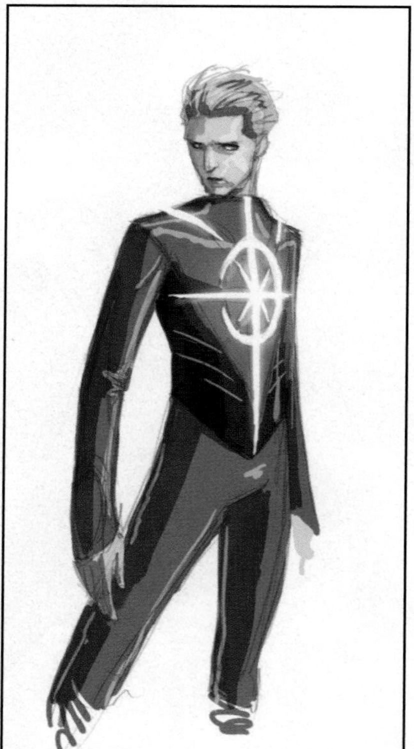

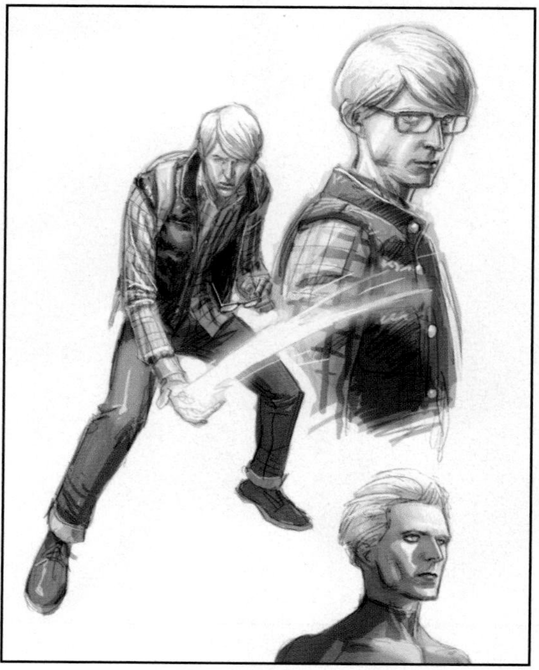

LAYOUTS & INKS: **DUSTIN WEAVER & JAY LEISTEN**

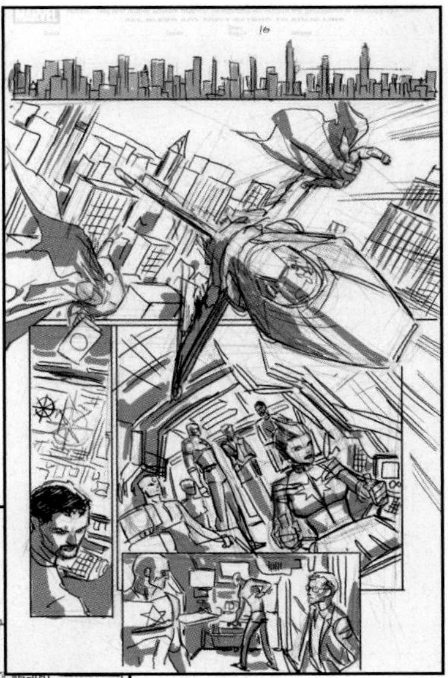

#7, PAGE 16

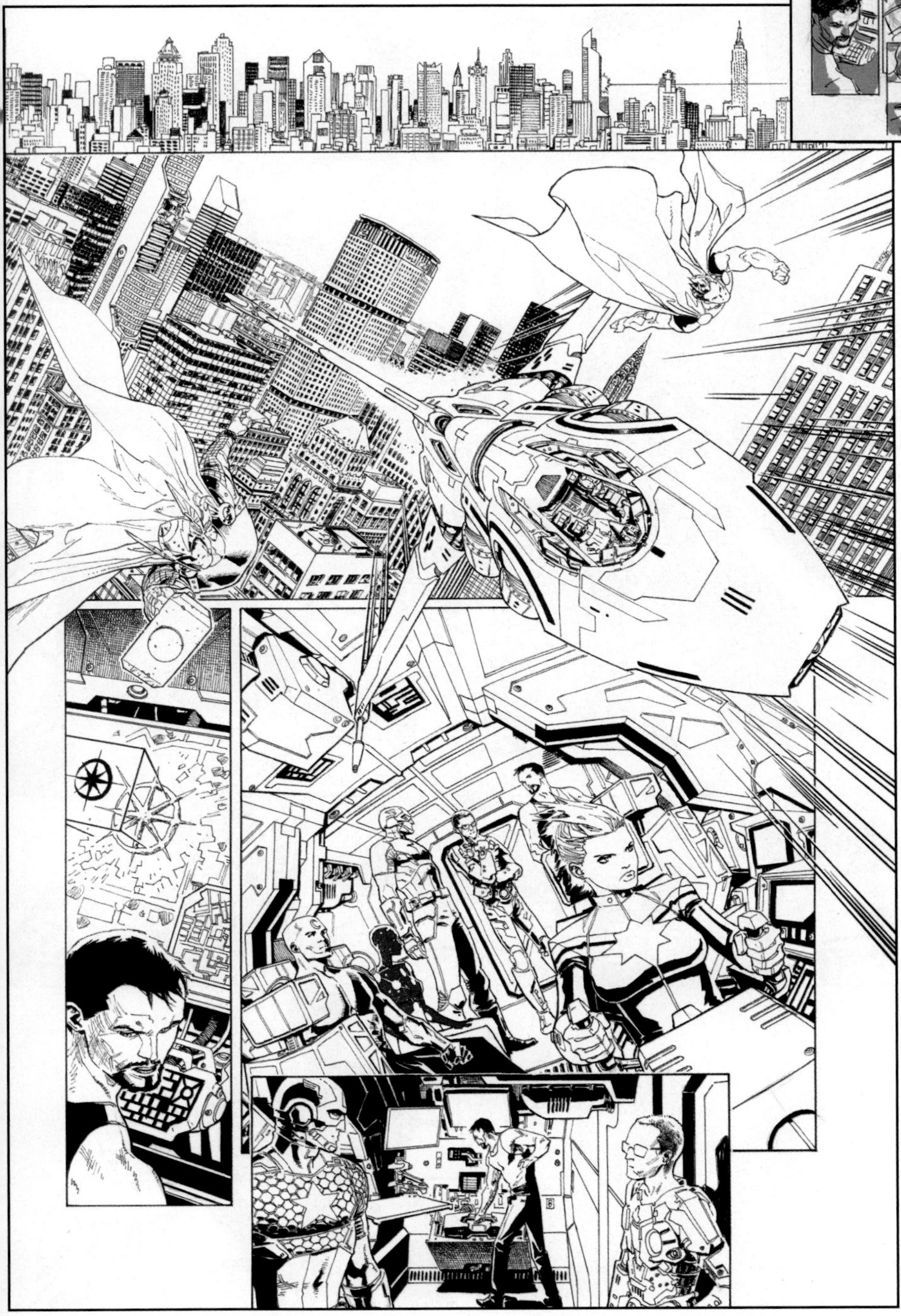

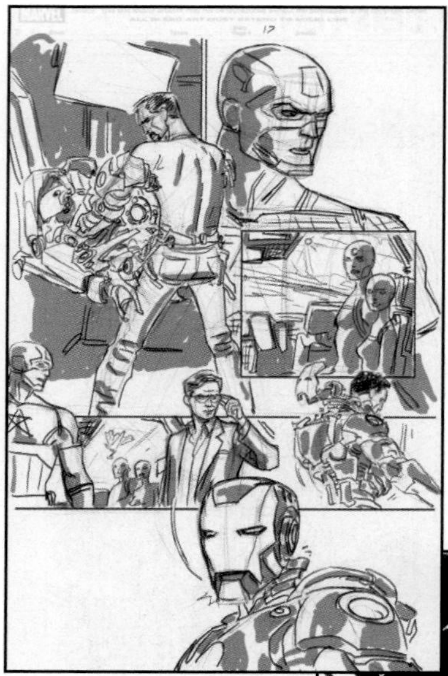

#7, PAGE 17

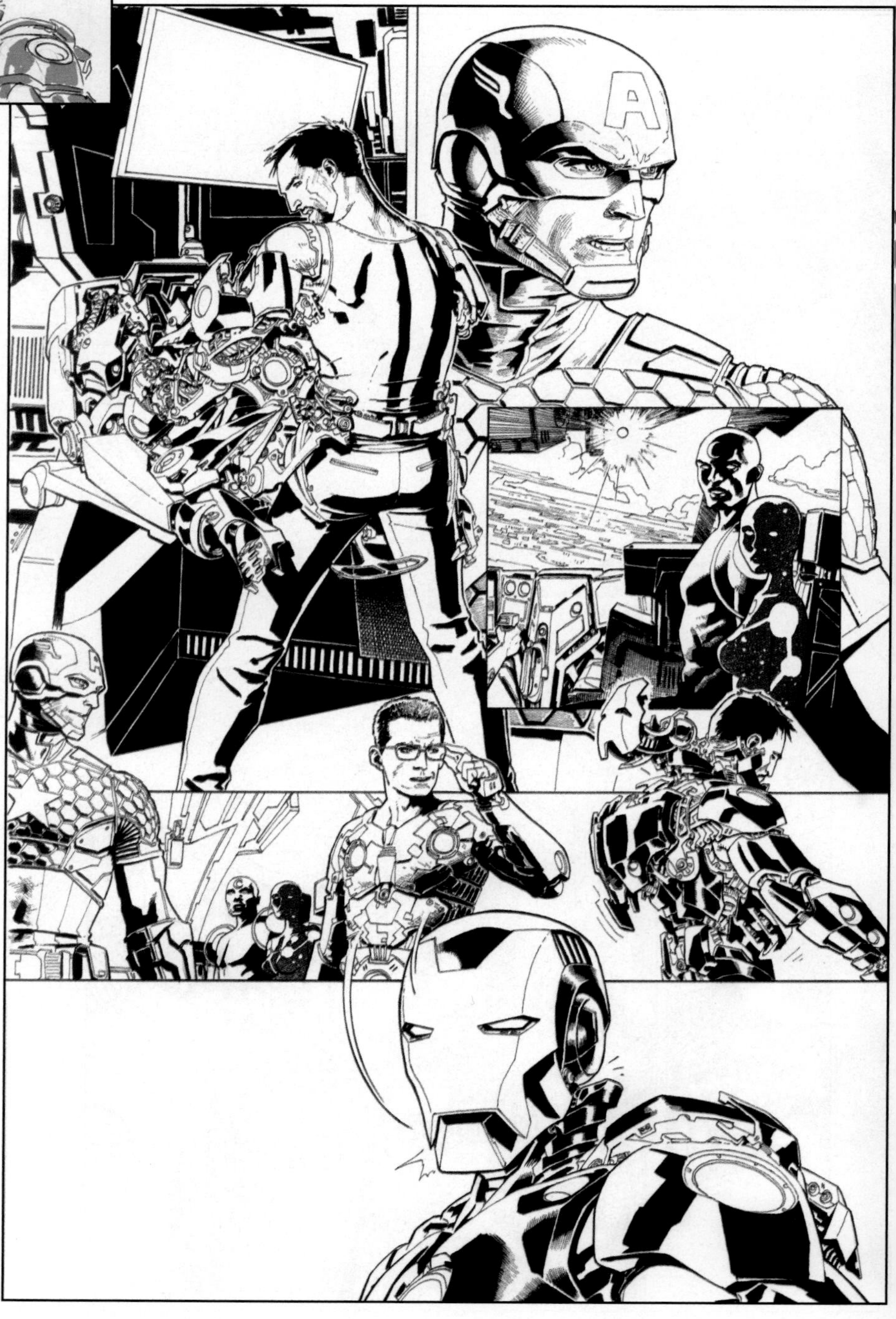

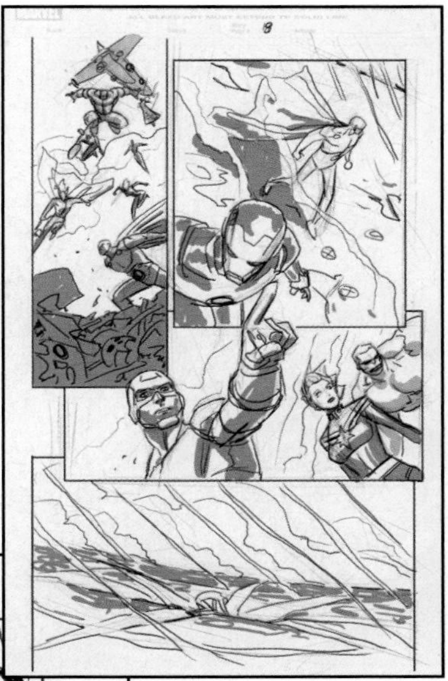

#7, PAGE 18

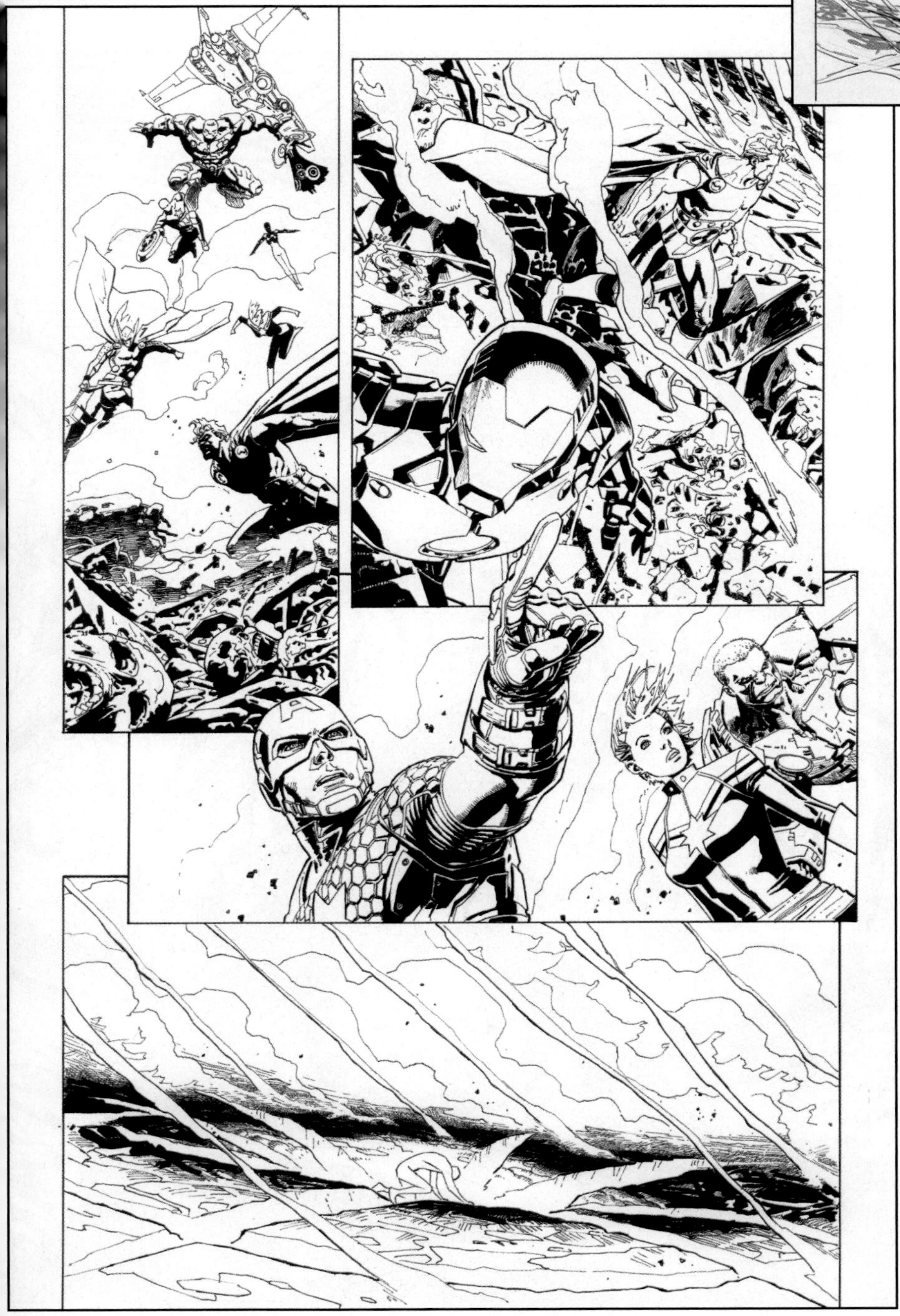

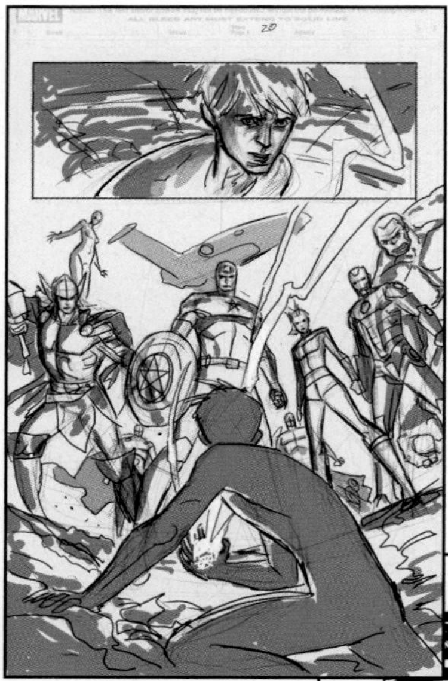

#7, PAGE 20

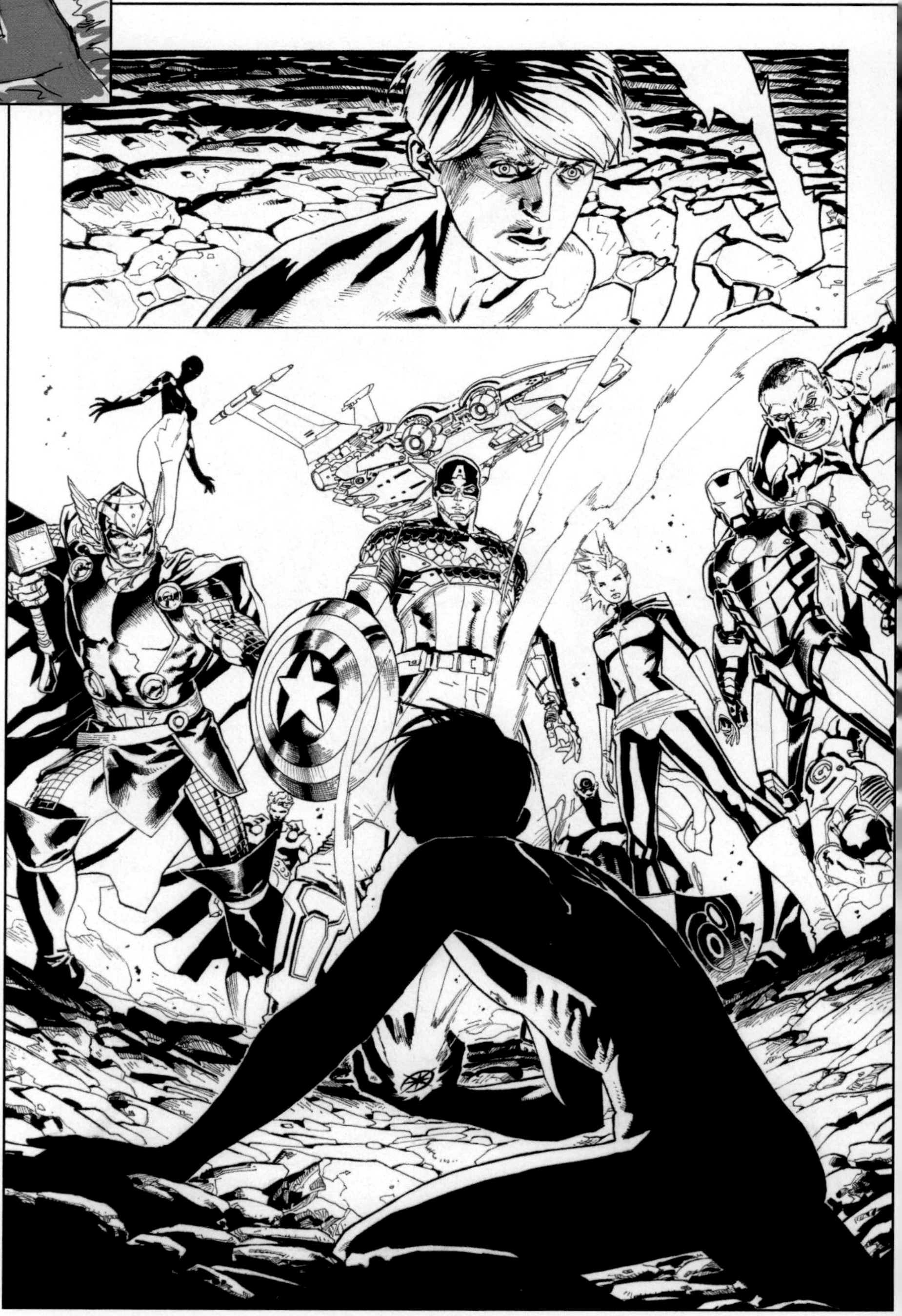

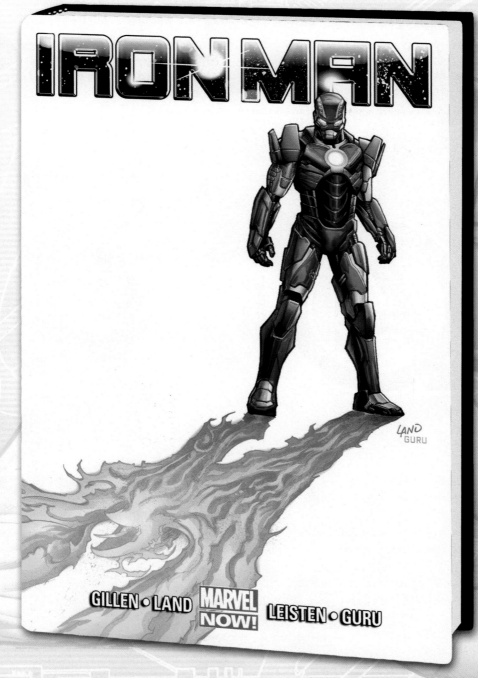

TO ACCESS THE FREE *MARVEL AUGMENTED REALITY APP* THAT ENHANCES AND CHANGES THE WAY YOU EXPERIENCE COMICS

1. Download the app for free via
   marvel.com/ARapp
2. Launch the app on your camera-enabled Apple iOS® or Android™ device*

3. Hold your mobile device's camera over any cover or panel with the **AR** graphic
4. Sit back and see the future of comics in action!

*Available on most camera-enabled Apple iOS® and Android™ devices. Content subject to change and availability.

AVENGERS

AR INDEX

TO REDEEM YOUR FREE DIGITAL COPY
USE THE CODE BELOW:

AVGV2HC72J9S

1. GO TO MARVEL.COM/REDEEM. OFFER EXPIRES ON 7/10/15.
2. FOLLOW THE ON-SCREEN INSTRUCTIONS TO REDEEM YOUR DIGITAL COPY.
3. LAUNCH THE MARVEL COMICS APP TO READ YOUR COMIC NOW!
4. YOUR DIGITAL COPY WILL BE FOUND UNDER THE *MY COMICS* TAB.
5. READ & ENJOY!

YOUR FREE DIGITAL COPY WILL BE AVAILABLE ON:

MARVEL COMICS APP
FOR APPLE® iOS DEVICES

MARVEL COMICS APP
FOR ANDROID™ DEVICES

MARVEL